T R A V E L E R S ' T A L E S

pilgrimage

ADVENTURES OF THE SPIRIT

TRAVELERS' TALES

pilgrimage

ADVENTURES OF THE SPIRIT

Edited by

SEAN O'REILLY AND JAMES O'REILLY

Series Editors

JAMES O'REILLY AND LARRY HABEGGER

TRAVELERS' TALES

SAN FRANCISCO

Art Direction: Michele Wetherbee
Cover design: Carin Berger
Interior design: Susan Bailey and Kathryn Heflin.
Photography: © Photonica
Painting: Scala/Art Resource, New York. Noli me tangere (detail). Fra Angelico (1387–1455).
Page layout: Cynthia Lamb using the fonts Bembo and Boulevard.

Distributed by Publishers Group West, 1700 Fourth Street, Berkeley, California 94710.

Library of Congress Cataloguing-in-Publication Data

Pilgrimage: adventures of the spirit / edited by Sean O'Reilly and James O'Reilly.— 1st ed.
     p. cm.
  Includes bibliographical references.
  ISBN 1-885211-56-2 (alk. paper)
   1. Pilgrims and pilgrimages. I. O'Reilly, Sean. II. O'Reilly, James.

BL619.P5 P515 2000
291.3'51—dc21   00-041787

First Edition
Printed in the United States of America
10 9 8 7 6 5 4 3 2 1

Keep knocking, and the joy inside
will eventually open a window
and look out to see who's there.

—RUMI

Table of Contents

Part Two
IN THE PILGRIM'S HEART

Pilgrimage: An Introduction

In May 1987, I gathered with friends and colleagues at the Director's Guild Theater in Hollywood to premiere the documentary film we had been working on for several years, *The Hero's Journey: The World of Joseph Campbell*. After the screening, several of us gathered on stage for a discussion with Professor Campbell. Near the end of the session we opened up for questions and comments from the audience. When someone thanked him for his comments on Sam Keen's documentary, *The Faces of the Enemy*, Campbell responded by contrasting the demonizing of other cultures, especially during wartime, with the perennial purpose of the spiritual life.

"The main awakening of the human spirit," he said, "is compassion. The main function of propaganda is to suppress compassion."

At that point, our moderator, Richard Beban, asked, "What do you see as the way out?"

After spending years in the editing room looking over seventy hours of film footage and videotape, I thought Campbell's response would be along the lines of "Read more Greek myths." Later I learned from his wife, Jean Erdman, that she thought he'd say, "Go back to the Upanishads. That's what saved me."

Instead, the maven of mythology startled us all with a koan-like answer.

"Tourism. I see the way out as tourism."

The theater erupted in laughter.

I nearly fell off my chair.

His wife was in shock. She sat stock-still in her front-row seat, waiting for an explanation or at least a qualifier.

Campbell waited, like the old Irish raconteur he was, allowing for the laughter to subside. Then a certain gravitas descended into his voice. "Go somewhere and meet somebody else," he continued. "Perhaps even learn another language."

Later that month I telephoned Campbell at his home in Honolulu, and we spoke about the film premiere and my upcoming journey to Paris. I confessed how surprised I was with his comments about tourism. He countered that he was serious about his recommendation.

"But if we do go somewhere," he added, "we should learn as much as we can about the place, including the language, the arts, the myths." That's how we learn to see past the artificial divisions of nations and cultures, he went on to say. When we discover what we have in common with others we learn how to demystify the stranger—and may even stop turning our neighbors into enemies. Eventually we can learn compassion, which is the real teaching in all of the wisdom traditions.

Those words resounded in me through my long stay in Paris, and for years afterward as I continued my own travels around the globe. The notion that tourism can do more than bring pleasure and provide escapism has helped me have more patience with the often aggravating elements of the travel business—the still rampant colonial mentality of the rich tourist lording over the poor locals, or the pandering for the almighty tourist dollar. I've learned that even your basic tourist trap has the potential for helping people pull out of their tortoise shell of provincial thinking.

The Campbell koan came back to me in the mid-nineties when I saw the first news items about the "swords-into-ploughshares" transformation taking place around the globe. By the year 2000, I read, the travel industry would surpass the armaments and automotive industries as the biggest business in the world. Moreover, as the decade drew to a close, another phenomenon was emerging. More people were embarking on pilgrimages than at any time since the Middle Ages. Millions of seekers were setting forth on spiritual journeys down the ancient pilgrim roads from Santiago de Compostela to Mecca, Rome to Jerusalem.

Curiously enough, pilgrimage is something I've taken for granted all my life. Raised in a French Catholic home outside

Detroit, I was familiar with the pious tradition of arduous journeys to holy sites, but being the son of parents who also loved the arts I was equally comfortable with the notion of following in the footsteps of writers, painters, even ballplayers, to pay my respects. For me the task of tasks of our lives is to see for ourselves how the sacred is all around us, even if, ironically, we have to go halfway around the world to learn how.

So it's not a long stretch for me to regard pilgrimage as one of those life-hints Kurt Vonnegut, Jr. had in mind when he said, "Strange travel suggestions are dancing lessons from God."

No doubt, pilgrimage can be a rote experience, like anything else in life, but at its most genuine I believe it to be a spiritually transformative journey. As evidenced by the roots of the word pilgrim (from the Latin *per agrum*, meaning "through the fields") there are sublime depths to the ancient tradition. The word-picture evokes a traveler with a spiritual purpose walking over sacred ground. What this really means is getting off the bus, off the train, away from the chamber of commerce sites. If real travel is travail, then pilgrimage is ordeal. By definition any journey is physically difficult, but pilgrimage is also spiritually challenging. It demands that we follow our spiritual compass and put the soles of our shoes to the soul of the world. It means getting back in touch with our earth, our roots, ourselves.

There are as many forms of pilgrimage as there are proverbial roads to Rome.

There are journeys to fulfill religious obligation, journeys of thanks, journeys of curiosity, homage, and serendipity, even journeys of penance ("Say three Our Fathers, three Hail Marys, and walk to Rome, my child"). All are journeys of renewal.

As pilgrims we go back to find something we lost; we return to the source to be restored, rejuvenated, revivified. I've traveled as tourist, traveler, adventure tour guide, and writer, and have been overjoyed to see things with new eyes, and as Pico Iyer writes, been forced to "shake up [my] complacencies." But it has been as a pilgrim—to Angkor Wat, Easter Island, Chartres, Pablo Neruda's house in Valparaiso, Chile, Rumi's tomb in Konya, Turkey—that I have felt most alive. Something happened at each of these sites that vitalized me and helped clarify my deepest thoughts.

The bona fide soul journey echoes John Muir's realization at Yosemite a century ago, "I only went out for a walk, and finally concluded to stay out till sundown, for going out, I found out I was really going in."

As if brought to light by the lantern of a pilgrim circumambulating the shrines of an ancient landscape, the stories that comprise this marvelous anthology reveal the simultaneous inner and outer nature of the spiritual journey. The adventure that renewed the traveler now renews us through the telling of the tale. What comes to mind when I think about these stories is passion. Every one of these tales is brimming with passion for pilgrimage, the journey grounded in spiritual wonder.

In Tara Austen Weaver's story about her pilgrimage around the island of Shikoku, she revels in the ordeal of hard cycling for which she wasn't prepared. "Mountains became my challenge," she writes, "a physical mirror of my inner struggles." Initially she feared that her journey was a mere escape, as many pilgrims do, but she came to realize that it was indeed an authentic search when it dawned on her she had "found the peace and knowledge I was looking for." Michael Wolfe's account of his arrival in Mecca evokes the ecstasy often associated with sacred travel. "The first sight of the shrine was literally stunning," he writes of the Ka'ba. Men and women wept the rarest sort of tears. "I also felt an urge to escape my skin," he goes on, "to swoop through the crowd like lines in a Whitman poem, looking out of every pilgrim's eyeballs." Then he heard the cry, "We made it! We made it!"

Beyond the epiphanies of the lone traveler, pilgrimage also offers as one of its perennial attractions what the anthropologist Victor Turner calls *communitas*. Pilgrimages are often provoked by feelings of spiritual isolation. Alone in our beliefs, we embark on a journey and encounter kindred spirits, which can strengthen the sense of community. In his account of a journey walking in the footsteps of the Buddha to Bodh Gaya in India, journalist Nicholas

Shrady writes with grace about the numinous scenes he encounters. But he also reports with unusual candor the lesson he learned sitting under the Bodhi tree among a swarm of other seekers and ascetics. "Better to be overcome with humility, I thought, than to be greedy for enlightenment." In the excerpt from Roger Housden's book about his travels in Algeria we follow the writer as he retraces his own footsteps back to a mysterious caravanserai called Tam, deep in the Sahara. There he finds "many young men in search of a real life," and is haunted by the comparison with friends he left behind. "Most people I know in Europe have money and trappings but are in search of a real life, as these men are. I had come here, to the Sahara, because I too wanted to feel the real life that once again seemed to have slipped away from me." Ann Hood's dramatic story of her journey to El Santuario in Chimayo, New Mexico, in search of a cure for her dying father reminds us that pilgrimages are really "miracles of inner transformation." Mark Matousek's tale is a fine example of the "accidental pilgrim," to paraphrase Anne Tyler. Through a series of serendipitous adventures he meets Mother Meera in Germany, where he compares his experience of *Darshan*, the bliss of her sheer presence, to a moment of awakening where you are "turning and stepping out the back door of your own mind."

Many accounts from pilgrims remind us that the sacred is as much "out there" as it is "in here." James D. Houston writes movingly of his journey to Hawai'i that he had "the urge to consecrate the moment" of his arrival, and felt that "I touched the place and the place touched me." He adds that, "These sites that call forth reverence and awe and humility and wonder, we make them sacred, and the ancient ties are never lost, the oldest voices calling from within (stones)." In her story about a journey to Khembalung in Nepal, Anne Armbrecht Forbes writes, "...what the pilgrims see along the way depends on what they are capable of seeing." And later, "At the moment I felt most alone I realized I was never alone. The sacred is always there waiting to wake us and be seen by us, like a tree waiting to greet our newly opened eyes." Along a similar path, Rabbi David A. Cooper writes about

Jerusalem itself as an opening into the spiritual dimension. There it became clear to him that the message of all great religions is essentially the same: separate identity is an illusion, everything is finally connected. "One day," he writes, "I hope to celebrate the unification of all humanity."

As the intrepid travelers in this inspiring collection attest, pilgrimage represents a model for all journeys. Ideally each one is as contemplative as it is adventurous. The boon of pilgrimage, we see here, is the revelation that the ground around our own backyard can be regarded as sacred as any famous site. This truth, known to many pilgrims, is beautifully portrayed in Ruth Kamnitzer's parable-within-a-story of her journey to the hilltop temple of Murugan at Palani, in India. There she learns of the mythical contest that Shiva and Parvati conjured up for their sons Murugan and Ganesh. "Whichever son managed to go round the world first would win the piece of golden fruit," she writes. While Murugan dashed off on his peacock, Ganesh merely walked around his parents, saying, "You are my world."

These spellbinding stories also remind me of the wisdom of Chaucer's invocation in the *Canterbury Tales*. The innkeeper at the Tabard Inn asks the departing pilgrims to tell two tales to strangers on the way to Canterbury, and two tales on the way home. Chaucer knew that the community at home needs stories as much as it needs food and water. We need tales of the stranger, as Campbell saw, to help us appreciate our common humanity. But we need news of other worlds and customs, much as William Carlos Williams described our need for poetry, because "the world dies every day for the lack of it." News that people are crossing borders not just on the map, but in the heart and soul. Strangely, I'm also inspired by the tales in this collection to recall that we may also need to be occasionally reminded about how much we don't know about why we travel. An old Zen story captures the spirit.

The wandering monk Fa-yen was asked by Ti-ts'ang,

"Where are you going?"

"Around on pilgrimage," said Fa-yen.

Ti-ts'ang asked, "What is the purpose of pilgrimage?"
"I don't know," replied Fa-yen.
Ti-ts'ang nodded and said, "Not knowing is nearest."

What memorable tales from the old pilgrim roads give us is the gift of the courage of our convictions. They remind us that at the crossroads moments of our lives perhaps we should, as the Buddha reminded his followers with his last words, "Walk On." Walk on, contemplating, ruminating, meditating, observing what is sacred in and around us.

—PHIL COUSINEAU
North Beach, San Francisco

Phil Cousineau is a writer, filmmaker, photographer, and adventure travel guide. His twelve documentary film credits include The Hero's Journey: The World of Joseph Campbell, Ecological Design: Inventing the Future, *and* The Peyote Road. *Cousineau is also author or editor of more than a dozen books, most recently the best-selling* The Art of Pilgrimage: The Seeker's Guide to Making Travel Sacred, The Book of Roads, *and the upcoming* Once and Future Myths. *He now makes his home on Telegraph Hill in San Francisco.*

PART ONE

ON THE
PILGRIM'S ROAD

RABBI DAVID A. COOPER

✦ ✦ ✦

Old City, Jerusalem

A city holy to three religions gives the pilgrim
a taste of unexpected joy.

BEHIND THE MOUNT OF OLIVES, THE SKY UNFOLDS SOFTLY IN
tints of rose and lavender as an unseen artist applies thin streaks of
melting light onto an ever-moving canvas. The golden Dome of
the Rock stands at the heart of the city—some say the heart of the
world—reflecting the changing hues like a great beacon calling
out to the soul of humankind. Jewish mystics believe that every
prayer uttered to God flies from around the world to this point on
the planet—the Temple Mount—from where it is released to
heaven. Now in the awakening dawn the reverse occurs: the celes-
tial response to all our prayers flows through the sacred stone
mound beneath this golden orb, and radiates out for all who are
willing to hear.

Jews, Christians, and Muslims each believe God's response to
the call of humanity is directed specifically to them because of
their devotions. Over the centuries they have fought to control this
particular piece of earth in the Middle East, as if somehow holding the keys is a divinely imposed obligation. Passions are strong
and even violent on this issue; the subject does not lend itself to
reason. There is no room for compromise.

I sit in meditation on the roof of an apartment building in the

3

Old City of Jerusalem as the calm of early dawn gives the impression of peace and harmony. The Muslim call to prayer ended a while ago, and large flocks of chattering birds have performed their sunrise ritual, skimming just overhead in the direction of Silwān, to the southeast. Each morning I have noticed thousands of these little birds passing over al-Aqsa Mosque—at the south end of the Temple Mount—as they fly toward the rising light on the horizon.

In Arabic, the Temple Mount is called Haram al-Sharif (the Noble Sanctuary)—and it is the third holiest place in the world for Muslims, the others being the Ka'ba in Mecca and the Mosque of Muhammad in Medina. It is not the Temple Mount itself that is important, but the consecrated stone lying beneath the Dome of the Rock.

After crossing the silver dome of al-Aqsa Mosque, the birds fly near the City of David, just outside the current Old City walls. These are ruins of the original Jerusalem conquered by King David three thousand years ago. Some say that the prophet Gad revealed to David that this city would be the home for God's sanctuary on earth. David set his heart on building the house of God, the first Temple, but his son Solomon was destined to perform this work. Still, it was called the House of David because according to Rabbi Ishmael, "Since David was with his whole soul devoted to it, wishing to build it, it is named after him."

The birds continue in their flight, and from my vantage point, they seem to land somewhere around Hezekiah's Tunnel, built 2,700 years ago to assure a steady supply of water for the city when it was under siege. At one end of the tunnel is the Pool of Shiloah, while at the other end is the Spring of Gihon. At the Pool of Shiloah are remnants of a church built over a thousand years ago to mark the spot where Jesus sent a blind man to be cured in those waters (John 9:7, 11). One Jewish tradition says that souls bathe in the water of Shiloah before presenting themselves to the heavenly kingdom, but most Kabbalists agree that souls must be purified in a river of fire before entering paradise.

Legend has it that Mary washed her infant's clothes in the waters of the Spring of Gihon. A biblical account tells us about another event that happened here a thousand years earlier than Mary—Solomon was crowned king. "[They] caused Shelomo [Solomon] to ride on King David's mule, and brought him to Gihon. And Zadoq the priest took a horn of oil out of the tent, and anointed Shelomo. And they blew the shofar; and all the people said. Long live king Shelomo" (I Kings 1:38, 39).

I envision these places from where I sit, knowing that in less than a half-hour's walk I can dip my hands in the waters of Gihon. The collective unconscious of Western tradition centers here, and I could easily spend many lifetimes studying the history, stories, traditions, and wisdom teachings related to sites within a couple of kilometers. Everywhere I look, spiritual contemplation beckons. It is no accident that this city is the cradle of Western tradition—the *kedusha* (holiness) is so dense, my feet are barely able to touch the ground.

The mystical center of Jerusalem is an outcropping of stone covered by the Dome of the Rock—it is about fifty feet across. Many teach that this rock was called by the ancients the *even shetiyyah*, the foundation rock from which the cosmos was woven, the hub of the universe, the navel of the earth. Some believe this is the site of the Holy of Holies, the innermost sanctum of the house of God, where once each year the Jewish high priest—in the time of the Temple (two to three thousand years ago)—would commune directly with God on the holy day of Yom Kippur. Nobody else was ever permitted to enter. When the high priest was about to go into the inner sanctuary, his assistants tied a long rope around his waist, for if he had the slightest impure thought while in the Holy of Holies, he would die instantly and the rope would be the only way to get him out.

Tales abound about this sacred rock. Adam and Eve lived here; Abraham came here to sacrifice Isaac. In the future, the fountain of total awareness will bubble forth from this place. In Islamic tradition, Muhammad stepped off this rock when he took his famous night journey to heaven. Local guides usually point out to tourists an indentation in the side of the rock that is reputed to be Muhammad's footprint.

The Holy of Holies was the resting place of the Ark of the Covenant, which contained the tablets inscribed with the Ten Commandments, brought down from Sinai by Moses. The Ark also held the Torah, the scroll of the five ancient books written by Moses, dictated by God. On top of the Ark were seated two cherubs made of solid gold facing each other with outstretched wings almost touching. Between these cherubs, God's presence was manifest, and all heavenly transmission was focused here. As one writer of the Kabbalah notes: "The space between them [the cherubs] was also seen as an opening into the spiritual dimension. In concentrating his thoughts between the cherubs on the Ark, a prophet was able to enter the prophetic state."

An interesting story is told in legend about how Solomon selected the physical location of the first Temple.

> He was long in doubt as to where to build it. A heavenly voice directed him to go to Mount Zion at night, to a field owned by two brothers jointly. One of the brothers was a bachelor and poor, the other was blessed both with wealth and a large family of children. It was harvesting time. Under cover of night, the poor brother kept adding to the other's heap of grain, for, although he was poor, he thought his brother needed more on account of his large family. The rich brother, in the same clandestine way, added to the poor brother's store, thinking that though he had a family to support, the other was without means. This field, Solomon concluded, which had called forth so remarkable a manifestation of brotherly love, was the best site for the Temple, and he bought it.

There are thousands of stories about the *even shetiyyah*, the Temple Mount, the first and second Temples, and all that has taken place in that location during the two thousand years since the destruction of the second Temple. Despite the rich lore that is attached to this location, traditional Jews today are forbidden by religious law to set foot on the Temple Mount, because anyone in the proximity of the Temple sanctuary requires specific rites of purification defined in the Talmud—and these cannot be performed in our day.

Many Jews pray for the rebuilding of the Temple. Traditionalists mean this literally—take down what is there and put up a new structure. Mystics view the Temple not so much as a physical building, but as a level of God-consciousness. For them the legend of Solomon gives us an important clue: that is, coexistence was a principle upon which the Temple was founded and is a necessary condition for its rebuilding. Almost everyone agrees that building the third Temple will require a miracle—but Jerusalem is the home of miracles.

One of the ten miracles of the first Temple was that although the physical space available within the boundaries of the Temple walls was not sufficient to accommodate the hundreds of thousands of pilgrims who came to Jerusalem each year, still everyone was able to get inside the walls by pressing closely together. This in itself was miraculous. But the miracle recorded by the sages was that when ritual required all present to prostrate themselves flat on the ground, which meant taking up at least four times as much space as standing, there was still room for the multitudes to lie side by side on the ground! No teaching could be more clearly symbolic: there is always sufficient space in any situation, if the level of devotion is sincere, even though the results may defy all logic.

Life in Jerusalem awakens a new inner cadence; it is not something that could be measured with biorhythms, rather it is in another realm, which I have labeled pneumarhythms, the mysterious flow of spiritual source into the breath of life. And in the process, I am gaining fresh understanding of the nature of the Divine. My rational, pragmatic approach to life served me well in the material world, but it had not provided a clear sense of purpose. This is now changing, but not in any way that I can explain, for the entire experience is beyond the limits of reason.

I have fallen into an "in-between" world as I separate from the past but do not have a clear orientation to the future. Nothing fits as it should. I continuously wear a yarmulke, the head covering

worn by a traditional Jew, but I still feel on the fringe. I do not
dress in pressed pants and light shirts of respectable Orthodoxy, the
black suits of Hasidism, or
the rainbow colors of the ex-
flower children who have
found their way back into
traditional practice. In truth, I
continue to have difficulties
with organized religion,
Jewish or any other.

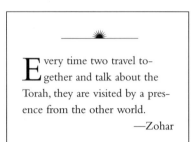

E very time two travel together and talk about the
Torah, they are visited by a presence from the other world.
                              —Zohar

*My quest is spiritual and
mystical. The religious life does not interest me as much as the potency of
faith; I am not drawn to the ritual, but to the primal forces that are awakened. It is a search for the Soul: my soul, the soul of humankind, the soul
of the planet and of the universe.*

The Old City of Jerusalem is surrounded by walls of stone, hundreds of years old, massive enough to stop a modern tank. On the
west side, Jaffa Gate opens into the Armenian and Christian quarters; to the south, Zion and Dung Gates provide passage into the
Jewish Quarter; Lions' Gate opens to the east, and Damascus Gate
to the north, giving access to the Muslim Quarter. These gates,
plus a few others, are the only passageways through the majestic
stone blocks of the Old City fortress.

Every day crowds of residents, tourists, and military platoons
pass through the walls of Old Jerusalem in a steady flow.
Sometimes, when the heat rises in the summer, life inside this
stronghold begins to feel like a pressure cooker. The intensity
builds, and the people inside must soften and become pliant, or the
valves will blow. Whenever that happens, the scalding steam whistles out rapidly in a shriek that is often heard around the world.

Our first six months in the Old City were focused on integrat-
ing with the Israeli lifestyle. As we had experienced a year and a
half earlier in Bayit VeGan, our social lives centered on the Sabbath
meals. There were also gatherings for every *simchah* (joyous event),

including engagements, weddings, births, brits (circumcisions), bar mitzvahs, and other special events, like naming a daughter, moving into a new home, or completing an important piece of study. *Simchahs* are frequent occurrences—rarely a month passes without at least one or two of these special celebrations.

We had celebrated Rosh Hashanah, Yom Kippur, Sukkor (one week long), Shemini Atzeret, and Simchat Torah on our first trip; in addition are the Holy Days of Hanukkah, Purim, Passover (one week long), and Shavuot. There are also some important observance days, including Tisha B'Av (mourning for the destruction of the First and Second Temples), the Fast of Esther (the day before Purim), and Tu B'Shevat (the festival of the New Year of Trees), in addition to many minor days of commemoration or fasting. Moreover, every new moon is a special day, the entire month of Elul (at the end of the summer) has significance in preparation for Rosh Hashanah, and there are forty-nine days of counting the Omer between Passover and Shavuot. Add to all this the national holidays, which include Independence Day and Jerusalem Day—one wonders how anything gets accomplished in between all the festivities.

It is difficult for people outside Israel to relate to the richness of the Hebrew calendar. In the USA, we celebrate Easter, Thanksgiving, and Christmas, along with a half dozen or so national holidays. We may have a few *simchahs* in a year, but some years pass without any. We occasionally have guests for a meal, and try to go out for dinner and entertainment as often as possible, but most of our time is spent with the television, newspapers, or magazines.

Life in the Old City, on the other hand, was like having a close family of a couple of hundred cousins, aunts, and uncles all living within a mile. One day a week—Shabbat—was specifically set aside for family affairs. No business discussions, travel, or outside entertainment was allowed on this day—the family sat together around meals, in prayer groups, or in study sessions where the primary topic was invariably one of religious contemplation.

This was also a close family in other ways. Whenever there was a birth, and there were many, the new parents could usually rely on having their meals prepared by neighbors. In times of illness, a steady flow of visitors and helping hands would appear magically. Child care was widely shared, and there were many layers of potential support for the multitude of minicrises that arise in everyday life.

Our major effort at the time was to learn the language. It was slow going, made worse by the fact that almost all of our close friends were native English speakers. Although we worked intensively in language school for four months, we did not make much progress. Our difficulty with the language was a constant source of frustration that was never resolved.

Daily life during this first year was intense. Fortunately, I had developed a regular meditation schedule, and continued to take three- to seven-day retreats throughout this period. These days of inner silence provided my spiritual grounding despite the highly charged lifestyle of the Old City community. In many ways, my time of solitude was necessary to assimilate the incredible flow of information that overwhelmed us, and it was, as well, an important source of nourishment for the transcendental being that lived within—a being that was becoming ever more familiar to me through my constant inward practice.

The image stood by my left side, whispering into my ear, "What do you want, David?" I answered, "I want to be stripped of my conceit."

Two masked executioners appeared. They began to peel away my skin. It was terrifying but painless. I watched in horror as they ripped away layer after layer. Finally, I was merely bone from the neck down, but my large head remained. There were also two jewel-encrusted shields, one covering my chest, the other my back. They were some kind of body armor, each an elongated diamond shape. I held on to them fiercely. I did not fight the stripping of the flesh, but these body shields I wanted or thought I needed.

The hooded ghosts persisted in pulling away the shields. I let go reluctantly. I now looked really awful. I cried out for help to cover my nakedness, and was provided with a simple cloth of homespun cotton, like Gandhi used to wear. It was humble cloth, secure, and it had a glow of its own.

"Are you satisfied?" the whispering voice asked. I said that I felt terrible, vulnerable, frightened—and I asked about the shields. "Pride on the front and insecurity on the back," it said. "The front one is the direct link to conceit, the other is the real cause of most bravado."

I felt helpless, but strangely calm. The voice said, "You can have it all back, if you want." I declined and sat shivering, seeing myself on a block of ice floating in an enormous sea. The ice was slowly melting, and I waited for the inevitable. But when my bony feet touched the water, it was warm. I floated away on the gentle sea; it was a new form of flesh, translucent, without boundaries. I now knew that I was completely safe.

"What is this?" I asked.

The voice responded: "The Nowhere of Selflessness."

Three weeks were spent cleaning the house in preparation for Passover. During this period traditional Jews do much more than a normal spring cleaning; they search for *hametz*. Literally, *hametz* is fermented dough, which includes anything made of five specific grains: wheat, barley, oats, spelt, or rye. Mystically, this represents a process of inner purification, removing anything that leads to pride—which is any quality of thought that isolates us from the awareness of our spiritual connections. According to the rabbis, pride "prevents us from performing the will of God."

Thus, the entire house had to be meticulously cleaned. Every piece of clothing was examined to make certain not even a crumb of bread or morsel of cracker was caught in a pocket lining. All books were taken down and fanned to check for any food particles. Drawers were pulled out, rugs turned over, and the entire kitchen was carefully scrubbed.

The prohibitions concerning *hametz* include any pots, pans, dishes, or cutlery that have been used during the year—in principle, it is as if they absorbed the essential quality of the *hametz*. Thus all religious Jewish households have an entirely separate set of dishes and everything else needed to run a kitchen during the week of Passover. This first year we bought a couple of plates, a pot, and a few pieces of silverware—just enough to survive.

Although unleavened bread, matzah, is the symbol many people associate with Passover, the most engaged spiritual work of the holiday is done in the purification process prior to the actual seder, the meal in which the matzah is eaten. The constant physical cleaning, down to the minutest speck, invariably gives rise to irritation with trivial details and wasted time. To do the job well requires enormous patience and discipline, which are two primary ingredients of spiritual practice.

In addition, there is the study of a bulky catalogue of religious law related to Passover that must be reviewed and integrated during the weeks of preparation. It includes what may or may not be eaten, how food may be prepared, the specific details of the seder ritual, and the general principles that apply to the entire period of the weeklong observance. The weight of all these precepts packed into an event like this is usually sufficient to break the will of newcomers. The lengthy process required distinct surrender, another vital ingredient for spiritual development.

The night of the seder continued into the early morning hours. When we finally reached the words "Next year in Jerusalem!" marking the culmination of the long ritual, I leaned on my cushion and closed my eyes. Countless faces arose out of a silver mist, tumbling over each other, faces of many designs, but the eyes were all similar, expressing mixture of anticipation and pleasure. I could not but contemplate how many tens of millions of seders had been conducted over thousands of years, in which people were searching for a release from the constriction of their own enslavement, the limits of the mind, the snares of language, the boundaries of thought, the constraints of concepts and notions about who we are and what life is all about.

The story and ritual of Passover celebrates the possibility of escaping a prison that has infinitely high, impassable walls. How can we escape the limitations of our own minds through thinking? This is like asking the warden for the key. We must rely on something outside of ourselves to engineer the breakout. Thus, Passover celebrates the Jewish understanding that the ultimate path of enlightenment is revealed through the hand of God—not because we are deserving, but because the Divine Source imparts in some way, beyond all understanding, a supreme level of freedom.

This Passover was the first time I recognized the extent to which I was entangled in a web of my own making, a complex edifice of self-identity and conditioned responses. I was shocked to realize the enormity of this jumble of perceptions, attitudes, and opinions. Until now I had not fully appreciated the predicament; like a slave who is blind and deaf, I had simply done what I thought was expected of me. Suddenly my eyes and ears were opened, and the potential moved my soul; I knew with a certainty never before experienced that there was something else, something more, a truth that could shatter the prison of my own mind.

We require higher tasks, because we do not recognize the height of those we have. Trying to be kind and honest seems an affair too simple and too inconsequential for gentlemen of our heroic mould; we had rather set ourselves to something bold, arduous, and conclusive; we had rather found a schism or suppress a heresy, cut off a hand or mortify an appetite. But the task before us…is rather one of microscopic fineness, and the heroism required is that of patience. There is no cutting of the Gordian knots of life; each must be smilingly unravelled.

—Robert Louis Stevenson,
A Christmas Sermon

A couple of days after the seder, at 2 A.M. Easter morning, I walked through the city's subtly lit corridors of carved stone walls and listened to my steps ricocheting loudly in the hollow night. Cats' eyes gleamed from moving shadows, as the animals stalked an unseen quarry hidden behind loose rocks. The shadows fell upon my approach, well out of striking range, following the ancient wisdom of the jungle— unknown may be dangerous.

At its quietest in these early-morning hours, the Old City is the most regal. Mundane street chatter awaits the signs of dawn, and the city is given a respite from human traffic in the marketplace, the gas fumes of tractors, and the tons of trash dropped by throngs of tourists. Thus Jerusalem sighed quietly in the night as I crossed

from the Jewish Quarter into the Muslim Quarter on my way to
the Church of the Holy Sepulchre in the Christian Quarter.

The general consensus is that the Church of the Holy
Sepulchre marks the hill called Golgotha, and that the site of the
Crucifixion and the last five Stations of the Cross are located under
its large black domes. Marble stairs lead down under the church,
where there are caverns containing burial tombs, and many believe
that this is where Jesus was buried two thousand years ago.

All day Good Friday, a foreboding, sonorous bell in this church
had tolled every couple of minutes. It was compelling, the inter-
vals between the bells being just long enough to allow one to forget the sound so that each bell jolted the awareness anew. As I
walked, the power of the bell vibrated an inner chord—something
portentous had happened long ago and was still happening.

Fortunately I had visited the church before, or I would not have
been able to find it in the darkness. It is not on a main street, and
the only way in is to push through unmarked gates that open on
its courtyard. It was quiet and I was alone; but soon I was standing
before the huge doors leading into the main dome.

The church was dark, dingy, Byzantine; the carved stone pillars
were obscured behind water stains and mold. Lanterns with colored glass created an eerie feeling, like being in the bowels of a
medieval castle, awaiting the black knight to appear from around
the corner. A number of priests were gathered at an altar, dressed
in black, carrying long, tapered candles and a huge incense burner
spewing out clouds of pungent myrrh and frankincense. They did
not look happy.

I walked around slowly in the dark. The church was filled with
priests and portly middle-aged women dressed in black, with black
scarves pulled tightly over their foreheads. Few of the altars were
being used; it was quiet and solemn.

A dim light glowed in one of the stairwells, drawing me down
to explore the lower caverns. After I had descended a few steps, the
light began to brighten, glowing more radiant as I continued
down. And then I heard melodious voices and knew that I had
found what had pulled me out of bed in the middle of the night.

This was not a dream, not a vision in my meditation—I was really here, this was really happening.

Rounding a corner, I saw a group of nuns, dressed all in white, dancing in a circle, singing a delightful hymn. There were about two dozen of them. Off to one side were four men dressed in white—I'm not sure what to call them: brothers? monks? priests? One song ended, and the next began; this time the men joined in.

I stood there transfixed, my heart thrilled to their music. It was like Sufi dances I had experienced. These people were ecstatic; the entire group glowed in the whiteness of their habits and the joy of their devotion. They continued like this for an hour, and I was so filled with emotion I could hardly breathe.

Then they stopped for a while and performed an initiation or an induction of two men and one woman who had been standing on one side, dressed in ordinary clothes. The two leaders, a middle-aged bearded man, and a lovely middle-aged woman, stood before the group and administered vows in French. The young woman was initiated first. And then the two young men together, each lying prone on the floor with arms outstretched. When they stood up, they were given white robes, which the congregation helped them put on over their street clothes.

The dancing began again, with renewed strength and jubilation. Everyone was dancing together, and the hallelujahs rebounded throughout the caverns and subcaverns that were normally the domain of the dead, but were now fully bathed in light. On they went, singing, whirling, the most beautiful faces I have ever seen in a religious gathering—or anywhere, for that matter.

And then, suddenly, one of the young men glanced at his watch and looked up with tears streaming down his face, whispering something—and then shouting for all to hear: *"CHRISTO RESURRECTE! CHRISTO RESURRECTE!"* ("Christ is risen!")

Something surged within me, and I shouted back: "YES!"

Then the rest of the group joined in, the men crying out, *"Christo resurrecte,"* while the women circled them singing hymns of praise in a state of intense passion and ecstasy. One man ran up the steps toward me, saw my yarmulke, but also my smile, and we hugged, he whispering, "*Christo resurrecte*," and I responding, "Amen, brother, amen."

This was an affirmation of life. The purest, sweetest mystery of death and rebirth. I suddenly understood the parallels between the secret of resurrection and my newfound understanding of the profound meanings of Passover. They were virtually identical; the process of transformation from the limitations of constriction into the enlightened state of the Spirit. This is what is meant by messianic consciousness, the breaking of the bonds of Egypt and making the Exodus to the Holy Land. It was clear to me in those moments that the mystical message of Judaism, Christianity, and Sufism were all the same. The Paschal Mystery, the teaching of Christ as the sacrificial lamb, holds its epiphany in the realization of our illusion of being separate identities, and breaks through to Life, the mystical union with the Divine.

Clearly this is not the way religious traditionalists interpret these transformative events. Indeed there are obvious distinctions in outward expression and practices in different religions, but I was convinced more than ever that *Christo resurrecte, Allah Hu-Akbar* (Arabic: God is great), and *Shema Yisrael* (Hebrew: Hear O Israel) all come from the same source and speak to the same source, the Divine revealing itself to itself.

At the peak of this ecstasy and euphoria, dark shadows appeared on the stairs. We had been making too much commotion, sharing too much love, broadcasting too much light in the affirmation of the most significant message of Jesus Christ: Live! And the plump little women in black pushed the heavyset, sagging-jowled priests in black toward a confrontation with light. The message was clear—bright light reveals dust and cobwebs in the corners; uncontained joy interferes with solemn ritual. Thus, the congregation of light was asked to leave.

We all walked out together, quietly elated. The nuns glided down the road ahead, still in their habits; the men changed back into street clothes, and were indistinguishable in the early-morning light. I watched the nuns walking away, and when it was too late realized that I had no idea where they worshipped or lived, or how I would ever find them again—but I hoped one day to dance with them once more, celebrating the unification of all humanity in messianic consciousness.

Rabbi David A. Cooper has been a student of mysticism for more than thirty years, traveling and studying extensively the mystical elements of a variety of traditions. He spent almost ten years living and studying in Jerusalem before moving to the Colorado Rockies in 1991. This story was excerpted from his book, Entering the Sacred Mountain: Exploring the Mystical Practices of Judaism, Buddhism, and Sufism.

JACK HITT

* * *

On the Road to Santiago de Compostela

The author encounters dogs, lightning,
and questions of sanity.

AFTER A MONTH OF WALKING THE ANCIENT ROAD TO SANTIAGO, Spain, a pilgrim loses his mind—not in the psychiatric sense, but like an obsolete appliance. Think of an eight-track tape player permanently misplaced in the cellar. It's useless and unnecessary, but should its function ever be needed again, you can always retrieve it. When I walk, I stare at the ground sliding beneath my feet, and I am speechless, lost in a hot pulsing haze. To look me in the eye, you'd see the milky cataracts of an aged ox strapped into his traces, lugging his burden.

I set out one late spring to retrace the medieval pilgrimage route that once bound Europe in a belt of traffic. The old network of roads converges into one just over the Pyrenees; today I am halfway across Spain on the 500-mile path that once accommodated millions and still carries a few thousand each year to Santiago, in that panhandle notched just above Portugal. Like many my age, I had effortlessly cast off the religion of my parents as if stepping out of a pair of old trousers. So I hit the road to Santiago because I had read of its tradition of welcoming those with feeble motives. A twelfth-century document at one pilgrims' shelter says: "Its doors are open to all, well and ill, not only to

Catholics, but to pagans, Jews and heretics, the idler and the vagabond and, to put it shortly, the good and the wicked." I believe I can find myself in there somewhere.

On the road today, time is a long silence, and that is why I say a pilgrim begins to lose his mind. I just don't need it. I've spent entire afternoons slogging through a trench cut so deep into a wheat field that I am invisible to all except the birds. Central Spain is nothing but wheat fields, and wheat, it seems, finds me fetching. Mosquitoes inexplicably prefer some people. I've never had a problem with them because apparently I am spoken for by the plant kingdom. I am beloved by wheat. Their stalks bend toward me in the wind, anxious to propel their seed my way. They have mistaken me for rich topsoil (not so surprising after a month of pilgrimage). Wheat burrs assault me from all directions, hitting me in the face, once swiftly—whoa—plugging up a nostril. They gather into harvest decorations in my hair and burrow into the wrinkles of my filthy clothes. After a morning's walk, my legs are dense congregations of future generations of wheat.

When the road occasionally veers out of the wheat fields and overlaps with a highway, I enter a sphere all my own. The cars zoom by so fast, I am but a blur to them, as they are to me. I have left that dimension. My only acquaintances are poor farmers puttering on tractors or families piled onto old hay wagons drawn by mules. These people always greet me kindly. I am one of them.

This morning, as I begin a seventeen-mile leg into the plains of Castile, an old man on a moped stops to talk. He is small and frail with a transparent face and a wheeze like a child's rattle. He smokes constantly as he speaks in the nearly indecipherable, all-vowel nose-speak of a rural man. "You must be careful up ahead," he advises.

"Careful?"

"There is much danger up ahead on the plains of Castile."

"Danger?"

"Yes, and great torments and evil."

In Spanish, the words ring medieval. *"Hay tormentas y mal tiempos."* Great, I am thinking. At last, some action. "What should I do?" I ask.

"You should just be ready. I don't know what pilgrims do. Perhaps you shouldn't walk."

"Are the plains always full of torments and suffering?"

"No, but when it comes, it's bad," says my bony mystic.

"How do you know this?" I ask.

He pauses, a bit sad. "I saw it on television."

I am marveling at this surreal answer, a charming mix of folklore and technology. In my mindless fog, it is a good hour before I open my pocket dictionary and learn that these words mean "rainstorm" and "bad weather." My shaman was quoting the television weatherguy. Every pilgrim claims a saint to serve as a guardian spirit. Saint Groucho of Marx, watch over me.

★

For centuries there were miracles and apparitions to be seen at every turn of the road to Santiago: you could meet angels, beggars, kings, and status-seekers—the Plantagenet king Edward I on horseback, St. Francis of Assisi walking barefoot, and a certain Flemish wayfarer who is reputed to have carried a mermaid around with him, in a tub.

—Frederic V. Grunfeld,
Wild Spain: A Traveller's Guide

The only relief from the wheat field is a tiny village named Hornillos. It means "little stoves" and was founded in 1156 to provide my ancient predecessors with a cooked meal before walking into the vast emptiness of the Castilian plains. The stoves are long gone. There is no restaurant here. The only refuge is a tilted shed beside the church so infested with flies that I skip my daily siesta and walk on. Three widows, in elaborate black lace, sit at the end of town in the pose of eternal silence.

I nod my head to acknowledge them.

"Beware of wolves," volunteers one.

"Wolves?"

"On the plains, there are wolves," says another.

"Wolves?"

"Sharpen your stick," she says.

"Wolves?"

"May Santiago protect you," she says.

These words sound eulogistic.

The famous plains of Castile are misnamed. They should be called the plateaus. A few miles outside of Hornillos, the road zigzags up a fierce incline until arriving at a level lip and opens to an infinite vista of…wheat. Wheat and more wheat, as far as the eye can see. Dorothy's poppy fields on the outskirts of Oz hold nothing to this view. I have never seen this much of the planet in one take.

I had frequently been warned about the heat and emptiness of the plains. Not the slightest smudge of shade. Not even a shed. The occasional farmer comes up to plow, but not today. There is no one.

No matter how far I walk, the horizon unwinds like a scroll, laying out more wheat fields. The stalks are sickly thin and translucent up close; no more than eighteen inches high, struggling amid tough clods and rocks the size of fists. The larger rocks and boulders were plucked out centuries ago and gathered into unintended cairns. They are blanched an unnatural white and pitted with hollows by centuries of wind blasts and hot sun, like monuments of skulls.

Pilgrim diaries testify to the terror of the Castilian plains. In April 1670, an Italian pilgrim named Domenico Laffi left Bologna for Santiago. He saw many odd things along the way; on the plains of Castile, he saw a pilgrim attacked and eaten alive by a swarm of grasshoppers.

The narrow channel of dust that scores these wheat fields is so dry that the ground has cracked open in places. Why hadn't I noticed these before? Did these fissures yawn open a few moments ago? These are bad signs. My gaze goes downward, oxen-eyed and cautious.

Hours pass, and the wheat fields unroll. Big clouds bound in— Steven Spielberg props, cottony bales that hang so low I imagine that on tiptoe, I could finger their dark feathery bottoms. Some remnant of childhood superstition keeps my eyes on the ground as if that will keep them from breaking open and soaking me with rain. In the far distance, there's a sound like someone moaning.

About ten feet in front of me, a small brown bird wings its way out of the clouds and falls leadenly on the road in front of me.

Oh, come on.

I am jabbering aimlessly to myself. I sing every song and recite every poem I know. Movies that I have visually memorized, *Diner*, for example, play from beginning to end out here in the whistling expanse of the spacious Castilian Gigantoplex. A few weeks ago, the wind bore only the Doppler squeal of a phantom car. That was then; today it's an hallucinatory open house. I hear singing in the wind, four-part harmonies of Renaissance madrigals, shopping mall renditions of Christmas carols, all the Top 40 hits fried onto my synapses before I left (the opening mandolin riff of REM's "Losing My Religion" perversely floats up every ten minutes like a human rights violation). I hear arguments and complaints—my mother frets again about my quitting my job, a high-school bully apologizes for beating me up, an old girlfriend confesses she can't live without me. It's an auditory Rorschach out here.

The horizon never changes—a thin black line drawn between the brown wheat and darkening clouds ahead. From time to time, the fields betray a slight upward incline. But one mild hump merely leads to another, more wheat, more stones. In the middle of this new field, three dogs scour in the distance. I open my pocket-knife and sharpen the point of my stick.

A pilgrim gets to know dogs pretty well. Dogs are everywhere in Spain. Each yard has a savage dog chained to a stake. Every village is overrun with skinny strays. They snake around the corners of buildings and nose up the alleys prowling for scraps. Tailless cats with slack bellies scramble in their wake.

Dogs generally keep their distance. They aren't particularly brave unless there's enough of them. A pilgrim learns to translate the idiom of a dog's bark as fluently as a parent comes to know the meaning of a child's cry.

Barking is a similar language. A healthy throated sound, deep in the bass register, is a statement of territory. A declarative sentence and nothing more. But there are other grammars. Skinny dogs, desperate from hunger, can let rip with a mean scraping sound. In the syntax of the wild, these are the irregular conjugations. Be very afraid.

As I approach their parallel, the dogs send up a few introductory barks. I have no fear because I read them perfectly: territorial claims, nothing more. Suddenly, all three break into a furious sprint, tearing at the air with snapping howls, straight for me.

I can see that they bear the marks of wild Spanish dogs. They all are plagued by mange. The largest one has a dead ear, permanently bent over. The small leader runs a little sidewise, crablike; his backside is rubbed raw, absolutely hairless in bleeding patches. These are seriously ugly dogs.

The three pull up and trot side by side, as one. I walk slowly but deliberately. They circle me, heading out in front on the road. They stop and I inch closer. The lead dog rips with a frightening bark, a fierce shredded blast. I read him clearly.

A strange fear overtakes me, and it's one I have never felt. Of course I'm scared of three dogs attacking me, alone, on this empty plateau. But that's not it. This is a new fear. I am scared because I know that I am prepared to kill them. I have my knife in my left hand and my stick in my right. My breathing is rapid. My pupils must be pinholes. We are locked in direct eye contact. My frontal lobes have shut down and handed off total control to that reptilian stub in the base of the brain. Nerve bundles that haven't been tickled since the Pleistocene epoch have taken over my main features. My mouth is pried open, and my teeth are bared. Sounds gurgle in the back of my throat. I am almost standing on the outside watching when it happens.

On the plains of Castile, I bark. I didn't know humans made a noise the way birds of prey caw, cats caterwaul, or coyotes bay. But humans have their noise, and you can't really appreciate the human ululation signifying the will to kill until you've felt it pour out of your very own face. It is a ragged, oscillating sound (Tarzan isn't that far off). Strangely, it's rather high up the register—pubescent, even comical, in its bestial ineptness.

A force sweeps through me and I fly directly at my enemies. My knife is gripped underhanded, and my spear waggles in the air. And then I bark—again and again. It originates somewhere in a sleeping pocket of my solar plexus and screeches through my vocal cords with the force of a childhood vomit. My entire body convulses with explosions: "*La-lulalulaluaaaaaa.*" More or less.

The dogs jerk forward, but the force propelling me toward them won't let me flinch. As with any good bluff, you can't let up on your pose, no matter what. My face is squeezed into a Nordic mask of blood-red fury. I lunge and bark. The effect is a threat that roughly translates: I will slice open your bellies, smear your entrails in this dust and perform grand pliés in the viscera.

And without further linguistic exchange, they signal their comprehension of my remarks by bolting in full ignoble retreat, hiding amid wheat.

My hands are shaking. My pulse, which is usually high with all the work of walking, is racing. The succubae who have haunted me all day redescend, and a new, exacerbated spookiness consumes me. I am carrying on a delightfully stupid but vaguely reassuring conversation with myself when a grand blast of thunder rolls across the plains. The clouds are now in full costume dress, big black tumblers wheeling from left to right across the Castilian stage. They have dropped in altitude, now brushing my hair with static. A sweet metallic aroma fills the air. I vacantly ponder its meaning.

Vast sheets of rain explode from the clouds as I frantically pull out my poncho, logically located at the bottom of my pack. The wet plastic sticks to my skin, and the dripping cowl obstructs my view. I want to see because I need to count. On the horizon, a broad streak of light flares as if someone had flashed a spotlight. It's sheet lightning, well known to be harmless. But I count the seconds—thousand one, thousand two, thousand three, thousand four, thousand five, thousand six. A peal of thunder sounds. I remember my father teaching me this trick when I was a little boy. Each second between the blast of light and the sound of thunder represents a mile. This is part of the lore of storms we learn as children. I am dredging up a good deal of that lore just now.

A jagged white line—*not* sheet lightning—impales the horizon. Thousand one, thousand two, thou...

Not a good sign.

Another flash of light momentarily drains all the color from the landscape. I see this one *hit* the ground—far up the road but inside the field before me. What was that other bit of lore? Lightning strikes the tallest object. My eyes sweep the panorama of endless wheat fields—midget stalks stretching to two feet at best.

I am six foot one. Lore is surfacing unbidden: never stand beneath a tree.

Lightning is just a gathering of static electricity.

Lightning doesn't come down to earth, but actually moves up....

A bolt explodes directly in front of me, maybe fifty yards away. This is a network of bolts—a tick-tack-toe grid of light and heat. Thunder bellows at once. Should I turn around and back away from the storm? Can I outhike a storm? Should I curl in a little ball and try to hide like a wild dog in the wheat? Should I stand still?

I decide to run in a forward direction, and I choose to augment this plan with a bit of heartfelt shrieking and babbling. Encumbered by a pack, this strategy is neither graceful nor effective. I can't scare away lightning like dogs. This really is some kind of message. The dogs failed, so they wheeled out Zeus's old-standard never-fail legendary deus ex machina.

I can't believe that I am going to die out here, struck by lightning. Bolts are now blasting on both sides of me like bombs. I can see them clearly. I can smell them. In my mind, each spot is marked by charred wheat stalks and a modest puff of black smoke. I run for fifteen minutes. Run and scream, to be accurate. Run and scream and hoot and howl and hoo-wee, to be even more accurate.

I am surrounded by illusions. Lightning is exploding at my side. Voices scream in the wet wind. I hear pursuing footsteps. Up ahead, the horizon suddenly telescopes, drawing itself toward me.

As it does, the earth cracks open at the edge, and a small black cross erupts from the muddy ground. Following behind it, a small stone pyramid forces the cross higher until it is clear and visible and lovely—an optical illusion that has probably comforted pilgrims for a millennium. Shortly, an entire church pushes its way up out of the earth and into view. Other buildings crowd around its side and rear up. A town in a valley.

As I turned to go I noticed something moving in the far distance. I knew what it was: I had seen it in movies. It was the swimming headlights of a train refracted in the warm air and smoke, and it was slowly approaching. I had no ticket and there was no one else in the station, so I put out my hand to stop it, and slowly it came into the station and drew to a halt. I was so happy I did not even realise that this was cheating. I smiled at the people in the carriage and sat down. It would take us about half an hour to get to Astorga; it would have taken me a day to walk it. I had placed myself in the company of rogue pilgrims of medieval times who surely must have cheated too.

—Colm Tóibín, *The Sign of the Cross: Travels in Catholic Europe*

The pilgrim's path suddenly plunges into an alley of stone. I can hear the rumble of cattle and the cackle of fowl. Welcome to Hontanas. The rain gathers and sluices through this street, softening the manure into a sludge of slippery offal and freeing pent-up odors. I appreciate their reassuring aromatic complexity, like a glass of red wine. At the church, I run to its wall to try to get out of the downpour. An open doorway across the street reveals four old women playing cards.

"Pilgrim, would you like a sandwich?" one of them offers in Spanish.

"Yes, yes, please, please, yes."

"I will bring you one."

I call out a thank you from under the slight eaves of the church.

"You were caught in the rain," another says.

"Rain!" I blurt in my awkward Spanish. "Beautiful ladies. Rain! Dogs! Death! Birds! Hell! Fear!"—I am capable only of uttering nouns for the moment—"Rain! Yes, rain, but also"—I can't call forth the word for lightning storm—"How do you say in Spanish when light comes down from the sky?"

"*¿Tormentas?*" one of the women answers.

"*¡Tormentas!*" I cry. "Yes, yes, that is the word, isn't it?" A convulsive laughter seizes me. "*Tormentas, sí, sí, tormentas. Tormentas grandes. Muchísimas tormentas.*" I am laughing the laughter of idiots. I can't stop until I am tranquilized by the sight of the old woman carrying food. Half of Spain lies ahead. Another month on foot takes me through the tall meadows of Frómista, across the dead rivers of León, over the craggy hills of Ponferrada, up the alpine mountains of Galicia and then into the comfort of the valley of Santiago. The sandwich is huge—ham and a Spanish omelet on a baguette the size of my arm. I tear into it like a jackal.

Jack Hitt is a contributing editor at Harper's Magazine *and* Lingua Franca, *and writes regularly for* The New York Times Sunday Magazine. *A native of Charleston, South Carolina, he had just reached "the Dantean age of thirty-five" when he decided to walk the 500 miles to Santiago. This story was adapted from his book* Off the Road: A Modern-Day Walk Down the Pilgrim's Route into Spain, *and first appeared in* The New York Times.

✦ ✦ ✦

In Search of Miracles

Sometimes the greatest miracles
are not the most obvious.

THE DAY MY FATHER WAS DIAGNOSED WITH INOPERABLE LUNG cancer, I decided to go and find him a miracle. My family had already spent a good part of that September chasing medical options, and what we discovered was not hopeful. Given the odds, a miracle cure was our best and most reasonable hope. A few weeks earlier, while I lay in a birthing center having my daughter, Grace, my father had been in a hospital across town undergoing biopsies to determine the cause of the spot that had appeared in his mediastinum, which connects the lungs. Eight years before, he'd given up smoking after forty years of two packs a day and had been diagnosed with emphysema. Despite yearly bouts of pneumonia and periodic shortness of breath, he was a robust sixty-seven-year-old, robust enough to take care of my son, Sam, to cook, and to clean the house he and mother had lived in for their forty-seven years of marriage.

We are a superstitious family, skeptical of medicine and believers in omens, potions, and the power of prayer. The week that the first X-ray showed a spot on my father's lung, three of us had dreams that could only be read as portents. I dreamed of my maternal grandmother, Mama Rose. My cousin, whose own father had died when she was only two and who had grown up next door to us with my father stepping in as a surrogate parent for her, dreamed of our great-uncle Rum. My father dreamed of his father for the first time since he'd died in 1957. All of these ghosts had one thing in common—they were happy. A few days later, my father developed a fever as the two of us ate souvlakia at the annual Greek Festival. The X-ray they took that night in the emergency room was sent to his regular doctor. Nine months pregnant, I arrived at my parents' house the next morning with a bag of bagels. My father stood at the back door with his news. "The X-ray showed something," he said dismissively. "They need to do a few more tests."

For the next month he underwent CAT scans and –oscopies of all sorts, until, finally, a surgeon we hardly knew shouted across the hospital waiting room: "Where are the Woods?" I stood, cradling my newborn daughter. "Hood," I said. "Over here." He walked over to us and without any hesitation said, "He's got cancer. A fair-sized tumor that's inoperable. We can give him chemo, buy a little time. Your doctor will give you the details." He had taken the time to give my father the same information, even though as he was coming out of anesthesia it had seemed like a nightmare to him.

When someone died in our family, my father pulled out his extra-large bottle of Jack Daniels. It had gotten us through the news of the death of my cousin's husband, my own brother's accidental death in 1982, and the recent deaths of two of my own forty-something cousins, one from melanoma and one from AIDS. That late September afternoon, my father pulled out the bottle for his own grim prognosis. As the day wore on, we'd gotten more news: only an aggressive course of chemotherapy and radiation could help, and even then the help would be short lived, if it came at all. "Taxol," the pulmonary specialist had told us, "has given some people up to eighteen months." But the way he bowed his head after he said it made me realize that eighteen months was not only the best we could hope for, but a long shot. My sister-in-law, a doctor, too, was harsher. "Six months after diagnosis is the norm," she said.

Sitting in the kitchen that once held my mother and her ten siblings, their parents and grandparents, every day for supper, I did some quick math. Was it possible that the man sitting across from me sipping Jack Daniels would not be alive at Easter? A WASP from Indiana, he had married into a large, loud Italian family and somehow become more Italian than some of his in-laws. At Easter, he was the one who made the dozen loaves of sweetbread, the fresh cheese and frittatas. He shaped wine biscuits into crosses and made *pizzeles* that were lighter than any my aunts produced. At six-foot-one and over two hundred pounds, cracking jokes about the surgeon, he did not look like someone about to die. He was not someone I was going to let die. If medical science could only give him a year and a half tops, then there was only one real hope for a cure. "There's a place in New Mexico with miracle dirt," I announced. "I'm going to go and get you some." "Well," my father said with typical understatement, "I guess I can use all the help I can get."

Perhaps for some people the notion of seeking a miracle cure is tomfoolery, futile, or even a sign of pathetic desperation. The simplest definition of a miracle that I know is the one that C. S. Lewis proposes in his book *Miracles*: an interference with nature by supernatural power. But even that definition implies something that many people do not believe—that there is something other than nature, the thing that Lewis calls the supernatural. Without that other power, there can be no miracles. For those who cannot buy into the notion of this other power, miracle healing belongs back in the Dark Ages, or at least in a time before the advent of modern medicine. To believe in miracles, and certainly to go and look for one, you must put aside science and rely only on faith.

For me, that leap was not a difficult one. My great-grandmother, who died when I was six, healed people of a variety of ailments with prayer and household items, such as silver dollars and Mazola oil. The source of a headache was always believed to be the evil eye and was treated by my great-grandmother by pouring water into a soup bowl, adding a few drops of oil, then making circles on the afflicted person's palm while muttering in Italian. Curing nosebleeds involved making the sign of the cross on the person's forehead. Around our hometown of West Warwick, Rhode Island, she was famous for her ability to cure sciatica. In order to do this, my great-grandmother had to go to the person's house on the night of a full moon and spend the night, so she could work her miracle at dawn the next day. There was a time when she had a waiting list for her services

Most miracles occur through the intercession of a saint. If one wants a favor, one prays to a particular saint to act on one's behalf. My great-grandmother was no different. She had prayers to various saints to help find lost objects, answer questions, heal. Her prayers to Saint Anthony could answer important questions, such as, Will I have a baby? Does he love me? Will my mother be all right? The prayer was in Italian. She would go into a room, alone, and ask the question. If she was able to repeat the prayer three times quickly and without hesitation or errors, the answer was a favorable one. But it the prayer "came slow" or she couldn't remember the words, the outlook was dire.

The legend goes that my great-grandmother learned all of these things as a young girl in Italy. She was a shepherdess on the hills of a town outside Naples, near a convent. The nuns took a liking to her and passed on their knowledge. Her faith was sealed years later when my grandmother came down with scarlet fever. The doctors said she would not live through the night. My great-grandmother bundled up her daughter and walked all the miles to the convent. There, the nuns prayed in earnest to the Virgin Mary to spare this child. By morning, she was completely well except for one thing: her long dark curls fell off at the height of her fever. My great-grandmother took her daughter's hair and gave it as an offering of thanks to the Virgin Mary. When my grandmother's hair grew back, it was red, and it remained red until the day she died, seventy years later.

I grew up with this story, and others like it. I never questioned it. Like the story of the day I was born or the day my parents met, I accepted it as fact. But when I shared the story with a friend recently, he said at its conclusion, "But, of course, that's not true." Startled, I asked him what he meant. "Why, that never happened," he said, laughing. "It couldn't happen. Maybe her fever simply broke or maybe the doctors thought she was sicker than she was. But she wasn't cured by the Virgin Mary, and her hair probably just turned more red as she got older." Therein lies an important distinction between one who believes in miracles and one who doesn't. A believer accepts the miracle as truth, no questions asked. Although I didn't accept my friend's explanations of our family lore, I also knew I could not dissuade him from believing them.

That was how I came to take my ten-week-old daughter an hour northwest of Santa Fe, New Mexico, up into the Sangre de Cristo Mountains, to the little town of Chimayo and its El Santuario. The area had been a holy ground for the Tewa Indians, a place where they believed fire and water had belched forth and subsided into a sacred pool. Eventually, the water had evaporated, leaving only a puddle of mud. The Tewa went there to eat the mud when they wanted to be cured. Sometime around the year 1810, during Holy Week, a man called Don Bernardo Abeyta is said to have been performing the Stations of the Cross in the hills at Chimayo. Suddenly, he saw light springing up from one of the slopes. As he got close to it, he realized the light was coming from the ground itself. He began to dig with his hands and there he found a crucifix. He ran to the Santa Cruz church, which was in a nearby town, and the priest and parishioners went with him and took the crucifix back to their church. The next morning, the crucifix was missing. Somehow it had returned to the place it was found. The same thing happened two more times, so they decided to build a chapel—El Santuario—at the spot. This chapel contains the hole, called *el pocito* (the well)—with the healing dirt.

Like many sites that claim miracles, Chimayo is difficult to reach. Grace and I flew from Boston to Albuquerque, changing planes en route. There, we met my longtime friend Matt, rented a car, and drove for over an hour to Santa Fe. The next morning we rode into the mountains on what is called the High Road to

Taos, along curving roads covered with snow. Signs are few, and even getting to El Santuario requires a certain amount of faith. Along the way, we had to stop more than once so I could breast-feed the baby. Despite all of this, I never once grew discouraged. Before I left, my father had hugged me and said, "Go get that dirt, sweetheart." No matter what, I would get it for him and bring it safely home.

Chimayo is called the Lourdes of America because of all the healings that have been associated with it. When one thinks of miracle healing sites, Lourdes is probably the place that first comes to mind. If I hadn't already taken a serendipitous trip there fifteen years earlier, it is probably where I would have gone. In 1982, when I was working as a flight attendant, I was called to work a trip one day while I was on standby. It wasn't until I hung up that I realized the only destination I had been given was "Europe." This was unusual.

I was twenty-five years old and at a point in my life where I had abandoned many of my childhood ways. I had moved from my small hometown in Rhode Island to live in Manhattan. I was working at a job that was not usually associated with someone who had graduated sixth in her high school class and with high honors from college. Instead of the young lawyers I had been steadily dating, I was now madly in love with an unemployed actor. And, perhaps most important, I had given up not just on the Catholicism with which I was raised, but on religion altogether. Like many people I knew at that time, I liked to say that I believed in God, but not in organized religion. The truth is I didn't think much about God back then, except in sporadic furtive prayers for my immediate needs: *Don't let me be late, Please have him call, Help me decide what to do.*

When I arrived at Kennedy Airport and looked at my flight schedule, I was delighted to see that the first part of the trip in-volved deadheading—flying as a passenger—to Paris that evening and staying overnight. The next day, at Charles De Gaulle Airport, I spotted several other flight attendants waiting for the same Air France flight. They all looked glum. After introductions, I asked if any of them knew where we were headed. "Didn't they tell you?" one of them moaned. "We're going to Lourdes!"

It was Easter week, when upward of a hundred thousand people go to Lourdes, and the streets were clogged with people with varying degrees of illness and deformity, nurses and nuns in starched white uniforms, tourists with cameras snapping pictures of the dying prone on their stretchers, the cripples atrophied in their wheelchairs, the blind with their white canes. But none of this prepared me for what was to come.

It took us almost four hours to board the flight back because of all the wheelchairs, stretchers, and medical equipment. Already the doctor on board had administered emergency care to a dying man. A mother told me that her daughter, seventeen years old and blind, had a rare disease in which her brain was destroying itself. "There's nothing to be done," she whispered.

I had arrived in Lourdes on a late night train and discovered to my horror that all the monetary exchanges were closed. This was in the days before ATM machines and certainly before I had the wherewithal to obtain a credit card. I was a rebellious student intent on debunking the miraculous aura of Lourdes, and clearly I was not being welcomed by the higher powers. I made my way to the Grotto and found that it was still crowded though the hour was late. Despite its beauty I found it vaguely repellent, as if something very sweet emanated bad odors. I went outside and took solace from the river and the night sky. Not being a particularly devout pilgrim, the Virgin repaid me in kind, for I spent a miserable night on a stranger's front porch and took the first train out of town.
—Sean O'Reilly, "Night Train"

"This was our last chance." The girl sat beside her, staring blankly from eyes the light blue of faded denim. When I placed a meal tray in front of a sixty-year-old man suffering from multiple sclerosis, he grunted, gathered all his strength, and threw it back at me, his eyes ablaze with anger. "It's not you," his wife apologized, her head bent to hide the tears that streamed down her cheeks. "He's angry at everyone."

I sought out the priest who had led a group of a hundred people from Philadelphia. "Do you believe that any of these people will be cured by a miracle?" I demanded. I was young and jaded and arrogant, a stranger to death or illness.

"A miracle," he said, "is usually instantaneous. But some of these people have things that it will take X-rays and tests to see if they are cured."

I looked at the young girl with the brain disease. Certainly then she had not had a miracle.

"The church has physicians," he explained, "who study alleged miracles." He told me about the process, how a miracle case must be proved by a medical history and the records and notes of everyone who has treated the person. Scientific evidence such as X-rays and biopsies are examined. "And," he added, with what I interpreted as skepticism, "the cure must be a total cure. No relapses or recurrences."

"How many of these instantaneous cures have happened at Lourdes?"

He averted my eyes. "I think three," he said. "But you're missing the point," he said. "This is all they have left to do. Miracles come in unexpected ways."

It seemed to me a sad journey. Especially when out of the approximately forty cases a year investigated by the Consulta Medica, only about fifteen are deemed miracles. (The Consulta Medica is the Catholic Church's official body for investigating miracle claims.) Such a statistic in 1982 would have made me even angrier that these people had gone so far, with such hope, only to be disappointed. But by the time I went to Chimayo, I was a different person, and the statistic actually bolstered my belief that the dirt there might cure my father.

I was no longer the skeptical, arrogant young woman who had left Lourdes in a self-righteous huff. Just three months after my trip there, my brother died unexpectedly, and I found myself wanting to find faith somewhere, to believe in something more solid than my fleeting encounters with Buddhism, the Quakers, Ethical Culture, and the Unitarian Church. Over the years between then and my father's illness, I'd been married and divorced, suffered a miscarriage, lost jobs, changed careers, remarried, given birth to two children, and moved back to my home state of Rhode Island. And I'd returned to church, though not the Catholic Church of my childhood.

When I arrived at El Santuario, I had the fear of my father's death to motivate me and an open heart, a willingness to believe that a cure—a miracle—was possible. Matt had come with me to bring back dirt for his friend, who was dying from Hodgkin's disease. Not even the signs posted everywhere—NOT RESPONSIBLE FOR THEFT—could deter us. Here was a small adobe church with a dirt parking lot, a religious gift store, and a burrito stand called Leona's, which was written up as the best burrito place in New Mexico in all of my guidebooks.

We proceeded under an archway and through a courtyard where a wooden crucifix stood, then into the church where the altar was adorned with brightly painted pictures by the artist known as the Chili Painter. But we hadn't come to see folk art. We had come for a miracle. So we quickly went into the low-ceilinged room off the church in search of the *pocito*. What we found first was a testimony to all the cures attributed to this place. The walls were lined with crutches and canes, candles, and flowers, statues of saints, all offerings of thanks for healings. Despite the signs asking people not to leave notes because of the fire danger around the lit candles, and not to write on anything except the guest book, the offerings had letters tucked into their corners. One statue had a sonogram picture pinned to the saint's cloak. Another had a letter in Spanish "Thank you for the recovery of our little Luis. Our baby boy is now well. *Mil gracias.*"

Against one wall of this room sits a shrine to the Santo Niño, who is believed to walk about the country at night healing sick children and wearing out his shoes in the process. As a result, an offering of shoes is given to him whenever a child is healed. The shrine at Chimayo is full of children's shoes, handmade knit booties, delicate silk christening shoes. Roses and letters of thanks adorn the statue, which is seated and holds a basket of food and a gourd to carry water.

In this small room, I began to tremble. I felt I was in a holy place, a place that held possibility. I had not felt that sense of possibility in the hospital and doctors' waiting rooms that had dominated my life these past few months. Even when a surgeon promised to remove my father's tumor if "the sucker will only shrink some," I didn't get the sense of peace I had as I stood surrounded by these testimonies to faith. One, from Ida P. of Chicago, stated that her husband still had six more radiation treatments to go when, on a Sunday, she brought him the dirt. On Monday the tumor was gone.

Ducking our heads, Matt and I entered the even smaller room that housed the *pocito*. It was just a hole in the dirt floor. The walls were covered with offerings, including a note that said: "Within this small room resides the stillness of souls that have discovered peace. Listen to their silence. JK, New York." Matt and I knelt in front of the *pocito* and scooped the dirt with our bare hands into the Ziplock bags we had brought. I cannot say what Matt was thinking as he dug. But I had one prayer that I had repeated over and over: Please let my father's tumor go away.

Unlike other sites attributed to miracle healings, Chimayo is not associated with any particular saint. At Lourdes, people believe that Saint Bernadette intercedes on their behalf. Four years before my visit to Chimayo, I went on a long weekend trip to Montreal, Canada. One of my stops was a visit to Saint Joseph's Basilica, where a priest named Brother André was said to have healed people through prayer and oil from a particular lamp. The cures were frequent and often spontaneous. For the year 1916 alone, 439 cures were recorded. "I do not cure," Brother André said. "Saint Joseph cures."

But I did not visit Saint Joseph's Basilica for a cure. I went because the relic displayed there is a particularly gruesome one:

Brother André's heart. I've always attributed my love of the more grotesque aspects of Catholicism to my Italian upbringing. My memories of my first trip to Rome are dominated by the various bones and pieces of cloth that churches display. The notion of viewing a heart was especially appealing. However, once I entered the ornate basilica and viewed the heart in its case, I decided I should also see the place where people go to pray to Brother André for a miracle. The walls of this room, too, were lined with offerings, the canes and braces of those who have been healed.

In many ways, I was even more of a cynic than I had been when I'd visited Lourdes. The death of my brother and the emotional havoc it wreaked on my family had left me in a spiritual vacuum from which I had not yet recovered. More recently, a love affair had gone bad, and I was questioning not just my spiritual beliefs, but also my ability to trust and love again.

That day in Montreal, I was not in need of a physical healing, but I had been in turmoil for several months, a turmoil that it did not seem would have an ending anytime soon. For someone who had entered the basilica on a lark—to view a human heart—I was strangely moved by the place, and by the people around me who knelt and prayed. Their conviction was obvious, and in many ways I envied their ability to believe in the power of prayer, or saints, or miracles. I knelt, too, and thought of all the events that had led me to this dark time I was living. At its core was a betrayal in love, a broken promise, a broken heart. A decision—whether to trust this person again—seemed unreachable. I replayed the past months like someone watching a home movie, and then I asked for resolution.

Resolution came. Not that day, or even that month, but, many months later. I would not even now claim that the resolution came from the moments I spent praying in Saint Joseph's Basilica. What I gained there was a peace of mind, a calming of the soul, without which I could not have reached a decision. Perhaps more important is that I also began my journey back to faith through that visit. Although the Catholic Church excludes such healings from consideration for miracles, as they do the cures of any mental disorders or diseases that have a high rate of natural remission, I believe a healing of some sort began there. Three years later, as I stood in El Santuario de Chimayo hoping for a miracle of the physical sort, I remembered that day in Montreal and the feeling that overtook me there. As WK from California wrote after her own visit to Chimayo: "It didn't cure me, but then it's God's will. Peace of mind is sometimes better."

Buoyant from our time spent at El Santuario, Matt and I went off to find one of the weavers that live in and around Chimayo. Carefully following the signs for Ortegas, we ended up at a small store that sold carvings and local folk art, not rugs. "Is this Ortegas?" we asked, confused, when we entered. Matt was as certain as I that we had followed the signs exactly and turned in where they pointed. The ponytailed man behind the counter, Tobias, smiled at us. "You've been to get the dirt," he said. Later, Matt and I would both comment on how gentle his face was. Perhaps it was this gentleness that led me to tell him why I had come and the particulars of my father's disease. He nodded. "He'll be cured," he said. "I've seen it myself, the healings."

He told us the story of a couple who had arrived at his door— "like you two!" The man was grumpy, angry at his wife for insisting they come all this way from Los Angeles when her doctors had told her a cure was hopeless. Sympathetic toward the wife's plight, Tobias invited them to dinner. Reluctantly, the man agreed. As they sat eating on the patio of a nearby restaurant, a strange light began to emit from the woman's breast. Soft at first, it grew brighter and larger until it seemed to encompass her entire chest, like a cocoon. Then it slowly dissipated. It was the skeptical husband who spoke first. "Did anyone else see that?" Each of them had. "My tumor is gone," the wife said confidently. Although Tobias did not know what kind of cancer the woman was suffering from, he was certain then that it was breast cancer, and that she had been cured. He was right on both accounts. Back in California, baffled doctors pronounced her completely free of breast cancer.

"It works," Tobias said.

Matt asked him how, with thousands of people visiting the *pocito*, the dirt was never depleted.

"Oh," Tobias said, "the caretaker refills it every day. Then the priest blesses it."

This mundane refilling disappointed me. The story I had heard about the dirt was that it replenished itself in some inexplicable way.

"It's not the dirt," Tobias told us. "It's the energy of all the people who come and pray into that *pocito* that makes miracles happen."

Of course, there is no real explanation for what makes miracles happen. But there are plenty of explanations that attempt to disprove them. Just as my friend gave many reasons why my grandmother lived through her bout of scarlet fever, skeptics use scientific, historical, and geographic data to explain away "miracles." Simply put, people either believe or don't. In my own search to understand miracles, I came across books and articles in support of each side.

Joe Nickell, the senior research fellow for the Committee for the Scientific Investigation of Claims of the Paranormal, has written an entire book debunking everything from stigmatas to the Shroud of Turin. On miracle healings, he believes that some serious illnesses, such as cancer and multiple sclerosis, can undergo spontaneous remission, in which they go away completely or abate for long periods of time. Nickell also cites misdiagnoses, misread CAT scans, and misunderstandings as explanations for miracle healings. He reports that as of 1984, 6,000 miracles had been attributed to the water at Lourdes but only 64 of those had been authenticated as miraculous. Those 64 miracles, he claims, were most likely spontaneous remission, as in the case of a woman who was "cured" of blindness, only to discover she was suffering from multiple sclerosis and the disease had actually temporarily abated.

In response to such skepticism, Dr. Raffaello Cortesini, a specialist in heart and liver transplants and the president of the Consulta Medica, told Kenneth L. Woodward, the religion editor of *Newsweek* magazine and the author of *Making Saints*, "I myself, if I did not do these consultations, would never believe what I read. You don't understand how fantastic, how incredible—how well-documented—theses cases are. They are more incredible than historical romances. Science fiction is nothing by comparison." Believers in miracles do not even need such substantiation.

Still, advances in medical science have made the number of accredited miracles decrease over the years. Pope John Paul II, in his address to a symposium of members of Consulta Medica and the Medical Committee of Lourdes in 1988, agreed that medicine has helped to understand some of these miraculous cures, but, he added, "it remains true that numerous healings constitute a fact which has its explanation only in the order of faith...." Because proving miracle cures has become so difficult, the Church has lightened its requirements on miracles for canonization. It is true that historically, miracles were much more commonplace. In the thirteenth century, Saint Louis of Anjou was responsible for a well-documented 66 miracles, including raising twelve people from the dead. Obviously, today's doctors might easily disprove not only many of Louis of Anjou's miracles but also a good number of those that came before and after him. That still leaves us with the ones that no one—not even Joe Nickell—can explain that have occurred since the advent of modern medicine.

Other skeptics point to geography as a factor in alleged miracles. Since many miracles depend on the intervention of saints, and since most saints are European, a high number of miracles occur there. Certain countries, such as Italy, boast more miracles than others. Physicians from Italy—southern Italy in particular—believe so strongly in miracles that they are more willing to accept a cure as miraculous. The culture there is such that saints and miracles are a part of everyday life. As I drove through southern Italy recently I was struck by how common statues of saints were. They appeared on roadsides, hanging from cliffs, in backyards, on city street corners, virtually everywhere. Almost always there were offerings at the statue's feet, flowers, bread, letters. This was where my own ancestors came from, and I can attest to our family's openness about letting miracles into our lives.

But other cultures share this openness, this willingness to recognize the miraculous. Rather than disproving miracles, I wonder if it doesn't support their existence. It was Augustine who claimed that all natural things were filled with miracles. He referred to the world itself as "the miracle of miracles." I saw this acceptance of daily, small miracles when I visited Mexico City during the Feast of the Virgin of Guadalupe. It was there, in 1553, that a local man named Juan Diego, while walking outdoors, heard birds singing, saw a bright light on top of a hill, and heard someone calling his name. He climbed the hill and saw a young girl, radiant in a golden mist, who claimed to be the virgin. She told him she wanted a church built on that spot. When Juan Diego told the bishop what he had seen, the bishop asked him to go back and demand a sign as proof that this was really the Virgin. When he returned, the apparition made roses miraculously bloom, even though it was December. Convinced, the bishop allowed a cathedral to be built there. More than 10 million people annually visit the shrine in Mexico City, making it the most popular site, after the Vatican, in the Catholic world.

Although it was an impressive sight to behold when I made the walk to the Basilica of the Virgin of Guadalupe along with people, many on their knees, who had come from all over Mexico, that spectacle of adoration was not what struck me about Mexico and its relationship to the miraculous. Rather, it was the way the culture as a whole viewed miracles that impressed me. Street vendors everywhere sold *milagros*, the small silver charms that mean, literally, "little miracles." The charms take the shape of body parts—arms, legs, hearts—and are pinned to saints in churches, to the inside of people's own jackets, everywhere. When I told a vendor that my mother had recently broken her hand, he gave me a *milagro* in the shape of a hand, at no charge.

Throughout Mexico one can also view *retablos*, paintings made on wood or tin that request favors for everything from curing someone of pneumonia to asking that children not fall out of windows or that a woman have a safe childbirth or that a house not catch on fire. Although many churches have glorious collections of *retablos*, these painting also adorn the walls of shops and homes, humble requests for miracles large and small. "Oh, yes," a friend of mine who lives in San Miguel de Allende told me, "here in Mexico it is a miracle if someone's oxen do a good job or if it doesn't rain on a special day. Miracles happen every day here."

As if to prove her point, we encountered one such miracle the night before I left Mexico City. Several of us climbed into a cab to go to a restaurant, but the driver was unfamiliar with the address. Everyone studied the map and planned the route, but still we couldn't find the street. Several times we stopped and asked direction. We still couldn't find it. After forty minutes and yet another set of directions, the cab came to a screeching halt. "We're here!" our driver exclaimed happily. "It's a miracle!"

Perhaps, then, part of understanding what a miracle is comes from one's openness to the possibility that they exist and occur regularly. It could be argued that one has to be Catholic to have this ability, since predominantly Catholic countries and cultures claim to have such an attitude. There are many Catholics who would agree that they believe in miracles simply because of their religion. Since I haven't actively participated in Catholicism since I was a young teenager, I would not have credited Catholicism with my own belief in the miraculous. But in retrospect, the roots of that belief must be in my Catholic and Italian upbringing, a combination that certainly indoctrinated me into believing of a general kind.

In fact, the connection between miracles and healing stems largely from the miracles attributed to Jesus. One could, then, broaden the definition of who more readily accepts miracles to include all Christians. Yet I suppose that someone could believe in miracles without believing in the teachings of Christ, or even without believing in God. Conversely, one can believe in God without believing in miracles. What seems most likely is what Kenneth Woodward explains: "To believe in miracles one must be able to accept gifts, freely bestowed and altogether unmerited." Once one has the ability to do that, it is a small leap to then accept that these gifts have come because someone has intervened on your behalf. Woodward goes on to say that "in a graced world, such things happen all the time." If one presumes that the world

is without grace then one cannot accept any gifts, especially those
that come from prayer.

When I made my pilgrimage to Chimayo, I had reached a
point in my life where I believed in a graced world. I believed that
the birth of my son was miraculous, that the love I shared with
my husband was a gift, as was my ability to shape words into
meaningful stories. Of course I credited hard work, talent, and
character, too. But I had come to believe in Augustine's view of
the world as the "miracle of miracles." When I arrived back in
Rhode Island with the dirt from El Santuario, I felt that anything
could happen.

Twenty-four hours after my father held the dirt, he was in respiratory failure and was rushed to the hospital by ambulance. It was
Christmas Eve, three months after his diagnosis. Although it would
have been a crisis of faith, quite the opposite happened. I simply
believed that he would survive. What happened next surprised me
more than his bad turn of health.

While he was in the hospital, his recovery from what turned out
to be pneumonia deemed unlikely, his doctor performed a CAT
scan, assuming the tumor had grown. My father had only had two
treatments of chemo and he needed five before there was any hope
of the tumor shrinking. Visiting him, I asked if he was prepared for
the CAT scan.

"Oh, no," he said with great confidence, "the tumor is gone."
"Gone?" I said. He nodded. "I sat here and watched as cancer left
my body. It was black and evil-looking and came out of my chest
like sparks, agitated and angry." I was willing to believe the tumor
might disappear, but such a physical manifestation was more than
I had considered. True, Tobias had told us of a light enveloping a
sick woman's chest, and it had seemed miraculous. But here was
my father, a practical, no-nonsense Midwesterner, telling me a
story that hinted of science fiction.

The next day my mother called me from the hospital. "Ann," she
said, awed, "the CAT scan shows that the tumor has completely
gone. It's disappeared." In the background I heard my father chuck-

ling, and then my mother made the doctor repeat what he had said when he walked into the room with the results: "It's a miracle."

Here is the part where I would like to say that my father came home, tumor-free, cancer-free, miraculously cured. The part where I would like to tell you that, well again, he traveled with me to New Mexico, to El Santuario de Chimayo, to leave his CAT scan results in the little low-ceilinged room beside the baby shoes and notes of thanks and crutches and braces and statues and candles.

Instead, my father went home, had one more dose of Taxol, and the next day was once again rushed by ambulance to the hospital in respiratory failure. He spent almost two weeks in intensive care, diagnosed with double pneumonia. From there, he was moved onto the cardiac ward for a week and then into rehab. Weakened by his near-death illness, he moved around using a walker and had no memory of his days in

In the Western world, we believe that scientific truth lies in the objective observation of events—or, as it is commonly put, that "seeing is believing." But it must be obvious that there is a great deal of confusion in this area. After all, almost everyone believes that the Earth goes round the sun, and we are fairly well convinced that the solar system is on the outer edge of a spiral arm of a huge galaxy, despite the fact that most of us haven't seen these things. We accept them not because they have been demonstrated to us, but because we believe they could be. In other words, someone has been able to convince us of their existence. Most of us take this to mean that their existence has been "proven." We believe science advances by demonstrating the existence of previously unknown or unexplained phenomena, when in fact it reformulates our view of the world in a way which allows us to accept them.

—George Simon, "Some Epistemological Considerations in the Study of Non-Verbal Communication" the ICU. My family remembered it all too well, however: the all-night vigils by his side, sleeping on chairs, waiting for doctors and tests and change. Once he was in rehab, his doctor repeated the CAT scan, suspecting a recurrence of the tumor. But there was none, and a date for his release was set.

Two days before he was to come home, he spiked a fever and acquired a cough that proved to be the onset of yet another bout of pneumonia, this one a fungal pneumonia common in patients undergoing chemotherapy, and usually fatal. The doctors prepared us for the worst. "He will never leave the hospital," his pulmonary specialist told us. His health failing, my father instructed us on how to prepare the Easter breakfast specialties that he had been in charge of for the last twenty-five years—how to turn a frittata so it doesn't break, the secret to making light *pizzeles*.

The day before Easter he began to die. His oxygen supply was so low that his legs grew blue and mottled. A priest was called and administered the last rites, now known as the sacrament of the sick. But when the priest walked away, I grabbed my father's hand and sought a miracle yet again: "Daddy," I said, "please come back. For me and Sam and Grace." At the sound of my children's names, my father struggled not only to open his eyes, but to breathe, a deep life-sustaining breath. By that evening, he was sitting up. "I thought I was a goner there," he joked. Easter morning he told my mother that her frittata was too dry. I stayed with him all day. We watched a movie that night, and then he went to sleep.

The doctor suspected the cancer was back and had spread to my father's brain. He did CAT scans on his bones, lungs, and head. But my father remained tumor-free and cancer-free. Despite this, he died a week later, from the pneumonia he'd caught because of a compromised immune system. More than once since then I have found myself wondering not *if* I got a miracle or not, but whether I prayed for the wrong thing. Should I have bent over the *pocito* and asked for my father to live rather than for the tumor to go away? What I am certain of is this: I got exactly what I prayed for on that December afternoon at El Santuario de Chimayo.

✳

Around the world, at Lourdes and Fatima, on the Greek island of Tínos and in a municipality called Esquipulas on the far eastern part of Guatemala, in Montreal and Chimayo, people are making pilgrimages, asking for miracles to save their lives or the lives of their loved ones. At least, that is what they believe they want, and they will settle for nothing less. After my father died, I still wanted to find someone whose miracle had happened, who had prayed for God to spare their loved one, and for God to have answered.

In my search I traveled to the remote Italian town of San Giovanni Rotondo on the Monte Gargano, the "spur" of the Italian boot that divides the plains of Apulia from the Adriatic Sea. There, a Capuchin monk known as Padre Pio is said to have performed miraculous cures, even after his death in 1968. No ordinary man, Padre Pio had the stigmata, the gift of transverberation (a wound in his side like the one Jesus had), and the ability to bilocate—to be in two places at the same time.

On our way from Naples to San Giovanni Rotondo, an all-day car ride through mountains and rugged terrain, I read the story of Padre Pio aloud to my husband and our eight- and four-year-old. My husband kept rolling his eyes. More than once he whispered to me, "The guy was a kook." But when I'd finished, I asked the children if they believed that Padre Pio was capable of everything the book said. Did they believe he could heal people, too? "Oh, yes!" they both said without hesitation. He was, they concluded, a very special person.

It was a brutally cold March afternoon when we arrived at the cathedral there. The wind blew at over fifty miles an hour. But still the church was packed. I made my way downstairs to Padre Pio's tomb, where the kneelers around it were full of pilgrims with offerings of roses. A father stood beside his young son, who sat hunched and twisted in a wheelchair. As they prayed, the father lovingly stroked the boy's cheek. Watching them, I was convinced that the boy would not walk out of here, leaving his wheelchair behind. I did not believe that the boy would ever walk. But rather than feeling anger at this, as I had years earlier at Lourdes, I felt a sense of peace, a certainty that the boy and his father would leave here spiritually stronger, that they would somehow have the courage to deal with the disease the boy had been given.

True, Padre Pio has been given credit for many miracles. In one, a young girl was born without pupils in her eyes. Her grandmother prayed to Padre Pio without any results. A nun urged her to make a pilgrimage from her small town to San Giovanni Rotondo. There, the monk touched the girl's eyes, and she could see, but she still had no pupils. As in all places where miracles are said to happen, the legends of the healing are whispered among those who go. They are written about in the small brochures one can buy for a few dollars at the church. But it is only the hopeful, the desperate, who crowd around the water, the dirt, the heart, the tomb.

As I stood to leave Padre Pio's tomb, a middle-aged man and his mother hurried into the room. The woman held a statue of the Virgin Mary, an offering. But what I saw on their faces was a look that I recognized too well, a look I wish I was not familiar with. They wore the shocked and grief-stricken expressions of those who know they are about to lose someone they love. Perhaps they had just received the news. Or perhaps the person had taken a turn for the worse. They had come here because the doctors had told them there was nothing else that could be done. It was a matter of days or weeks or months. The only thing left to do was ask for a miracle.

Despite the fact that I am a woman who is firmly rooted in the physical world, practical and realistic, and skeptical about many things in life at the end of the twentieth century, I still traveled across the country with my newborn daughter, believing I could bring home a miracle for my dying father. Almost a year to the day that my father died, I went back to El Santuario de Chimayo. Father Roca, who has been the parish priest there for forty years, talked to me in his tiny office inside the church. I had written to him months earlier and told him my story. In person, he is a man who dispenses smiles and stories as easily as holy water; several people came in while I was there and, without missing a beat, he blessed their medals and crucifixes, sprinkling holy water, murmuring prayers.

"I have reread your letter many times," he told me. "I am so happy for your family." Thinking he was confused, I said, "But my father died." Father Roca shrugged. "It was God's will. The tumor went away, yes?" I nodded. "Do you know who came here one month before he died? Cardinal Bernadin. From Chicago. He came here and asked me to take him to where the dirt was. I led him to the *pocito* and then left. Fifteen minutes later he emerged, smiling, at peace. 'I got what I came for,' he said." "He wasn't cured," I said. Father Roca smiled. "I know."

I spent about twenty minutes with Father Roca. He told me about the crucifix that was found here. He told me about the miracles he had personally witnessed: the woman who was so sick that her son had to carry her to the *pocito* but who walked out on her own; the young man who came to pray en route to throwing himself off the mountain in despair, but after praying at the *pocito*, decided to return to his wife and baby. To Father Roca, the miracles of El Santuario de Chimayo are not just physical. Rather, they are miracles of inner transformation. "There is," he told me, "something very special about this place."

Later, I returned to the small room with the offerings, and the smaller room with the *pocito* that the caretaker refilled every day. I prayed there, a prayer of thanks for the miracles that had come my way since I'd last visited Chimayo: good health, the love of my children and my husband, the closeness of my family, and, finally, the courage to accept what had come my way. If someone at the shrine on my first visit had told me the miracle I would receive was peace of mind, I would have been angry. But miracles come in many forms, both physical and spiritual. Before I left El Santuario, I again removed a Ziploc bag from by pocket and filled it with dirt. Back at home, my aunt had recently been diagnosed with lung cancer. She needed a miracle, too.

Ann Hood is the author of seven novels including Somewhere off the Coast of Maine, Waiting to Vanish, Places to Stay the Night, *and* Ruby. *She has also written numerous short stories, essays, articles, and the non-fiction book* Do Not Go Gentle, *which is based on her essay "In Search of Miracles." She lives in Providence, Rhode Island.*

✦ ✦ ✦

Darshan with Mother Meera

*The unintended pilgrimage can be
the best journey of all.*

ALEXANDER HAD A SURPRISE FOR ME. SHORTLY AFTER MY ARRIVAL
in Paris, he informed me that we would be stopping en route to
India to visit a woman he knew in Germany.

"Who is she?" I asked.

"The less you know, the better," he said.

It's a testament to how completely I'd put myself in Alexander's
hands that I let it rest at that.

In the meantime, Alexander showed me his odd Parisian life,
which surpassed in Proustian detail the one he had described in his
novel. There was the miniscule jewel-box flat in Saint-Sulpice,
filled with Russian icons, Hindu sculpture, incense, and clutter;
nightly dinners with millionaires and baronesses (once, when the
buzzer rang, he actually said, "Oh shit, it's the empress of the Holy
Roman Empire," and it was); long, slow walks across the Seine to
the haunted Place Georges Cain; drunken dinners at the Cafetière;
visits to the Indian collection at the Musée Guillemet; strolls
through the Tuileries to watch the queers weave in and out of
bushes in various states of undress.

I was impressed, and slightly confused, by Alexander's mixture
of mysticism and worldliness. When I asked him how he could be

so wild *and* on a spiritual path he reminded me not to be fooled by appearances. He assured me that the sacred and profane are all the same in the eyes of God, that it is all part of the same feast. Hungry to absorb what I could of this new outlook, overjoyed to be free of my life in New York, I took Alexander at his word, and was swept along by the whirlwind of his passion with absolutely no idea what would happen next.

We took a train to Frankfurt and arrived at twilight in the non-descript village of Thalheim, dominated by a church steeple just like a thousand others in the German countryside. Herbert, the huge, bespectacled man who met us at the train station, drove us to a modest house overgrown with vines and warned us not to talk as we entered. *Darshan*, whatever that was, had already begun.

The Baal Shem Tov, a Hasidic master who lived 200 years ago in Poland, once compared the moment of his awakening to turning and stepping out the back door of his own mind. At 7:30 P.M. on August 24, I stepped through the back door of my own. With absolutely no preparation, I was shaken to the core, changed—in seconds—from a man who thought he knew the world to a man aware that he knew nothing.

As I crossed the threshold into the foyer, my ears began to ring. I rubbed them hard to make the sound stop, but the buzzing continued, like a swarm of bees or static on the radio, breaking the room's otherwise eerie quiet. I looked at Alexander, who pointed to his own ears and nodded his head, indicating that I should follow him up the stairs.

Then I saw her. Peeking over the top of the banister, my eyes fell on a tiny Indian woman in a vermilion sari, sitting on a chair, her eyes closed, holding the head of a kneeling child between her fingers. Her dark face was serene—her shoulders slightly hunched as she touched the boy's temples, the two of them frozen in a strange tableau as he held her feet. Neither of them moved at all as I watched. Finally, the woman opened her eyes, released his head, and sat back, gazing straight into the boy's eyes. Her expression was fierce and unwavering, her head rocking slightly forward as she examined him another minute, until finally she lowered her eyes and gazed down at her hands. The boy touched his forehead to the ground and returned to his chair, making way for an old woman, who hobbled to the carpet and knelt with difficulty, the whole process beginning again.

I was mesmerized by the sight of her. I knew immediately, without knowing how I knew, that this woman was unlike any human being I'd seen before—qualitatively different—as if she belonged to another species. I recognized viscerally, not logically, as one would recognize a taste or a smell, that she was something other. Her stillness, her silence, the curve of her shoulders in silhouette, or, more than that, the atmosphere that surrounded her, reminded me of something enormous and ancient, like a mountain.

I sat on the stairs and closed my eyes. Immediately, the background of my inner vision turned golden orange and I felt myself sinking into a kind of trance, my body heavy, my head light. Against this glowing background, the woman appeared, flying in slow motion, taking me up with her, bouncing me through space like a seal with a ball. I was aware that I was somewhere outside myself, observing from an odd remove as she soared back and forth, teasing me, pulling me further and further from my ordinary mind.

Alexander touched my shoulder. I opened my eyes and saw her sitting alone. It was my turn—she was waiting for me—I wanted to run in the opposite direction. Alexander tugged at my arm; finally I stood up and walked to the carpet in front of her. Feeling awkward and vaguely ridiculous, I knelt and lowered my head. I felt her fingers on my temples, her thumbs locking onto my head on either side of my fontanelle, finding their place and gripping like a vise. Touching her feet through the silk of her sari—they were cold and small, like a child's—I stared at the lines of gold in her hem. Strangely, other than the embarrassment of putting my head into the hands of someone I had never seen before and bowing in front of another person for the first time in my life, I felt nothing as I knelt there. I tried not to breathe too loudly and counted the seconds until it was over.

Finally she released my head and I sat back on my heels looking into her dark eyes. Her face was blank and expressionless. The pupils of her eyes—which nearly filled the entire oval, like a cat's—licked back and forth as she stared at me, as if they were seeing through me. I had the sense that she was actually *doing* something as she stared, as steady as if she were boring through a wall. It took every ounce of my strength not to look away. Finally she lowered her eyes and I returned to my place on the stairs.

She waited a minute more. When no one came forward, she stood—bringing all of us automatically to our feet—and without raising her eyes from the floor, slowly climbed the stairs to the top of the house, followed by an older Indian woman who had been sitting at her side.

> Come and I will show thee the cosmic curtain which is spread out before the holy one…Into this are woven all the generations of the world and what they will do until the end of generations.
>
> —Metatron to Ishmael,
> *Hebrew Book of Enoch*

The house emptied in minutes. Alexander led me down a narrow staircase to the kitchen in the basement and told me to wait there. My head was spinning, and as soon as I was alone, I began to invent explanations for what had happened to me on the stairs. I was overanxious, tired, stressed. I was succumbing to Alexander's otherworldly influence. I had been swept up by the strangeness of the woman sitting there silently. Holding people's heads in her hands. Alexander interrupted my thoughts.

"Mother Meera will see you now," he said, smiling in the doorway. "Follow me."

We climbed the stairs to the room where the woman had been earlier. She was standing perfectly still—no more than five feet tall—her attendant by her side, a sweater covering her sari. She gazed modestly at the floor.

My mind went completely blank. The four of us stood in

silence for several minutes. Finally Alexander came to my rescue. "Mark just escaped from New York, Mother," he said. "His friends are dying. He may be sick too. He doesn't know anything about God. He needs your help."

I tried to think of something to say, but in this woman's presence, words seemed somehow superfluous. I looked up, and at that moment, she flashed me a knowing smile, her face becoming radiant. Our eyes met for a second, and then she looked away.

"You are welcome in the Mother's house," the other woman, Adilakshmi, said in singsong English.

"Thank you," I whispered. Mother Meera looked at me once more, smiled gently, and nodded her head, as if to confirm that explanations were unnecessary. She muttered several foreign words in a strange, growling voice to Adilakshmi.

"Mother says you will sleep tonight!" she translated. Then they turned and disappeared up the stairs.

Alexander was right when he said that I knew nothing about God.

Nominally we were Jewish, but we were bad Jews, fallen Jews, assimilated Jews—indistinguishable, except for the occasional Yiddishism, from the goyim. What our Jewishness meant, in practical terms, is that we ate twice as much pork as our gentile friends, got extra days off from school, and decorated a Styrofoam Star of David at Christmastime instead of a tree.

At Passover, my pious Russian grandfather stood at the end of the table, rocking in his tallis and yarmulke, reciting prayers that no one understood, while we fidgeted. My mother sucked on a Pall Mall, flicking ashes onto the carpet.

"Enough, already, for Chrissakes, Dad," she'd interrupt when we got to the plagues. "Flies, locusts, cattle disease," she'd mutter, rolling her eyes as we dipped our pinkies into the Manischewitz and dripped it, scourge by scourge, onto my grandmother's good china.

God was a nonissue in suburbia, a myth no one cared about, like Bigfoot. When the thought of a Creator did happen to float across my consciousness when I was a boy, it was immediately countered by cynicism. "What kind of a sick God would create such a world?" I asked. "What sad excuse for a God would live here?" Still, being inquisitive, I couldn't help but wonder sometimes about the source of things, beginning with me, Between the ages of five and ten, I spent most of my free time locked in the bathroom, sitting on the sink, staring at myself in the mirror, looking for answers. I would gaze into my eyes for hours on end asking: Who are you? What are you? Where did you come from? Why are you here? No matter how long I sat there waiting, though, I got no response to my questions or to the deeper mystery: what was watching me from inside my eyes, this spark that made me see in the first place.

When I was twelve and three-quarters, I did a crash course in Talmud to please my grandpa, and at my Bar Mitzvah six months later, recited half an hour of Hebrew I didn't understand. Afterward, I walked around the reception hall with an empty shoe box, collecting twenty-five dollar checks. Except for weddings and funerals, it was the last time I ever set foot in a temple.

The night of my Bar Mitzvah, my mother took me out to Dino's Pizzeria for a private dinner—"Just the two of us," she said. It was the first time I could remember her leaving my sisters at home to be alone with me, and it seemed odd. My mother put on lipstick and got all dolled up the way she did for Willy, and walking from the T-bird into our favorite restaurant, took my arm like a girl out on a date.

Inside we ordered sausage heros. My mother asked for a "screwdriver without the screw," meaning mostly vodka, lit a cigarette, and looked at me across the red checkered tablecloth, her eyes shadowed by candlelight.

"What's up?" I asked her.

"Nothing," she answered. "Can't a mother take her son out to dinner without something being wrong?" She said it coyly, gazing at me with the strangest mixture of pride and pleasure and something else I couldn't quite put my finger on.

Finally, after my mother had finished her drink, she asked, "How do you compare to the other boys at school?"

"What do you mean, compare?"

"Down there," she answered, looking at her lap.

I felt like she'd stuck her hands down my pants. "Why?" I asked.

"Because there's something you should know."

I wasn't sure I wanted to.

"Your father was enormous," she said, mouthing the syllables slowly. "In all my life, I never saw that much man. Till the last time we did it, it hurt me." The moist look in my mother's eyes was positively indecent.

I didn't respond—I was too confused, not only by this unsolicited piece of information, but my mother's interest and the implication of her message. Although I had always been sexual, this was the first time I'd thought of my penis as something to be measured, something separate from me. This led me to another conclusion as well—that man was measured by his sex—and since no one had been around to teach me otherwise, I lit on this image of plundering, pillaging cocksman as an ideal to shoot for. After that, sex had become my substitute for God, my "prayer gone awry." The fervor I channeled into getting laid was like a seeker's passion for truth, driven by the same desperate thirst for union. Instead of reaching for love, unfortunately, the impulse was slightly twisted in me, trying to be the kind of grandiose god my mother wanted, the kind my father was—enormous.

When I arrived in Thalheim, that was all I knew about a higher power. Except this: that if by some miracle I was ever to believe in God, it would have to be on radically truthful terms. Under no circumstances would I be seduced by some kind of spiritual cover-up that told me pretty lies, like I was blessed when I was sinning, safe when so many I knew were dying, loved when there was so much hatred everywhere. Dignity, in my view, meant facing the hard facts of life with as little fantasy as possible. These hard facts would never break me, I promised myself—God-hunger would never break me either, even if I wanted more than anything else for such an entity to exist. The possibility was almost too beautiful to imagine; so beautiful, in fact, that this longing became the knife that made the gash that made the scream that made my life.

My first night in Thalheim, in a room directly under Mother Meera's quarters, I slept for fifteen hours.

It was a sleep unlike any I'd experienced before, dominated by vivid, clear dreams. Again, as in my trance on the stairs, Mother Meera appeared, flying around in various costumes, changing shape and color. Pink first, she gently stroked my head, tucked against her soft breast; next she was a demonic red, her eyes cruel, fangs protruding from her mouth, fingers tipped with claws like a bird of prey. Blood dripped from the corner of her mouth and she tore savagely at my belly with her talons, ripping at my entrails. I screamed and clutched my stomach, to protect myself, but I was powerless, and finally, exhausted, surrendered to her fury, floating limply in midair like a doll with its stuffing torn out.

When I woke, Alexander had his arms around me and I was sobbing. He rocked me while I cried for two hours, curled up in the blanket. A grief no therapist had come close to evoking had been unleashed; like a cyst that had been lanced, the hardness in my belly poured out its poisons in spasms. Afterward, I took the first easy breath I could remember taking in years, and the crying stopped as mysteriously as it had started. I felt as clean and light and fresh as a child.

That afternoon, Alexander and I went for a walk outside the village, along a deserted road past the cemetery and fields where sheep and cows were grazing, up into the woods behind Thalheim. The lightness that followed my morning ordeal had not passed. I felt wonderful.

"Why didn't you warn me?" I asked Alexander. "Who *is* she?"

Alexander told me Mother Meera's story: The daughter of farmers, she was born Kamala Reddy in the village of Chandepalle, Andhra Pradesh, India, on December 26, 1960. Her family was not especially religious and she was not raised in any tradition. Her relationship with her family was never close; her real parents were the spiritual guides she met in visions, and it was to them that she turned for the love and help she needed.

Her spiritual evolution was rapid and complete. She had no human guru, read no religious philosophy, did no *sadhana*, or spiritual practice: her contact with the absolute was immediate and unmediated. At six, she had her first experience of *samadhi*, falling senseless for a day—an experience, she says, that taught her the detachment from earthly desires that others can spend a lifetime learning.

Two years later, at age eight, she was sent to work in the home of Venkat Reddy (no relation). Reddy had been having visions of the Divine Mother since childhood and had sat at the feet of several holy women during his spiritual search. They had, however, left him unsatisfied. When his uncle died, Reddy was forced to return to his village to manage his property. There he was immediately struck by the power emanating from young Kamala and, living in her presence, was soon convinced that she was exceptional.

In Reddy's story of his first experience with Mother Meera's psychic abilities, she had gone to stay fifty miles away.

> I was lying on my bed one evening. I heard her voice calling me and was amazed. How could she come all that way? I got up and looked for her. I could not find her anywhere, Later, I went to the city where she was. She said to me, "I came to you and you did not notice anything. I called out to you and you didn't hear." I asked her how she had come that far. She just said that there was "another way of traveling."

When Mother Meera's extraordinary gifts became impossible to deny, Reddy left his family and business affairs to dedicate his life to protecting her. For the next several years, Mother Meera related her experiences in other dimensions to Mr. Reddy. "She would often go into *samadhi* for fourteen hours without a break," wrote Reddy. "She would sleep and eat very little. Eventually, she would learn to be in a trance continually, which she is, with open eyes."

★

On our second afternoon, Alexander and I again walked up toward the woods behind Thalheim, along the muddy trail that bordered the pastures where black-and-white cows were grazing, past apple orchards and farmers in tractors, who nodded at us suspiciously, then turned back to their work, trying not to stare at the strange intruders in city clothes.

We walked across the field toward a stand of pine trees. As we approached, we stopped talking and, entering the grove, walked quietly, needles crackling under our feet, to a large stump, where we sat side by side to rest. It was an enchanted scene. The quiet sun was filtering down through the treetops in slants of light. I took Alexander's hands, and we sat there, staring, listening to each other breathe, watching the moisture rise up off the ground, coloring the panes of light like smoke.

I stared into the grove for several minutes and saw something so strange I could not believe my eyes. Mother Meera was standing thirty feet away, clear as day, twirling and dancing among the trees, trailing a pink, gauzelike fabric. My eyes were open; we had not been drinking or taking drugs; there was no sense of hallucination or even strangeness, just the figure of Mother Meera—about half the size she was in real life, but otherwise the same—turning and floating thirty feet away from where I sat. I blinked and watched, but before it could register fully, the apparition was gone.

Alexander believed in these visions. I did not and was becoming increasingly confused by what I'd seen since arriving in Thalheim.

"What *is* she?" I asked him, afterward, walking along the stream toward Dorndorf.

"What do you think she is?"

"I have no idea. I have nothing to compare her to."

"Mother is an enlightened being."

"What exactly do you mean by enlightened?"

"I mean that she is in direct contact at all time with God. I mean that she is fully conscious of, and operating at, many, many levels of reality at every moment. She is able to travel to other dimensions, to know what is in others' hearts, to see the soul with open eyes."

"How do you *know* this?"

"Because she has proven it to me time and time again. Can you explain what happened to you on the stairs? Or the sound in your ears? Your dreams or the vision you saw just now?"

I was forced to admit I couldn't.

"Of course you can't. All you can do is doubt. That's the ego's only defense against mystical reality: doubt, disclaim, deconstruct, destroy."

"You mean she's a guru?"

"In a sense," Alexander said, sitting on a bench overlooking the valley. "Guru means dark to light; anyone or anything that serves to enlighten is a guru. A book can be a guru, lightning can be a guru, a child can be a guru. In that sense, Mother is certainly a guru, a master, a teacher. But most human gurus work very hard for their own realizations; they do practice, they follow and impose rules. Mother has no discipline per se. She offers no discourses or religion. She gives direct spiritual help to whoever needs it."

I knew what he meant—merely seeing Mother Meera had awakened something in me, a sense or recognition, clear and unspoken.

Alexander continued. "In a certain sense, enlightenment is a relative quality. One person may be more enlightened than another. But it is not a finite quantity—as in, 'Now I'm enlightened'—it is a process without end, with its own road signs and hazards. Follow?"

"I think so."

"There are different levels of enlightenment or attainment, some more unusual than others. There are thousands of Buddhist monks around the world but only one Dalai Lama. There were thousands of Hindu monks around the world, but only one Ramakrishna. There were a thousand Christians after Jesus, but only one Saint Francis. Think of light: it is everywhere, but concentrated more intensely in some places than in others. Enlightened beings are concentrated sources of light. Each has his or her own unique personality, but behind this mask of difference, their motive, purpose, and essence are identical."

"But isn't that true of all of us?"

"Strictly speaking, yes. Fundamentally, we are all, in essence, enlightened beings waiting to realize it. But the difference between an ordinary person and someone in that state of consciousness is quantum. It's like the difference between a reptile and a bird: they have a common origin, but the bird has grown wings."

"And what about Mother Meera?"

"She is a particularly rare case because she was born already conscious. These powers come naturally to her. She has said that she knew, before she entered a body, who and what she was. It is extremely rare, but it can happen that certain individuals are born enlightened. History is full of examples. Mother Meera is one."

"And what about the rest of us?"

"We have to walk barefoot over glass to get there. We have to beg and weep and pound our chests. The art of awakening is like any other art: the only way to master it is through practice. A soprano does her scales, an athlete runs every morning; nothing worthwhile—least of all the spiritual life—happens without work."

"You make it sound like hard labor."

"It is," he insisted, "but not in the sense that you mean. Because in spiritual life, every step is also a joy and brings new strength, a deepening and broadening of the mind and heart. You are encouraged along the way by vision and bliss. You take one step toward God and God takes two steps toward you."

"And a teacher is necessary for this?"

"Absolutely. If you want to learn Greek, you've got to have a professor. You have to meet someone who is already enlightened to show you that such a state is possible. Occasionally," Alexander continued, "some other kind of shattering experience, illness or sudden grief, can blow the mind off its hinges and reveal the light of God. But for most of us, the first glimmerings of this enlightened consciousness come through contact with holy beings. That is how it happened for me with Mother.

"This contact is crucial. When you watch someone operating from a position of absolute love, something in your soul responds. Enlightenment is the natural destiny of human beings, the reason we're here, the missing link between chaos and order. Without understanding this, people understand nothing. Life is a meaningless series of births and deaths and excruciating pain without redemption."

"Part of me still believes it is."

"Of course you do. And you will continue to in some part of yourself for the rest of your life. You must be *dead honest* about this. Never pretend to be further along than you are. Spiritual hypocrisy is the worst hypocrisy, and your authentic doubt is your best friend, provided you understand that it is there to help you toward the light."

Alexander continued, without pausing for me to respond.

"Think about love," he said. "We use the word to mean everything it isn't, but what is love truly? It is action in alignment with nature, nature attuned to the force pulsing through your veins and the veins of the planet. People who are in that dimension of love are in God. They are illumined. Think of it as a form of genius. Everyone has a touch of it, but some have concentrated and harnessed it to the point where it bears fruit and spreads something wonderful in the world."

"So Mother Meera is a spiritual genius?"

"Of the highest kind. People like Mother are here, in a body, showing us that enlightenment is ordinary, tangible, that we are *not* the end of human evolution but merely a stage of it—thank God. I think that's why most people are so depressed. They think that this is the end of the line, that nothing is ever really going to change in the human condition. But the enlightened masters like Mother tell us not to worry too much about the bigger picture until we've actually perfected ourselves. It's better to keep it simple and keep your eye turned inward until it can see—and is softened enough to view the situation out there with the utmost compassion. If you observe Mother carefully, you'll see how gently she does everything; she never tells anyone what to do. The strongest are the most gentle."

"And the most silent."

"That's how it's always been. The wisest speak the least, and when they do, they speak in a few, well-chosen words, in simple speech, in parable. Unlike me!"

We had reached the top of the ridge and sat quietly for a long time on a bench overlooking Thalheim. "It's beginning to make sense," I said. "But I don't want to worship anyone."

"Don't worship, then. It's not your path. Scrutinize. But keep your eyes open and admit the truth of what you see."

Walking through the woods above Thalheim, I made a pact with myself: to believe nothing without experience, take nothing secondhand. I intended to observe, understand, and deduce for myself; to make use of all my powers of doubt and discrimination. Much as Alexander impressed me, I would not be seduced by his predisposition to faith. Driven by the fear of losing my mind and credibility, of becoming some kind of Shirley MacLaine woo-woo or God-I'm-gonna-die convert, I decided to err in the opposite direction: to keep my hard head, draw no conclusion, and wait.

In the days that followed, I watched Mother Meera like a hawk, waiting for some misstep, some indication that she was not the enlightened being Alexander claimed she was. But I could find no evidence that she was a fake. Whether giving darshan or walking to the bank, she was the same—self-contained, modest, and strangely noble, like a peasant queen.

She terrified me.

Outside of darshan, I did my best to avoid meeting her on the stairs or in the garden. When I did, my legs shook and I couldn't talk. To make matters even more confusing, Mother Meera did not act like a guru. She did not spend her days on a dais surrounded by flowers, having her feet oiled. As Alexander had said, she did not give discourses, nor did she dispense advice. She made no rules, created no dogma, belonged to no religion, allowed no ashram to form around her. When people wished to dedicate their lives to her, she told them to go home and keep the faith they were born into, returning every now and then when they needed her help. Alexander told me that rabbis and Catholic priests came to visit, also Buddhists, Hindus, Muslims, Sikhs, atheists, were all welcome—and Mother Meera never asked for anything in return. During the day, she was always working, mixing cement, hauling bricks, hammering shingles on the roof, sweeping the porch, watering flowers. Completely ordinary except for the silent force that seemed to surround her.

Darshan proceeded like clockwork. Every night at seven, as the church bells rang in the distance, a door opened at the top of the stairs and Mother Meera descended, eyes lowered. What had only days before seemed the oddest thing in the world now began to feel quite natural, yet at the same time otherworldly, sacred, unfolding seamlessly as a dance. Whatever this woman was doing, she was doing it effortlessly and with complete authority. It was, indeed, impossible to imagine someone *not* in some altered state of consciousness sitting here hour after hour, taking head after head into her hands without wavering.

One evening, I came forward and knelt in front of her. Her fingers grasped my head. My mind raced with thoughts. I felt absolutely nothing. I looked into her eyes, expecting some kind of recognition, but saw no one there. It was as if something were coming through her, watching me through her—or not me, but something within or beyond me. As Mother Meera stared, I noticed again that her pupils were indistinguishable, her face fixed like a mask, the irises vibrating back and forth. Afterward in bed, I read the following question and answer in a book about her:

> Question: *When we have done* pranam, *we look into your eyes in silence. What are you doing?*
>
> Answer: I am looking into every corner of your being. I am looking at everything within you to see where I can help, where I can give healing and power. At the same

time, I am giving light to every part of your being, I am
opening every part of you to light. When you are open,
you will feel and see this clearly.

I decided that Mother Meera was some kind of phenomenon,
a *lusus naturae*, a freak of nature, like the Amazing Kreskin or those
people with enlarged pineal glands who are able to move iron
carvings through glass with the tips of their fingers. There was *no*
doubt that she was extraordinary; what I did doubt was my ability
to believe that she was truly in contact with God. Even at this early
stage of my spiritual journey, I was noticing a disturbing reflex in
my psyche: every time I felt a kind of wonder, something in me
rose up to crush it. In a fit of frustration with my hardheadedness,
Alexander told me I had a mind like a meat chopper. He was right:
a part of me was too sharp, too eager to dissect, but that severity
was the result of a sincere desire to understand. If Mother Meera
was real, if this whole mystical worldview was real, it would break
through my defenses.

On the afternoon of our departure for India, Alexander
requested a private darshan for Mother to bless us on our trip. She
came downstairs in her work clothes, sat on the darshan chair and
took our heads in her hands. After she'd stared for longer than
usual into our eyes, Mother stood and said, "Have a safe journey."
Alexander left me alone in the room. There were two portraits
hanging on either side of the chair where Mother Meera had been
sitting: one of her as a teenager, an enormous red *tikka* dot in the
middle of her forehead, her face gentle and indulgent; the other a
painting of Mr. Reddy in a white Nehru hat. I stared into her photograph for a long time in the quiet dark of the room, then had
the impulse to place my head again on the pillow where Mother's
feet had rested. Making sure that no one was coming, I knelt
quickly in front of her chair and rested my forehead on the white
pillow. Immediately, my ears filled with the same electric buzzing
sound that had surprised me a week before. I stayed there, listening and asking inwardly to be shown what it was, imagination or

something real. "I need proof," I said aloud. "Please, if you have any power at all, help me change."

When I lifted my head from the cushion, it was burning.

Mark Matousek has written for Details, Harper's Bazaar, The Village Voice, Common Boundary, Poz, Utne Reader, *and many other publications. A former senior editor of* Interview *magazine, he is the author of* Sex, Death, Enlightenment: A True Story, *from which this piece was excerpted. He lives in New York City.*

✦ ✦ ✦

In the Footsteps of the Buddha

No one ever said the pilgrim's path was easy.

IN THE ELONGATED, EARLY-MORNING SHADOW OF A TAMARIND tree on the road from Varanasi to Sarnath, I came upon an ascetic sitting in meditation on a sinister bed of thorns. His body, rail-thin and withered, was smeared with ash; the pallor of his skin accentuated the wounds and scars of a soul bent on mortification. He was a devotee of Lord Shiva.

For an instant, I thought he was dead, but as I approached, he opened a pair of sunken eyes and stared ahead blankly. I laid some coins and fruit at his feet, but I had no desire to linger. My head was reeling with Vedic verses and images from esoteric rites, and my spirit dashed by a prolonged proximity to the dead and dying. I turned and continued on, leaving the ascetic to his austerities and the Hindu world behind. Before me lay a Buddhist geography, ruinous, but still spiritually charged, in which I longed to find a measure of peace.

When I had walked up the road a short distance, I looked back to see a vulture perched knowingly on a branch above the ascetic, craning its neck at imminent carrion.

Unlike the myth-inspired sacred sites of Hinduism, the stations of Buddhist pilgrimage in India trace the footsteps and spiritual progress of a historical figure. It is the story of Siddhārtha Gautama (563–483 B.C.), the son of an aristocratic Hindu chieftain (some say king), who abandoned his family and the rarefied life of the pleasure palace and walked into the night in search of Truth. His progress from renunciation to realization and from Enlightenment to Nirvana can actually be charted on the map.

Like the Christian pilgrim who wanders the hills and valleys of Palestine, the Buddhist strikes out on the dusty trails of the Gangetic plain to walk where the Buddha walked, to dwell where he dwelt. The paths and the holy places to which they lead—Bodh Gaya, where the Buddha reached Enlightenment, the deer park at Sarnath, where he preached his first sermon, or the remote village of Kushinagara, the lonely site of the Buddha's death—have come to form a sacred geography. It is to these and other sites, ancient and time-worn, but still resonant with the Buddha's message, that the pilgrim goes forth on both a spiritual and a physical journey, at times bowing the head in reverence, at others attempting to overcome the profane obstacles that relentlessly arise on the road. Had either the Buddha or Christ chosen a secluded, stationary life, there would be no footsteps to follow. As it was, they both exalted the peripatetic condition, and they both showed us a path. One path leads to Nirvana and the other to salvation and eternal life, two very different spiritual prospects. But in both cases, it is the pilgrim, the soul seeking enlightenment, who must set off on the journey. As the Buddha lay on his deathbed, he offered his followers a simple, if telling, imperative: "Walk on!"

They were waiting for me at a bend in the road, two diminutive figures clad in the stiff, yellow robes of recently ordained *bhikkus*, or Buddhist monks. Their finely shaven heads shone like gilded domes under the sun. They had traveled from Thailand in search of Buddha, and a mere three miles outside of Varanasi, halfway to Sarnath, they were aghast at what they saw. If, according to Buddhist scripture, the sight of an old man, a sick man, a corpse, a mendicant ascetic had spurred Siddhārtha to contemplate the root of human suffering, well, I was told, they had seen scores of all four. They wanted nothing so much as to return to the security and unwavering routine of their monastery.

"In Sarnath, we will find the Buddha's spirit," I said by way of encouragement, but they looked unconvinced and shuffled their sandaled feet in the dust.

"Buddha spirit also in the monastery," one said.

"Ah, but the Buddha was never in your monastery and he was in Sarnath."

This logic seemed to strike an emotional chord. An hour later, I walked into Sarnath flanked, rather ceremoniously, by *bhikkus*.

A vast excavated precinct revealed crumbling stupas, or reliquary mounds, the foundations of numerous ancient monasteries, and the odd remains of walls, pillars, promenades, pools, and courtyards spread out over a landscape of immaculate, emerald-green lawns. Hindu families were picnicking amidst the ruins; yellow-, saffron-, and maroon-robed *bhikkus* and *bhikkunis* (nuns) circumambulated the stupas; the day-trippers out from Varanasi snapped photos of the tame deer.

I sat beneath a banyan tree and tried to envision the scene at Sarnath as it might have been over two thousand years ago, when the teachings of the Buddha were still new and radical, the monasteries were thriving with eager followers, and the throne of the Mauryan Empire was occupied by King Ashoka (273–232 B.C.), a former warrior whose conversion to the dharma, or law of Buddhism, ushered in a golden age.

Yellow-robed monks and nuns would have been studying, meditating, walking, and discussing the Great Teacher's message. There would have been sculptors carving friezes and statues to adorn the stupas, and architects drawing up plans for yet another monastery. Pilgrims, patrons, merchants, and wanderers would have been entering the gates to listen to the word, pay homage to the Buddha, or test the dharma. Missionaries would have been setting off for China, Syria, Greece, Egypt, and Sri Lanka. Everyone would most certainly have read, or been made to understand, the fourteen edicts carved into the pillar erected by King Ashoka:

Edict 1 forbade the slaughter of animals for sacrifice.

Edict 2 detailed the cultivation of herbs and fruits for medicinal purposes and the building of roads and wells.

Edict 3 instructed *mahamatras*, or "officers of righteousness," to spread the dharma.

Edict 4 elaborated on Edict 3.

Edict 5 urged subjects to help the families of prisoners and criminals.

Edict 6 stated that Ashoka was available for counsel from any of his subjects.

Edict 7 called for self-control and purity of thought.

Edict 8 described Ashoka's pilgrimages.

Edict 9 denounced superstitious rites.

Edict 10 denounced fame and glory.

Edict 11 expounded on the beneficial effects of dharma.

Edict 12 instructed *mahamatras* to tolerate and encourage the principles of all religions.

Edict 13 apologized for the razing and slaughter of Kalinga.

Edict 14 summarized the previous thirteen.

Ashoka signed himself as Piyadasi, "the Humane"—and rightfully so.

It was at Sarnath that Buddhism was born, and after Bodh Gaya, where Gautama reached Enlightenment, it is Buddhism's most hallowed ground. This was the place where the Buddha chose to preach his first sermon, "Setting in Motion the Wheel of Dharma," to the five ascetics with whom he had fasted, meditated, and suffered austerities for six years before abandoning the mendicants and reaching Enlightenment at Bodh Gaya.

What the Buddha preached at Sarnath became the bedrock of Buddhism: the Middle Way, the Four Noble Truths, and the Eightfold Path.

Those foolish people who torment themselves, as well as those who have become attached to the domains of the

senses, both of these should be viewed as faulty in their
method, because they are not on the way to deathlessness.
These so-called austerities but confuse the mind which is
overpowered by the body's exhaustion. In the resulting stu-
por one can no longer understand the ordinary things of
life, how much less the way to the Truth which lies beyond
the senses. The minds of those, on the other hand, who are
attached to the worthless sense-objects, are overwhelmed
by passion and darkening delusion. They lose even the ability to understand the doctrinal treatises, still less can they
succeed with the method which by suppressing the passions leads to dispassion. So I have given up both these extremes, and have found another path, a middle way. It leads
to the appeasing of all ill, and yet it is free from happiness
and joy.

Buddhacarita, or *The Acts of the Buddha*

To follow the Middle Way, one must first grasp the Four
Noble Truths: the existence of suffering, the root of suffering, the
cessation of suffering, and the path that leads to the cessation of
suffering.

In turn, the Way, which leads to the cessation of suffering, is an
Eightfold Path: Right View, Right Thought, Right Speech, Right
Action, Right Livelihood, Right Effort, Right Mindfulness, and
Right Concentration.

It was a simple, if radical message—simple because liberation
could be had not from an accumulation of sacrifices or fortunes
of birth, but through the cessation of desire and separate self-
hood, and radical because it promoted morality without meta-
physics. Compared with the elaborate rituals, sacrifices, constraints, and overcrowded pantheon of Brahmanism, Buddhism
was a revelation.

Do not what is evil. Do what is good. Keep your mind
pure. This is the teaching of Buddha.

Dhammapada 183

I scoured the ruins. There wasn't a hint of a breeze, and the heat that rose from the baking Ashokan bricks was suffocating. There was, alas, precious little to see. Sarnath is less an evocative archaeological site than a heap of relentlessly plundered ruins. Were it not for the power of the message delivered here twenty-five centuries ago, the place would be hopelessly tragic.

I wandered over to the Dharmekha Stupa, which commemorates the spot where the Buddha preached his first sermon, and circumambulated in the company of saffron-robed *bhikkus* from Burma and lay Buddhists from Sri Lanka, Tibet, Japan, and China. The Tibetans turned their prayer wheels and beat diminutive drums; others chanted. I focused on the fifth-century Guptan reliefs on the exterior of the stupa. The only Indians I saw were a family sleeping off their lunch under a tree, and a group of Untouchable women squatting on a lawn nearby, patiently cutting the grass by hand.

I had often heard the disappearance of Buddhism in the land of its birth characterized as an enigma. To me, it was nothing of the sort. Between the merciless sword of the first Hunnish and later Muslim invaders and the animosity of Brahman priests and theologians, Buddhism scarcely had a chance.

The successive waves of Muslim armies that swept over northern India beginning in the eighth century treated the pacific Buddhists just like any other infidels—monks and nuns were murdered, monasteries sacked, and libraries burned. When the Muslim chieftain Bakhtiar Khalji entered Nalanda, the great seat of Buddhist learning, in 1199, he put over five thousand monks and nuns to the sword. There was no resistance. There couldn't have been—on the question of nonviolence, the Great Teacher had been unequivocal:

> If men speak evil of you, this must you think: "Our heart
> shall not waver; and we will abide in compassion, in loving-
> kindness, without resentment. We will think of the man
> who speaks ill of us with thoughts of love, and in our
> thoughts of love shall we dwell. And from the abode of

love shall we dwell. And from that abode of love we will
fill the whole world with far-reaching, wide-spreading, and
boundless love."

Moreover, if robbers should attack you and cut you in
pieces with a two-handed saw, limb by limb, and one of
you should feel hate, such a one is not a follower of my
gospel.

Majjhima Nikaya

The Buddhists died as submissively as the Christians in the
Roman circus, who went to their death empowered by Jesus's
injunction: "Do good to them that hate you."

To the Brahman hierarchy, the Buddhist message was as cata-
clysmic as the tenets of Christianity would be for orthodox
Judaism. Buddhism's rejection of the caste system and the existence
of a Supreme Being threatened the Hindu tradition at its doctrinal core. For at least three or four hundred years after the Buddha's
death, converts flocked to the Buddhist monasteries in droves,
especially during the reign of Ashoka, when Buddhism enjoyed
the status of a state religion.

The reaction of the Hindu pandits was nothing if not expedi-
ent—they absorbed the Buddha into their expansive pantheon as
an avatar of Vishnu and a reviler of the *Vedas*.

By the twelfth century, Buddhism had been all but erased from
India, a victim of Muslim fanaticism and the jealousies of the rival
Brahman creed. For nearly a millennium there was silence, until
British archaeologists started uncovering remains in the last cen-
tury, and Buddhist pilgrims began to turn up once again from
Japan, Sri Lanka, Thailand, China, Burma, Tibet, and the West,
from everywhere, indeed, but India.

There wasn't a bed to be had in Sarnath, not in the *dharamshala*,
the Government Tourist Bungalow, or any of the modern temples
maintained by the Buddhist nations of Asia. I settled on a patch of
grass among the Tibetan refugees, who had set up a makeshift
camp in the shadows of their temple. As night fell, I huddled in a
tea stall full of ruby-robed monks, novices, and their disheveled

countrymen and read from the *Dhammapada*, perhaps the most celebrated collection of aphorisms attributed to the Buddha.

> If month after month with a thousand offerings for a hundred years one should sacrifice; and another only for a moment paid reverence to a self-conquering man, this moment would have greater value than a hundred years of offerings.

> If a man for a hundred years should worship the sacred fire in the forest; and if another only for a moment paid reverence to a self-conquering man, this reverence alone would be greater than a hundred years of worship.

> Whatever a man for a year may offer in worship or in gifts to earn merit is not worth a fraction of the merit earned by one's reverence to a righteous man.

For over four days, I walked and rode in an occasional bullock cart through a landscape of rice paddies, wheat fields, and miserable red-clay villages before arriving at dusk in Bodh Gaya, the *axis mundi* of the Buddhist world.

At the Burmese *vihara*, or monastery, a young gatekeeper in wraparound sunglasses and a black mock-leather jacket led me through a courtyard, where mongrel dogs eyed me from the shade and monks sat bent over sacred books, to a spartan cell. In front of the cell next door, a rather bedraggled German couple, no longer young, was speaking in a querulous tone. When they saw me, they edged over to share their burden. It seemed a traveling companion of theirs had been missing for three days.

"He goes to Mahakala Caves for the day," said the woman, "but doesn't come back."

The gatekeeper looked unfazed.

"Have you gone to the police?" I asked.

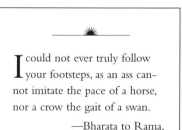

I could not ever truly follow your footsteps, as an ass cannot imitate the pace of a horse, nor a crow the gait of a swan.

—Bharata to Rama,
The Ramayana

"*Na ja, polizei*," said the man, "want dollars!"

"Have you gone off looking for him?"

"We are in meditation course. We cannot leave now," she said. "We are very close."

I wasn't quite sure what they were so close to, but it was clear that their meditation was more important than their friend.

The gatekeeper shuffled off without a word.

"Indians," said the woman in disgust as she watched him depart. "They are filthy people."

"Actually, he's Burmese," I corrected her. I didn't add that he looked a good deal cleaner than either of them.

They retreated into their cell to pursue their enlightenment.

I walked out of the monastery in the half-light, bound for the Mahabodhi Temple. It was a half-mile stroll to the temple complex. The unpaved road was lined with tented tea shops with names like Gautama Café and the Dharma Lounge. There were stalls selling beads, flowers, incense, and candles. The misnamed Shiva Travel specialized in bus tours of the Buddhist circuit. Rickshaw drivers rang their bells, pleading for a fare. Through the trees I could make out the black current of the Phalgu River.

When I reached the temple gate, I was set upon by a legion of urchins and beggars with unspeakable infirmities. A man with a leprous, half-eaten face tugged at my sleeve. I didn't stop. As soon as I crossed the threshold, there was calm.

The entire sunken temple precinct was aflame with the light from thousands of candles and tallow lamps, the "lake of fire" that E. M. Forster described on his visit here. The pyramidal, nine-storied temple spire soared from a broad plinth to a height of 180 feet; its surface was covered with carvings of lotus flowers, niches, string courses, moldings, and a multitude of miniature Buddhas. At the summit rose a gold finial. Buddhist lore attributes the temple to Ashoka, but archaeologists reckon the most ancient parts of the edifice date from the Kushana period (50 B.C.–A.D. 200). Its architect is unknown.

Spreading out around the temple, flickering in the light, was a studied landscape of flagstone alleys and paths that led to stupas and shrines where pilgrims walked, prostrated themselves, and sat in meditation. The whole numinous scene was accompanied by the low murmur of collective chanting.

I followed a group of white-robed pilgrims into the sanctum sanctorum of the temple and bowed, but didn't prostrate, before the golden image of the Buddha, depicted with his hand touching the ground, hailing Mother Earth to witness his awakening. The statue was flanked by vases full of peacock feathers and surmounted by a baldachin of rather cheesy gauze. From behind me someone whispered in my ear, "May the Buddha bless you."

At the rear of the temple, in a sanctuary enclosed by a finely carved sandstone railing, stood a papal, or fig tree, of the genus *Ficus religiosa*, a descendant of the Bodhi or "Enlightenment" tree under which Gautama sat and resolved not to stir until he had attained Enlightenment. In that night he grasped the insight at the heart of true Buddhist liberation: that impermanence and emptiness of self are precisely the conditions on which life depends. Gautama's liberation, his ascent to Buddhahood, and his brush with Nirvana inspired the two renowned, often quoted verses from the *Dhammapada*:

> I have gone round in vain the cycles of many lives ever
> striving to find the builder of the house of life and death.
> How great is the sorrow of life that must die!

> But now I have seen thee, housebuilder: never more shalt
> thou build this house. The rafters of sin are broken, the
> ridgepole of ignorance is destroyed. The fever of craving is
> past: for my mortal mind is gone to the joy of the immor-
> tal Nirvana.

I sat beneath the Bodhi tree amidst a bevy of Buddhists from Asia. They were all deep in meditation, except one elderly man who was chanting "*Om Mani Padme Hum*" ("Hail to the Jewel in the Lotus"). The trunk of the Bodhi tree was wrapped in gold fabric, and multicolored prayer flags were draped from its branches. The leaves were the shape of hearts. Propped against one of the roots was a sign that read: "Please do not pluck leaves from the sacred Bo tree." Evidently, overzealous pilgrims had been treating the tree to a slow death.

I crossed my legs and tried to meditate, but after a quarter of an hour or so, I gave up, not because of any external distractions—on the contrary, the scene was a picture of tranquility—but rather on account of some very persistent inner rumblings. To arrive at Buddhism's most hallowed ground, plant myself beneath the Bodhi tree, and attempt to meditate without rigorous preparation seemed to me, at best, fallacious and, at worst, positively fraudulent. I had, it's true, steeped myself in the sacred texts, and I found the message contained in the *Buddhacarita*, the *Dhammapada*, the sutras, and the Lotus of the Good Law, among other indispensable works, to be both ethically convincing and aesthetically appealing. It was not, however, enough.

Or maybe it was.

Better than a hundred years lived in vice, without contemplation, is one single day of life lived in virtue and in deep contemplation.

And so I sat in quiet contemplation. Better to be overcome with humility, I thought, than to be greedy for enlightenment.

When a caretaker came to lock up the enclosure for the night, I was alone. The sky was luminous with stars and a half moon, and all but a few isolated candles had been consumed. In front of the temple gates, the beggars lay wrapped in their shawls, sleeping in momentary peace. I emptied my pockets at their feet.

At first light I was back. It was too early for the tourists, but the temple compound was already teeming with *bhikkus*, lamas, and pilgrims. I wandered among the sites where the Buddha meditated following his Enlightenment. There was the Animesa Locana, "The Place of the Unwinking Gaze," where the Buddha spent a full week staring at the Bodhi tree without so much as a blink; the Cankamana, a cloister walk where lotus flowers carved into a raised platform indicate the spots where the Lord's feet trod; and the Ajapala Nigrodha, the banyan tree where the Buddha replied to the Brahman that only by one's deeds does one became a Brahman, not by birth. I liked this last shrine the most; its significance was not unlike the Christian message being spread to the Gentiles. Buddhism, like Christianity, arose as a light for all humankind, not merely for the twice-born or a chosen people.

As I sat taking notes in the cool shadow of a stupa, a tousled *bhikku* planted himself over my shoulder.

"You are Englishman?"

"No."

"Then you are Japanese," he said, offering a rather odd alternative.

"Also not. Guess again." But he seemed to have exhausted his possibilities and just stared at me plaintively.

"I'm American."

"Where is America?"

"Very far away."

"East or west?"

"It's just about equidistant."

"You are a Buddhist?"

"No, just an admirer of the Buddha."

"What God do you have?"

"A Christian God, I think."

Though a reformer, and perhaps from a priestly point of view a heretic (if such a word can be used in conjunction with a system permitting absolute freedom of speculation), the Buddha was brought up and lived and died as a Hindu. Comparatively little of his system, whether of doctrine or ethics, was original or calculated to deprive him of the support and sympathy of the best among the Brahmans, many of whom became his disciples. The success of his system was due to various causes: the wonderful personality and sweet reasonableness of the man himself, his courageous and constant insistence upon a few fundamental principles, and to the way in which he made his teaching accessible to all without respect to aristocracy of birth or intellect.

—Ananda K. Coomaraswamy and The Sister Nivedita, *Myths of the Hindus & Buddhists*

"You are not sure?"

"Sometimes not."

"I am a Buddhist. The Lord Buddha is my God."

"I didn't think that Buddhists conceived of the Buddha as a God."

"Buddha is my God!" he shouted in a very un-Buddhalike manner.

"I'm sure he is."

"You will give me money," he said, extending a filthy hand.

"No."

"Then you will give me your watch."

"I'm afraid not."

"Your camera."

This was becoming tiresome. I changed the subject.

"Where are you from?"

"I am from here, from Bodh Gaya."

"Ah, an Indian Buddhist."

"The Buddha was Indian! These people you see here, they are not Indians. This is our temple!"

Here, I thought, was all the ethnocentric prejudice of Hinduism draped in a saffron robe. When a group of Japanese pilgrims passed, he set on them with equal resolve.

"You are English?"

The Japanese took him for what he was, namely, deranged, and quickened their pace. I went off to practice some more tentative meditation beneath the Bodhi tree, the one place in Bodh Gaya where one is sure to be left in peace.

The revivification of Bodh Gaya and the restoration of its temple and shrines was made possible largely by the efforts of two men, Angarika Dharmapala and Sir Edwin Arnold, the former a Sri Lankan Buddhist and founder of the Maha Bodhi Society, the latter a Christian Englishman, poet, journalist, and adventurer. They were an unlikely pair devoted to the common cause.

On pilgrimage to Bodh Gaya in 1891, Dharmapala was shocked to find the temple in the hands of a Saivite priest, the statue of the

Buddha transformed into a Hindu icon, and the way barred to Buddhist worship.

> Reverently I visited the brick temple, built in the form of a pyramid, and examined the carvings on the ancient railing. But I was filled with dismay at the neglect and desecration about me. The *mahant*—the head of the Hindu fakir establishment—had disfigured the beautiful images. At the end of a long pilgrimage, the devout Buddhist was confronted with monstrous figures of Hindu deities. It seemed an outrage that this holiest temple of the Buddhist should be under the management of a man whose ancestors had always been hostile to Buddhism.

> I had intended to stay a few weeks and then return to Ceylon; so I had only a few rupees with me. But, when I saw the condition of the shrine, I began an agitation to restore it to Buddhist control. I communicated with the leading Buddhists of the world and urged them to rescue Bodhi Gaya from the Siva-worshiping Hindu fakirs. On May 31, 1891, I started the Maha Bodhi Society, to rescue the holy Buddhist places and to revive Buddhism in India, which for seven hundred years had forgotten its greatest teacher.

Today, the Maha Bodhi Society is the principal caretaker of the Buddhist holy places in India and a major charitable institution. At Bodh Gaya, the society maintains a primary school, a clinic, a library, and a pilgrim shelter.

The fakirs, however, are still in residence. Hard by the entrance to the temple they maintain a shrine and are fond of scandalizing the Buddhist pilgrims with Hindu rites and Vedic chants. On occasion, Buddhist and Hindu adepts have been known to come to blows.

If Angarika Dharmapala's appeal went out to his fellow Buddhist brethren, it was Sir Edwin Arnold who brought the Lord Buddha's message to the masses in the English-speaking West. In 1879, Arnold published *The Light of Asia*, an epic poem hailing the life and teachings of the Buddha. The work was an instant success both in England and America and won praise for its wealth of local color (Arnold had spent several years as a schoolmaster at the Sanskrit College in Poona, and he knew the subcontinent well). The poem did, however, have its detractors. Oriental scholars criticized its simplification of Buddhist doctrine. Devout Christians took offense at Arnold's analogy between the Lord Buddha and the Lord Jesus Christ. Through Arnold's flowery Victorian verse, however, masses of English-speaking readers got their first taste of the Great Teacher.

> Lo! The Dawn
> Sprang with Buddha's victory! lo! In the East
> Flamed the first fires of beauteous day, poured forth
> Through fleeting folds of Night's black drapery....

Like Angarika Dharmapala, Arnold too went on a pilgrimage to Bodh Gaya, and though he was no Buddhist, his sensibilities were likewise offended. Upon returning to England, he published an article in the *Daily Telegraph* entitled "East and West—A Splendid Opportunity," which revealed the lamentable state of Buddhism's most sacred sites. Suddenly the restoration of Bodh Gaya became a cause célèbre and funds and pilgrims followed.

Had it not been for Dharmapala and Arnold, Bodh Gaya might well have remained ruined and forgotten, its glory obscured by Brahman usurpers.

They warned me not to travel alone, especially on foot. In this, the *bhikku*-in-charge at the Burmese *vihara*, the taciturn gatekeeper, the proprietor of the Gautama Cafe, and the venerable Maitipe Wimalasara Thera, high priest of the Maha Bodhi Society, were all in agreement. Perhaps the last put it most plainly: "They will kill you." But he gave me his blessing anyway, as well as a copy of the *Visuddhi Magga, The Path of Purification*, an encyclopedic work on Theravada Buddhism that ran to 885 pages of excruciatingly fine print.

In fact, I was leaving Bodh Gaya reluctantly. Although I had not experienced any flash of enlightenment beneath the Bodhi tree or any moments of monumental insight, I was flush with the Buddhist message of compassion, mercy, love, devotion, serenity, meditation, and introspection. I found, gratefully, no harping on sin. Humans are not belittled in order to exalt the Buddha. Every individual, like the Buddha, has the potential for perfection. Nor was there any obstacle to joining the Buddhist fold, no status based on arbitrary bloodlines, no baptism, bar mitzvah, or secret initiation. It was enough to affirm the Three Refuges: "I take refuge in the Buddha, I take refuge in the Dharma, I take refuge in the Sangha."

When I walked out of Bodh Gaya, the German was still missing, a group of Taiwanese pilgrims, haggard and half asleep, was filing off a bus, and the dawn light had transformed the surface of the Phalgu River into molten gold.

It *was* dangerous to walk alone. Bodh Gaya, Rajagriha, my next destination, and many of the places where the Buddha wandered are located in Bihar (from *vihara*, or monastery), India's poorest state, its most illiterate, and as lawless a place as the world knows. In the first six months of 1996, Bihar reported 2,625 murders, 1,243 kidnappings, and over 60,000 other violent crimes—that's an average of 14 murders a day and 1 kidnapping every 4 hours.

The urgent, colorful prose of the *Times of India* painted the scene in Bihar thus:

Gangsterism and the mafia raj in Bihar are going full throttle, having acquired their full, turbo power. In West Champaran district, for instance, where kidnapping for ransom has become a cottage industry, blind hatred for the perceived enemy is the reigning ideology. This hatred is unfathomable and alive. Bhagad Yadav, Lalu Yadav, Ram Bhaju Yadev, Ram Singh, Allaudin Mian and Ram Basi Koeri are names which strike terror in the minds of young and old alike. In an atmosphere of lawlessness beyond any sense of proportion and shame, some crimes committed by them veer into the surreal.

The article went on to describe (with equal flair) tales of caste wars, murder, rape, and robbery and ended on a decidedly grim note: "Bihar has for decades symbolized the 'end of order.' That the State is slip-sliding into the abyss is no great news."

The Buddha spirit, it seemed clear, had most definitely been erased from the land of Gautama's ministry.

The countryside between Bodh Gaya and Rajagriha stretched out in a succession of palmyra palm groves, rice paddies, and fields of wheat and sugarcane. Tiger grass grew along the sides of streams, and tamarind and crimson-blossomed sal trees provided a measure of shade. Everywhere there was dust. On the horizon, the Barabar Hills rose in the haze. No traffic came along the road all day except for an occasional horse-drawn tonga or a bullock cart; their drivers stared at me, speechless, as they passed. When I came upon a group of village girls shaping dung cakes and singing by the side of the road, they covered their faces with their hands and ran into a field shrieking. Communication with the locals, I could see, was going to be tricky.

As the sun was dropping behind the crest of the Barabar, I made camp in a palm grove. It took me nearly two hours to gather enough wood for a fire. I fixed curry, sunk into *The Path of Perfection*, and listened to the whooping calls of a myna bird. Later, the night was full of wild dogs and jackals, and stars peaking through the fronds of the palms.

The following day, the road narrowed to a track and led through a series of mud-hut hamlets, where the men sat idly, the women worked tirelessly, and the children rolled in the dirt with the dogs and stray cattle. When I strolled through, all activity, such as it was, would come to a sudden halt. Then the mongrels would set on me, followed by the children, and finally the hollow-eyed elders. They would press around and gape.

In one of these cheery, nameless villages, I stopped for the night.

For all their initial suspicions, the villagers' mood changed abruptly when I asked, in halting Hindi punctuated by childlike gestures, to pass the night among them. At once, they became model hosts. The Sanskrit word for guest is *atithi*, "one who comes unannounced," and he is treated as a god, which in Hindu tales is very often what he is. I was led to the shade of a banyan tree, a place of honor in rural India, accompanied by a wizened patriarch. The other men and boys squatted around according to their place in the village hierarchy. A file of women, barefoot and bangled, brought me water with which to wash, a bowl of buttermilk, and a melon.

When I indicated that I was bound for Rajagriha, the name only elicited a vague wagging of heads. Nor had they ever heard of the Buddha. I don't think there was one among them who could read. They were of low caste and didn't own the land they farmed. They possessed nothing.

I spent the afternoon treating a number of sundry illnesses—cuts, burns, colds, and fevers—nothing that required anything more than aspirin, vitamins, antiseptic cream, or a clean bandage. Soon enough, however, an alarmingly long line had formed, and I went to great pains trying to tell them that I was, in fact, no doctor. It was useless; hope is eternal. An ancient man was led before me, his eyes milky white from river blindness. I shook my head in despair and pronounced the dispensary closed.

I had wanted to sleep under the banyan tree, but after dinner I was shown to a hut that had been vacated for my benefit. To refuse this sign of hospitality would have been unthinkable. Like everything else in the village, the hut was built of mud-brick and the thatched roof was covered in a tangle of squash vines. There was one door and no windows. Just outside the threshold stood the hearth. Inside, the earthen floor had been relentlessly pounded until its surface resembled polished Florentine marble. But for a charpoy on which to sleep, a blanket, some odd cooking utensils, and a modest shrine decorated with an image of Shiva torn from a magazine, there was nothing.

Before falling off to sleep, I read from the *Dhammapada* in the contrasting light of the Shiva lamp.

If on the journey of life a man can find a wise and

intelligent friend who is good and self-controlled, let him
go with that traveler; and in joy and recollection let them
overcome the dangers of the journey.

But if on the journey of life a man cannot find a wise and
intelligent friend who is good and self-controlled, let him
then travel alone, like a king who has left his country, or
like a great elephant alone in the forest.

Looming above me when I opened my eyes in the morning was
the figure of a grown man dressed in a woman's bathrobe printed
with a motif of delicate white roses on an electric blue background. I had, by chance, witnessed stranger things in India, but
usually not quite so early in the morning. And then I saw that he
had a gun, a steel-gray revolver with a grip wrapped in white medical tape. I was motioned to get up. There was another man standing in the threshold; he didn't have a gun, just a machete. I dressed,
shaking. No one said a word.

Outside, three more men, one of whom was holding a very
convincing sawed-off shotgun, stood surrounding the hut's owner,
a shriveled old man in a soiled *dhoti*. That he looked positively ter-
ror-stricken made me even more nervous. One kidnapping every
four hours, I thought, fourteen murders a day. Like a great elephant
alone in the forest, indeed. I recalled the voice of the high priest at
Bodh Gaya, "They will kill you." In my mind's eye I saw my sons
fatherless. I broke into a cold sweat.

The man in the blue bathrobe began to question the villager. I
couldn't follow a word of the exchange. But the gist, no doubt,
was, who was I? Where had I come from? And what was I doing
there? The villager stuttered his replies, never looking up. When
his interrogator didn't like a response, he waved his gun around furiously. Finally, the poor man fell to his knees and began to grovel.
It looked very much as if he was asking for mercy. The other men
laughed, and then they suddenly grew silent and looked at me. I
resisted falling to my knees. For a long time they just stared. When
I tried to help the villager up, I was pushed away.

One of the men went into the hut and came out with my backpack and a smaller day pack full of my books. The leader, clearly the man in blue, gestured for me to open the bags with the assured air of a customs officer. I set out my possessions neatly in the dirt. They began to pick at will. Their selections, I thought, were telling. They took all my food, a pot, a flashlight, and some tongs. Shorts and trousers didn't interest them although some lovely cotton material from Varanasi did. I imagined them fashioning some fine *dhotis*. Two of the men argued over some beads, and the leader snatched up all my tobacco. When I opened the pack with my books, they waved them away. At the sight of my stock of medicines, however, they were filled with quiet awe. Here, I hoped, was my chance.

I spread out the pills, creams, bandages, and rubbing alcohol on a clean white towel. I moved very slowly and methodically, like a priest preparing an altar for Mass. Over each item I mumbled something innocuous. I then motioned to the leader to sit by my side. He handed the revolver to one of his cohorts and squatted in front of me. Picking up a packet of aspirin as if it were some mysterious potion, I mimicked a splitting headache. With the vitamins, I first played fatigued and then inflated my chest and flexed my muscles. I held my stomach and doubled over to portray someone in need of an antibiotic. The dysentery sequence had them howling with laughter. But they were rapt. Only the day before I had been trying to convince the locals that I was not a doctor; now I had to assume the role of the most thoroughly competent general practitioner these men had ever set eyes on.

Gently, I took the leader's arm and played at taking his pulse. I had him roll his eyes, stick out his tongue, and expose his gums. I adopted a bedside manner at once informed and nurturing. I thought of Dr. Schweitzer among the natives. I questioned my patient, again by way of pantomime, about his bowel movements, his sleeping habits, his diet. All thoroughly professional. I proceeded to prescribe two multivitamin tablets a day, one aspirin after breakfast, and a toothbrush to clean his foul mouth. I dressed a nasty wound on his shin. By the time his visit to the "doctor" was through, the leader was smiling. He seemed genuinely grateful and it looked as if he felt better. And then, still smiling, he poked at my hip pouch as if to say, what have you got there? I withdrew a substantial wad of rupees. He caressed the bills from my hand; he was radiant. Now, he gestured, he felt much better.

I was confined to the hut. The shotgun toter squatted in the doorway. And my daintily clad captor went off to celebrate his recuperated health with some fresh currency.

I lay on the bed and considered my fate. Thus far, I had managed to hold on to my books, my clothes, and my life and, in the process, had adopted a new profession. The future, however, looked bleak, although some scenarios were clearly worse than others. I could be led off to some barren tract and, say, have my head severed from my body with a swish of a machete; that was the dire, pathological option. I could also be held for ransom, the economic option, and spend several months in living hell, never quite sure that the money would, in fact, turn up. I did not see my mother, God bless her, selling the family silver to get me out of India. Finally, there was the blessed, brotherly option; I could be set free unscathed.

The Buddhist broods on the body's impermanence, but I prayed long and hard to save mine.

I found it impossible to read, much less to write. I paced the interior of the hut, a diminutive five strides and a heel, until I was bouncing off the walls. All the while, my keeper watched me impassively. I looked into his dark, slightly feminine eyes and tried to determine whether or not this was the face of my executioner. He seemed hardly to blink or breathe or register any expression. I took this as a bad sign. A natural-born killer, I thought; he was probably dying to waste me.

Happily, the leader, this petty gangster of the mafia raj, as the *Times of India* might say, had a toothache. I was marched to the banyan tree to examine the patient. His mouth was flaming red from betel juice; still, I could see the rotten molar. He was, I was pleased to observe, in considerable discomfort. Nevertheless, ever the professional, I prescribed two aspirins and had him bite down on a third place atop the bad tooth, a wonderful technique to momentarily ease the pain and a treatment guaranteed to eventually rot the tooth beyond redemption.

I was given a bowl of lentils and unleavened bread. My patient alternately winced and watched me eat. When I had finished, he took a stick and traced a sickle in the dirt. So, he was not merely a thief and a tyrant, but a comrade! He passed the stick to me and motioned for me to define myself. This was a hard enough task even when I had the luxury of words; reduced as I was to semiotics, I found myself rather at a loss. Finally, I flattened a broad area in the dust with my hand and sketched a trident, an eight-spoked wheel, a cross, a Star of David, and a sickle moon; I then traced a generous circle encompassing them all. He studied my ecumenical doodling with an expressionless face. I had the uneasy sensation that my future might depend on this man's reading of ancient, sacred signs etched ephemerally in the dust of a godforsaken Indian village. After an insufferable silence he at last rose, stood above my sacred circle, and erased each sign in turn with a callused foot. He then delivered a coup de grâce, spitting a stream of betel juice into the dust at my feet.

As I was being escorted back to my prison-hut, I wondered if perhaps I should have included the hammer and sickle as well.

In the morning, villagers were peering in through the threshold and chattering excitedly. The blue-robed one and his merry band were gone just as quickly and quietly as they had come.

I felt like Daniel sprung from the lion's den. The locals, however, were morose. They referred to my captors as *dacoits*, roughly "brigands" or "outlaws" and made me to understand that they too had been robbed, not of rupees (they had none), but of food stores. What's more, I gathered it was a regular event. They were full of shame that I had been disgraced in their village. They wanted me to stay, to make it up to me. I wanted only to leave. I was free.

At my send-off under the banyan tree, the women sang and swayed. I was presented with three mangos and some delicate sweets wrapped in banana leaves. I bowed low, thanked them profusely, and bolted.

Nicholas Shrady is a writer whose work has appeared in The New York Times Book Review, Travel & Leisure, Town & Country, Architectural Digest, Forbes, *and many other publications. Born and raised in Connecticut, he now live in Barcelona, Spain. This story was excerpted from his book* Sacred Roads: Adventures From the Pilgrimage Trail.

MICHAEL WOLFE

✦ ✦ ✦

Making the Hadj to Mecca

An American Muslim fulfills the ancient and sacred duty.

I HAD CHOSEN MOROCCO AS THE STARTING POINT OF MY PIL-grimage because it was familiar territory. Previous visits over the years had accustomed me to its widely varied landscapes, its delicate peasant foods, and its ancient mores. I was able to bargain in the local language and count in dirhams in my sleep. I knew the alleys of the major cities. I had friends there.

In Saudi Arabia I knew nobody. I had never even been inside the country. I was only going now to perform a demanding set of rites whose complexities already made me nervous. I did not intend to add to this the task of measuring deserts or assessing its people. I would not be traveling, in any case. I would be almost exclusively in Mecca, Muhammad's birthplace and the least representative of Saudi cities. In light of Theroux's remarks about Saudi reserve, I could not expect to find very many friends there. Whatever waited at the far end of the runway would be very different and more impersonal. So I imagined.

As the airplane took off I steeled myself a little. Tedious hours aloft were relieved now and then by brief stops to change flights in Casablanca, in Tunis. That afternoon, for the last leg of the trip, I boarded a jumbo jet at the Cairo airport. The flight had originated in New York the day before, and its several hundred passengers looked bedraggled. Most were sleeping. Taking the last free seat beside a window, I glanced around only enough to see that nearly everyone wore pilgrim clothes. It was a short ride and oddly quiet. Scattered here and there across the aisles were the makings of a group of men with whom I was going to spend the next month in Mecca. But I did not know that yet. The sun rolled down behind us, tinting the Red Sea a violent orange. Nobody spoke.

We landed about eight o'clock P.M. at the hadj airport in Jidda and I followed a planeload of pilgrims down the ramps. The women among us were scarved and wore white kaftans. Every man had on the white *ihram*, two regulation lengths of seamless terry cloth that males approaching Mecca always wear. The lower wrap fell from my waist to my shins. The top half hung loosely off the shoulders. This sacramental dress, ancient and pastoral, is a common motif on Sumerian statuary dating to 2000 B.C.E. Against the airport's high-tech background we looked like shepherds emerging from a steam bath. The muggy Red Sea heat is legendary. I broke into a sweat leaving the plane.

We entered a stadium-size concourse full of hadjis. I stopped in my towels to gawk at the wing-spread roofs. Tented on all sides, they gave the effect of a Bedouin encampment. In overall area this is the world's biggest airport, containing a dozen enormous terminals. This year, in a period of six weeks, a million pilgrims were going to set down here, a jumbo jet every five minutes, four thousand hadjis every hour. It was also the world's only "annual" airport, its systems too specialized to handle normal traffic. At the end of the season, a few weeks hence, the whole complex would close until next year.

Our group divided and subdivided, moving down the mall. I passed through Customs, then joined a knot of three dozen pilgrims in a hallway. A Lebanese man with a curved stick took the lead. I had seen him on the airplane, wearing loafers and a Western business suit. His staff was a saw on a pole, for pruning trees. His name was Mohamad Mardini. Offhand, cherubic, in his thirties, he seemed to know more than the others where we were going. The saw, he said, was a gift for a friend in the city. Its blade was covered by a cardboard scabbard. Walking, I kept my eye on him in the crowds. If we fell behind, he raised the saw to direct us.

I fell behind twice. Once to take a drink of water, once to inspect a room that led off the hall. The size of a college gymnasium, brightly lit with shiny marble floors, the room was jammed with package-tour pilgrims, Malaysians in canvas slippers, turbaned Afghans, a few thousand white-clad Pakistanis. I had not expected to see so many women—young wives, sisters, daughters, matrons, crones—nor was I prepared for the dozens of languages. When I stepped back into the hall, my group had vanished.

I found them outside in a car lot, piling into vans with sliding doors. The sky was dark, but heat still welled up off the asphalt. A driver strapped my luggage to the roof. He wore a checkered head scarf and a *thobe*, the long white choir robe that Saudis favor. When the bags were secure, he jumped inside and revved the engine.

We moved into the foothills of the Hejaz. The name, meaning Barrier, pretty well described the escarpment we were climbing. Its western face walled off Mecca from the sea. Above lay the Tihama Plain. This road is called the Corridor of Dedication. Millions of hadjis have traveled it, trekking back into the peaks where Islam was conceived.

The night was moonless. Freeway lighting curtained off the land. Where it died away, I saw high desert dotted with scrubby thorn bushes and steppe grass. The road curved up through switchbacks, flattened to a plain, then climbed again. Isolated peaks poked up like islands. Now and then in fields beside the road we passed small herds of camels. Oddly formal looking in the headlights, they raised their heads from grazing as we passed.

As we rode along, the men began chanting the *talbiya:*

> *I am here to serve you, Allah, Here I am!*
> *I am here because nothing compares to you.*
> *Here I am!*
> *Praise, blessings, and the kingdom are yours.*
> *Nothing compares to you.*

These lines are the hadj's hallmark, as much as the *ihram*. I heard them repeated day and night for weeks. The fifth line, echoing the second, wrapped back on the first line like an English round. The Arabic is chanted:

> *Labbayk, allahumah, labbayk!*
> *Labbayk, la shareeka laka,*
> *Labbayk!*
> *Innal-hamda, wa n-ni 'mata, laka walmulk.*
> *La shareeka lak.*

Talbiya means "to wait, in a ready state, for an order or direction." One of its functions is to clear the mind, to prepare you for anything. In the van it began the moment we left the airport. Before long I would hear it in my dreams.

The *ihram* had a powerful impact on me, too. For one thing, it put an end to my months of arrangements. In a way it put an end to me as well. The uniform cloth defeats class distinctions and cultural fashion. Rich and poor are lumped together in it, looking like penitents in a Bosch painting. The *ihram* is as democratic as a death shroud. This, I learned later, is intentional.

Mecca lies fifty miles east of the Red Sea. It is a modern city of 1 million people, splashing up the rim of a granite bowl 1,000 feet above sea level. Barren peaks surround it on every side, but there are passes: one leading north toward Syria; one south to Yemen; one west to the coast. A fourth, a ring road, runs east to Taif. By day the hills form a volcanic monotony. At night they blend into the sky and disappear.

The first thing I discovered about Mecca was that I'd been spelling the name wrong. West of town we passed a fluorescent sign with glowing arrows and six letters sparkling in the headlights: MAKKAH. The orthography threw me. With its two hard *c*'s, Mecca is the most loaded Arabic work in the English language. Without them, what is it? No one here said MEH-ka. They said ma-KAH. The accent took getting used to, but English-speaking Makkan insisted on it. "Do you spell Manhattan, men-HET-en?" one of them asked me.

A title was linked to Makkah on every road sign: al Mukarramah, "the Ennobled." With its special laws of sanctuary, with its status as the birthplace of Islam, the city was sacred ground, however you spelled it. It was also strictly off-limits to nonbelievers. Another sign, at a freeway exit, read:

STOP FOR INSPECTION
ENTRY PROHIBITED TO NON MUSLIMS.

The van rolled to a stop beneath the sign. Two soldiers stepped out of a booth and played their flashlights through the cab. Visas were checked. The hadjis continued chanting. A few looked nervous.

Some Westerners think of Makkah as forbidden to foreigners. In fact, it exists to receive them and is largely composed of them. Most of the populace descends through thirteen centuries of migrant pilgrims who settled here after their hadj and did not go home. The result is a cosmopolitan city, where every nation and race has taken root. Naturally it is completely Muslim. Only a Muslim has any business being here.

The officers brought back our passports in a basket. We left the checkpoint and continued on. Hejazi landscapes are studies in barren grimness. It was hard to imagine a sanctuary among these mangled limbs of Mother Nature. Bare hills rose in the headlights—treeless ridges reminiscent of Death Valley. The skyline looked straight out of Stephen Crane:

> *On the horizon*
> *The peaks assembled;*
> *And as I looked,*
> *The march of the mountains began.*
> *And as they marched, they sang,*
> *"Ay, we come! We come!"*

At the top of a final ridge the road swept east and joined a freeway. The asphalt here was lit up like an airfield. Luminescence bathed the rubbled hills; then, at blinding speed, the van shot under a giant concrete book. I swung around in disbelief, staring back through the windows. There it stood: a sculpture the size of an overpass, an Oldenburg mirage of a huge arched cross beams supporting a forty-ton Qur'an. *Did you see that?* Then we came over the lip of the canyon. The light of Makkah lay fanned out in a bowl.

We stopped at the Hotel al-Waha, on a street lined with modern-looking buildings. A sign on the hill read UMM AL-QUARA ROAD. I left the van and waited at the curb to see what would happen. Glad to be standing, I busied myself helping the driver untie luggage. Before we finished, the other men were inside the hotel. Our shepherd, Mardini, stood in the doorway, waving me forward. "We're going to stay here for a while," he said.

I went into the lobby and lined up at the counter for my room key. The desk clerk, a fair-skinned Arab in a goatee, insisted on calling me Roy Thomas, I shook my head.

A man behind me laughed. "He thinks because you're from California, you must be Roy. I'm from California. This is not Roy Thomas, I know Roy Thomas."

"Who," I asked, "is Roy Thomas?"

"My professor." He was a boyish-looking man in wire-rimmed glasses. We exchanged a few words. His name was Mohamed Fayez, a graduate-student engineer from U.C. Berkeley, by way of Tunis. Fayez was slight with a quizzical brow reminiscent of Woody Allen's. We stood beside our bags, taking in the action.

Forty men in terry cloth filled the lobby, chatting, sitting on couches. Watching TV. Bolivia, Brazil, Guyana, Chile, Argentina, and Peru were well represented. Of the rest, a third were African-American. Others, like Mardini and Fayez, had roots in North Africa or the Middle East: an Algerian from Denver, a Ghanaian from Detroit, a Palestinian from Culver City. Together we formed a gallery of Islam's diaspora. We had the Western Hemisphere in common.

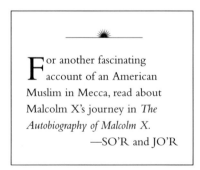

For another fascinating account of an American Muslim in Mecca, read about Malcolm X's journey in *The Autobiography of Malcolm X*.
                    —SO'R and JO'R

I said, "Which one is Roy Thomas?"

Roy Thomas was not here. A year ago, Fayez said, Thomas had formed a committee to welcome Nelson Mandela, the South African freedom fighter, to the Berkeley campus. Now that Mandela has finally been let out of prison and was coming to Berkeley, Thomas felt obliged to make good his word. A big reception was scheduled for tomorrow.

"It was supposed to have happened a month ago," Fayez said. "Now he's missed the hadj."

I said, "It's a pretty good reason."

"Allah decides everything," he said.

As the elevators began to work, a wave of exhaustion closed over me. The hands on my wristwatch were set for a different time zone. I jiggled my key, excused myself, and went upstairs.

I showered first, then turned on the TV. A constant stream of pilgrims passed under the windows. It was almost midnight and the streets were filled. The excitement was palpable. Touching my fingers together, they seemed to vibrate with a migratory throb. I slipped a belt around my waist to secure the *ihram*, folding two inches of cloth over the strap. I could now move freely and bend over.

A map of Iran filled the television screen, and an announcer in a *thobe* read from a clipboard. There had been a massive earthquake in Iran, in the mountains of Zanjan. Damage assessments were still coming in. Already a hundred villages lay in ruins. Aftershocks were being recorded, too, the nearest one 600 miles from Makkah.

The telephone rang.

I stubbed my thumb reaching for the receiver. It was the desk clerk.

"Mr. Thomas?"

I went downstairs.

Twenty minutes later we were climbing with the crowds up Umm al-Quara Road. Happily, this part of Makkah was set on bedrock. The buildings appeared to be carved into the hills, with a solid, quake-proof look about them.

At the top of the rise, where the street was closed to cars, a throng of 5,000 people moved up the pavement. Reaching the crest, I came up on my toes. Everyone knew what was down there, glowing at the bottom of the valley: the largest open-air temple in the world.

I fell in behind Mardini as we climbed. Soon I was being introduced to a Saudi guide named Sheikh Ibrahim, a professor of *Hadith* at the local university. I asked him what the Prophet had said about the mosque.

"Plenty," he chuckled.

Ibrahim was a gentle man, the most taciturn of the four guides attached to our party. A few blocks farther on I asked again.

He said, "Just remember: the Ka'ba is a sacred building. But not so sacred as the people who surround it," and pointing to the ground, he made a circle with his finger. "Whatever you do here, don't hurt anyone, not even accidentally. We are going to perform the *'umrah* now. We will greet the mosque, circle the shrine, walk seven times between the hills, like Hagar. Think of it as a pilgrim's dress rehearsal. Don't rush, don't push. Take it easy. Get out of the way if anyone acts wild. If you harm someone, your performance might not be acceptable. You might do it for nothing."

Sheikh Ibrahim's explanation of the *'umrah*—a pilgrimage of a more individual nature, the lesser, or minor, pilgrimage carried out at any time—was the longest single speech I would hear him make in the next four weeks. The view from the brown of the hill cut off further discussion. Behind a concrete overpass rose the biggest minaret I'd ever seen.

Down below, a mosque in the shape of a mammoth door key completely filled the hollow. Lit from above, roofless at the center, it seemed to enclose the valley bowl it covered. The proportions of this eccentric structure were staggering. The head of the key alone comprised a corral of several acres. In addition, attached to the east wall, the shaft of a two-story concourse ran on another quarter mile. For so much stone, the effect at night, beneath the banks of floods, was airy, glowing, tentlike. Seven minarets pegged down the sides.

This was the recent surrounding mosque that encapsulates a much older Ottoman courtyard. Ibrahim called it Haram al-Sharif, "the Noble Sanctuary." Its 160,000 yards of floor provided room, on a crowded day, for 1.2 million pilgrims. Galleries lit the second story. Parapets ran right around the roof. From the crest of the hill the minarets looked canted. I could not begin to guess the building's height. Its outer walls were faced in polished slabs of blue-gray marble, and the marine shades differed stone to stone. The veins shooting through them looked like ruffled surf. The minarets were spotlit. On every side the valley glowed.

I had never seen such a beguiling temple complex. Saint Peter's Basilica in Rome is roofed and open to tourists. Palenque covers more ground, but no one uses it. My aversion to sightseeing vanished before this pool of light and stone. All the must-see points were in one building.

We followed the road downhill beneath a bridge. Chunks of the mosque heaved into view as we went down, here a gallery, there a tower, shifting behind facades and concrete rooftops. Then the street curved sharply and the building disappeared.

A hot breeze swept down the hillside. Behind, the hum of traffic died away. The lots, where cars and buses parked at quieter times of the year, were occupied tonight by camping pilgrims. Fires burned low between the groups. Bedrolls lay open under bridgeheads. At the edge of the road we came upon a circle of Ghanaians reciting the Qur'an around a lamp. Most of the encampment was asleep now.

We entered the canyon lined with bazaars and food stalls. Where it leveled out, the mosque came into view. Its second floor had a Colosseum-like curve to the upper galleries. Across the road we stopped before a gate, forming a huddle. Ibrahim addressed us.

In the next few hours we were going to pay our respects to Islam's main shrines. The visit would have three parts. We would greet the mosque and circle the Ka'ba. We would drink from the Zamzam well. We would imitate Hagar's run between two hills in

search of water. There were fine points concerning these proce-
dures. Questions followed. Ibrahim or another guide replied.
When everything was settled, we waded into the crowds around
the mosque.

Most hadjis arriving at Makkah enter the *haram* through Bab al-
Salaam, "the Gate of Peace." Ibn Battuta went in by this gate; so did
Ibn Jubayr, his predecessor, who left a well-known account of his
pilgrimage in 1184 C.E. Tonight crowds on the stairs kept us from
fulfilling this tradition.

Mardini shrugged. We continued around the mosque to another
gate, Bab al-Malik. A shallow flight of steps let up to a foyer. We
deposited our sandals at the door and stepped across the threshold,
right foot first.

Inside we offered the formulaic greeting:

> *This is your sanctuary.*
> *This is your city.*
> *I am your servant.*
> *Peace is yours.*
> *You are salvation.*
> *Grant us salvation*
> *And guide us*
> *Through the gates of paradise.*

Crossing the foyer, we entered a series of pillared, curving halls.
In surrounding naves lit by chandeliers, fields of pilgrim families
sat on carpets, reclining, conversing, reading the Qur'an. Their
numbers increased as we moved deeper into the building. Books
on waist-high shelves divided quiet colonnades. Brass fixtures
overhead were interspersed with fans lazily turning. We continued
down an aisle through the crowds. The Ka'ba, Islam's devotional
epicenter, stood in an open courtyard dead ahead, but we could
not see it.

There were 300,000 pilgrims in the complex. Our walk from
the outer gate took fifteen minutes.

The colonnades enclosed an oval floor of about four acres. The oldest columns in the mosque flanked the perimeter, columns that Burckhardt, Burton, Al-Fasi, and Qutb al-Din all felt compelled to count and could never agree on. On the east wing they stood in quadruple rows; elsewhere they ran three deep into the building, making a courtyard portico.

I had read about this building and glimpsed it on Moroccan television, but taking its measure now was out of the question. Its proportions could not compete with its population, or with the emotional state of those I saw. To begin with, the aisles and carpets held an astounding racial microcosm: Berbers, Indians, Sudanese, Yemenis, Malaysians, and Pakistanis overlapped Nigerians, Indonesians, Bluchis, Bangladeshis, Turks, Iraqis, and Kurds. It was a calm crowd with almost no pushing. Our numbers did not result in agitation. The rush to reach Makkah was finished. The hadjis had arrived. Now the laws of sanctuary took over. This was the peace we had petitioned in the foyer. Everyone felt it.

Across the way a vigorous-looking Afghan in his eighties, six feet tall with burnished skin, stood praying into his open hands while big tears dropped onto his palms. A deep exhilaration knocked at my rib cage. Counting up columns in this became absurd.

As we walked, the aisles were subtly descending, conforming to the valley floor. We passed out of the covered portico and stepped down into the marble courtyard. This was the head of the key, the building's hub.

Moroccan mosques, to which I was accustomed, were all arranged in figures of four sides. The core of the mosque at Makkah is on the round, an open, roofless forum overlooked by tiered arcades. The marble floor is 560 feet on the long sides, 350 feet wide, polished to the whiteness of an ice rink. At the center of this hub stands the Ka'ba, a four-story cube of rough granite covered in a black embroidered veil.

This monolith is Islam's most sacred shrine. Thomas Carlyle, the Scottish historian, called it an authentic fragment of the oldest past. It was already ancient when Muhammad's grandfather restored it in 580 C.E. Its severe simplicity and black reflection lend the mass an upward rhythm. Tonight a light breeze ruffled its cover, and the slabs felt strangely cool beneath my feet. After acres of ceilings it was soothing to look up and see some stars.

We were fifty or sixty yards from the Ka'ba, moving around the outskirts of the forum. Knots of hadjis, stopped in their tracks, stood everywhere around. The first sight of the shrine was literally stunning. Men wept and muttered verses where they stood. Women leaned against columns, crying the rarest sort of tears—of safe arrival, answered prayers, gratified desire. I shared these emotions. I also felt an urge to escape my skin, to swoop through the crowd like lines in a Whitman poem, looking out of every pilgrim's eyeballs. I heard Fayez call out as he hurried past, "We made it! We made it!"

A doughnut ring of pilgrims ten rows deep circled the shrine, forming a revolving band of several thousand people. We kept to the edge of them, skirting the cube, and faced its eastern corner. Here a black stone in a silver bezel had been set into an angle of the building. This was its oldest relic, the lodestone of popular Islam. We faced the stone and stated our intention:

> *Allah, I plan to circle your sacred house.*
> *Make it easy for me,*
> *And accept*
> *My seven circuits in your name.*

Each hadji began at the black stone and circled the Ka'ba counterclockwise. This ritual is called turning, or *tawaf.* At a distance the wheeling pilgrims obscured its base, so that for a moment the block appeared to be revolving on its axis. As we came nearer, the shrine increased dramatically in size. On the edge of the ring we adjusted our *ihrams* and raised our hands to salute the stone. Then we joined the circle.

Keeping the shrine on our left, we began to turn. Ibrahim and Mardini went ahead, calling words over their shoulders as we followed. There were special supplications for every angle of the building, but not many pilgrims had them memorized. Now and then we passed someone reading set prayers from a handbook, but most people were speaking from he heart. I caught up to Mardini and asked him what was proper. The invocations all but drowned us out. "One God, many tongues!" he shouted. "Say what you want or repeat what you hear. Or just say, 'God is great.'" I dropped back into the wheel and did all three.

The first three circuits of *tawaf* were performed at a brisk pace called *ramal*. Richard Burton likened the step to the *pas gymnastique*. I had not imagined the hadj would be so athletic. Each time a circuit returned to the stone, it was all I could do to remember to raise my palms and shout, "*Allahu akbar.*" It was not the pace or the distance but the crowd that was distracting. On the perimeter of the ring I noticed wooden litters passing, on which pilgrims weakened by age or illness were being borne around. These pallets marked the circle's outer edges.

Coming around the northwest wall, we included in each circuit a half-circle of floor marked by a rail. Inside the rail lay two slabs of green stone said to mark the graves of Hagar and Ishmael. Directly above, a delicate golden rainspout protruded from the roof of the Ka'ba. The prayer at this spot alluded to the rainspout:

> *On that day*
> *When the only shade is yours.*
> *Take me into your shadow, Lord,*
> *and let me drink*
> *From the Prophet's trough*
> *To quench my thirst forever.*

The liturgy and the place were of a piece here.

We performed the quicker circuits near the Ka'ba, on the inside rim of the doughnut. When they were done, Mardini began taking side steps, distancing himself from the shrines as we moved along. I followed suit, working my way to the outer edge of the circle, where we performed our last four rounds at a leisurely walk.

As the pace fell off, space opened around us. I could see the black drape rustle on a breeze. It hung down the Ka'ba on all sides. Covering the cube in heavy silk. Its name is the *kiswa*. I later heard it called the shrine's *ihram*.

One had to perform the *tawaf* to comprehend it. Its choreographic message, with God's house at the center, only came clear to me in the final rounds. Orbiting shoulder to shoulder with so many others induced in the end an open heart and a mobile point of view.

The final circuit brought us back to the eastern corner. We saluted the black stone as we swept past, then washed up on an outer bank of marble, behind an underground copper enclosure the size of a phone booth. This was called the station of Abraham. Prayers offered here acquired special grace. We faced the Ka'ba and performed two *rak'ahs* together.

Our rite of *tawaf* was complete now, but the evening was not over. Next we descended a flight of steps to a cavernous room containing the Zamzam well. Cool air flooded the stairwell, cutting the night's heat as we went down.

In Ibn Battuta's day the Zamzam well was housed above ground in a large pavilion. Today the floor has been cleared of these installations. The water drawers and leather buckets have vanished, too, and the profiteers who place exorbitant fees on the concession. Even the well has been relocated, to a wedge-shaped amphitheater.

The air was deliciously damp the first night I went down there. The slanting stone floors ran with surplus water. Hadjis not content merely to drink dumped buckets of the liquid on their bodies, and strangers toweled off each other's backs. The atmosphere was like a friendly bathhouse. Here and there, on a dry patch, lay a solitary sleeper.

Rows of aluminum washbasins were arranged around the room. I took a sip from a public cup chained to a sink and was stepping aside to give Fayez room when a tremor ran through the basement. Beads of condensation shivered in the rafters. The *tawaf*? I thought, and then the vibration stopped. Fayez looked startled.

Makkah's most watchful Western chronicler, John Lewis Burckhardt, wrote this about the well in 1814:

The Turks consider it a miracle that the water of this well
never diminishes, not withstanding the continual draught
from it....Upon inquiry, I learned from one of the persons
who had descended in the time of the Wahabys to repair
the masonry, that the water was flowing at the bottom, and
that the well is therefore supplied by a subterraneous
rivulet.

Makkah would not exist without this well. Its appearance in the
bone-dry Hejaz is a fundamental wonder: the first condition of
desert urban life. For thousands of years it supplied the whole town
for drinking and ablutions. Seeing it, I understood why
Muhammad had linked water to prayer and installed a purifying
rite at the heart of his practice. Even in pre-Islamic times the well
was sacramental. Today pilgrims drink from it to fulfill tradition.
Minerals render it heavy, but I found the taste of Zamzam water
sweet, not brackish, and very, very cold (having passed through a
cooling system in the basement).

The legend of Hagar's arrival in this valley is related in the book
of Genesis:

The angel of God called to Hagar out of heaven, and said
unto her, "What ails you, Hagar? Fear not; for God has
heard the voice of the boy where he is. Arise, lift up the
boy, and hold him in your hand; for I will make him a
great nation." And God opened her eyes, and she saw a
well of water; and she went, and filled the bottle with
water, and gave the boy a drink. And God was with the
lad; and he grew, and dwelt in the wilderness, and became
an archer.

The Bible casts Hagar in a passive role. Weeping, lost in a
wilderness, she sits with eyes averted, unable to watch her child's
death. Muslim legend describes a more active agent. In these stories Hagar runs between two hills, passionately seeking water in a
desert. Her drive is emotional, physical, existential. At stake are
faith and her family's survival.

The course of Hagar's quest, I now discovered, is still in active use within the building. Our last labor of the night was a ritual jog between the hills. The rite, called *sa'y*, takes place in the concourse on the long side of the key. To reach it, we crossed the Ka'ba floor, saluted the stone, then walked out of the courtyard, heading south.

A series of arches led through cloisters to a gate. Here the head of the mosque and its shaft were joined, forming a marble lane called the *mas'a*. Later I heard one hadji refer to it as the race-course. I was unprepared for the length of this passage: a quarter-mile stretch of covered mall, split in two lanes for pilgrims coming and going.

The course began at the top of a hill called al-Safa, jutting from the base of Mount Qubays. It ended at the second hill, al-Marwa, in the north of the building. I had never seen hillocks housed inside a building; domes had been set in the ceilings to accommodate their crowns. A complete lap covered about eight hundred yards. Here, as around the Ka'ba, old age and illness were shown consideration. Down the center of the *mas'a*, on a median strip dividing the two lanes, frail pilgrims were being wheeled in rented chairs.

Saluting the shrine at the top of each relay, we completed seven lengths, or about two miles. My legs began to throb in the third round. The contrast between the mystical *tawaf* and this linear, headlong rush could not have been greater. Wandering loosely between fixed points, doubling back on itself around the hills, the rite expressed persistence and survival. The *sa'y* was not a circle dance. Its intent seemed to be to instill compassion for the victim-ized and the exiled. This was the mall of necessitous desire.

We finished our run and stepped down onto a ramp beside al-Marwa. By now our *ihram* towels were streaked with dirt and sweat. We had come through the *'umrah*. We were *muta 'ammirin*. As we stood shaking hands (Mohamed Fayez high-fived me), two self-appointed barbers stepped from the wings, offering their ser-vices. In order to put aside the *ihram* clothes, a pilgrim who plans to return to them for the hadj is supposed to have a desacralizing haircut. Generally this means a token snip of three or four neck hairs. When it is done, we returned to Bab al-Malik for our sandals.

Michael Wolfe is the author of books on poetry, fiction, and travel, including One Thousand Roads to Mecca: Ten Centuries of Travelers Writing about the Muslim Pilgrimage *and* The Hadj: An American's Pilgrimage to Mecca, *from which this story was excerpted. He is also the publisher of Tombouctou Books and lives in Santa Cruz, California.*

✦ ✹ ✦

The Fruitful Void

The desert has always been a crucible for the seeker.

CREAKY OLD STAIRS THEY WERE, THE ONES LEADING UP TO THE priest's flat; oak stained dark, lit at the top by a dim light seeping through one of those frilly little lamp shades that were fashionable in the fifties. Sister Paula was leading the way. She was the guest sister at Twymawr Convent in Wales. She pushed back the door at the top of the stairs. The wan light of a February morning filtered into the room through two windows and picked out the dust on the faded carpet. One wall was lined with bookshelves; on a table in the corner stood an electric kettle, a jar of instant coffee, and some tea bags. Along another wall, the one with the wooden crucifix nailed to it, was a single bed covered with a pink flock bedspread.

"You are most welcome to use the library." Sister Paula beamed a matronly grin.

"Thank you; I have brought my own books."

Already too late to bite my tongue. She meant no harm. She was being *a good guest sister*. But I was wary, on my guard. This was the first Anglican establishment I had set foot in since my childhood. It was 1975, and I was thirty years old, but already the taste and feel of the place were evoking images from my youth: the obsequious local vicar, the social hierarchy, the self-conscious hymn singing, the drone of the sermon that no one listened to, the keeping up of appearances, the call of duty. All so painfully bereft of passion, spirit, and meaning. Not just anxiety but arrogance fueled my quick response. I rather thought I knew something about genuine spirituality now, having spent some years as a self-possessed seeker; there could hardly be much for me of interest on those dusty bookshelves lined with fading tomes on saints and church history.

She backed out of the room and left me gazing over the convent lawn to the single oak tree at the far end. Under the tree several plain wooden crosses marked the remains of sisters who had lived and died here. Beside them, behind a low hedge, was a trailer, the home of the community's hermit. I had come here for a week because I wanted time for reflection at a period in my life when events were moving fast. The environment of a contemplative community seemed an ideal context, especially since I had been told I could follow my own schedule.

I had not accounted for the way a place can seep into the pores: the smell of the furniture, the view from the window, the bells, the frankincense that came floating up through the floor from the vestry below to announce each of the seven daily services. I had not bargained for what I would find when, on the second day, unable any longer to resist the lure of the frankincense, I found myself irrevocably drawn down to Compline, their last service of the day. The chapel was a high, narrow cave, lit that evening with candles along the pews. The chanting of the nuns, the presence they summoned, their quality of attention evoked an unusual beauty whose effect stayed with me as I walked back up the oak stairs after the service and sat in the chair facing the bookshelves.

The air in my room was sweet still from the censer below, a bird was scuffling somewhere in the eaves. I got up and surveyed the books lining the wall. Bernard of Clairvaux, Catherine of Siena, Meister Eckhart, Carlo Carretto, *The Anglican Church in the Nineteenth Century*. I took down Saint Catherine and opened the covers. *James Lovage, Trinity College,* it said. 1936. The words went round a small red crest in the middle of the yellowing title page. That night I spent in Siena. I followed Catherine, entranced, round the city streets as she tended victims of the plague, oblivious of her own safety; I marveled at her visions, at her furious faith that seemed to transform all adversity into an opportunity to praise her Beloved.

The next morning I took down an author I had never heard of before. Carlo Carretto, *Letters from the Desert*, a small paperback among the rows of stiff spines. In 1946 Carretto was president of Italian Catholic Youth Action; in 1948, with the direct support of the pope, he organized a rally of hundreds of thousands of young Catholics in Rome. A few years later, at the height of his political and religious authority, he left everything to become one of the Little Brothers of Jesus, a renunciate fraternity in the Sahara. His book paints the great space and silence, the way the desert returns man to essentials. Reading his *Letters*, I realized how I wanted that. A vision began to form in my mind. Two hours later, I had decided to go on my own journey to Sahara.

My love of the desert, then, began in a Welsh convent. In the summer of that same year I was on my way to Algeria, fired by a dream. My plane touched down at Tamanrasset airstrip in darkness. "Tam" was a tiny settlement then, in southern Algeria, not so far from the border with Mali. I spent the couple of hours before dawn in the little passenger building, talking to a mountain of a man with a handlebar mustache who was on his way to Chad to hunt rhinoceros. As the rocks began to glimmer in the first light of dawn, I clambered into the Jeep that was to take us to town. We bumped down the track, and within a few moments the Sahara was unveiled to my staring eyes, a vast rolling moonscape of red rock and dust, streaked with the purple and yellow of the emerging day. The sun that was rising over the farthest crags was larger than any sun I had ever seen. As it lifted itself higher into the gaping sky, the rocks burned redder and stood in stark relief against the canvas of blue.

The flight from London to Algiers had taken us the same distance as the flight from Algiers to Tamanrasset. The second flight, though, was over nothing but desert. The Sahara accounts for a quarter of the entire continent of Africa and is widening its borders every year. Tam is hundreds of miles from anywhere, in the land of theTuareg, a proud nomadic people who still fail to recognize the arbitrary national borders across their territory. In 1975, Tam was a few streets of low houses, an old French caravanserai, and a fort—all constructed in adobe.

The Jeep stopped outside the fort. I passed through the gate in the red walls and stood for a moment contemplating a tombstone with the inscription:

> LE VICOMTE DE FOUCAULD
> FRÉRE CHARLES DE JÉSUS
> MORT POUR LA FRANCE

This, the resting place of Foucauld, was the birthplace of the Little Brothers. Charles de Foucauld had died here from a stray shot fired by one of the locals he was trying to protect. He had built the fort in 1916 to shelter the local population from tribal raids.

As aristocrat, a graduate of the Saumur cavalry school, a dandy who loved the best cigars and flirtatious women, he was sent in 1880 as a lieutenant with the Fourth Hussars to Algeria. He excelled as a leader but was quietly sent back to France over an affair with a Frenchwoman. At the age of twenty-four, in favor again with his regiment, he went on a solo reconnaissance mission to Morocco, disguised as a traveling Jew. The first Christian to survive the arduous journey into the interior, he returned with notes for a book on the topography and the flora and fauna of Morocco, along with a deep respect for the all-pervading religiousness of the culture.

Back in the high society circles of Paris, his book on Morocco a great success, Foucauld the adventurer was questioning his life direction. It was then that he was introduced to a man whose presence and simplicity touched him deeply. Abbé Henri Huvelin told him that he had long since found the means to be happy.

"And what is that?" asked Foucauld.

"It is to be willing to forgo one's joys," replied the abbé.

Foucauld went to Huvelin in the confessional the next day. Leaning into the box, he whispered, "I have come to you for instruction."

"Kneel, and confess your sins," was the reply.

"I have not come for that. I have come for instruction."

"Kneel, and confess your sins."

Foucauld did so, pouring out the deeds and events of his whole life. He took Communion and left the church that day with a mission to bear witness to the presence of God in the midst of human life. He became a priest and spent most of the rest of his life living in the Sahara and serving the poor there, fired by the persistent dream of founding a community similar to that of the early Desert Fathers.

Foucauld's story was an epic one, and he had a part to play in my own presence here now before his tombstone. He had inspired many people to live in utter simplicity and anonymity among the poorest people in the world. Indirectly, through one of his brothers, he had inspired me to come to this fierce and lonely place for my own reasons. I have my own dream to live out, and I felt gratitude for his part in it.

I was a couple of days in Tam before I managed to find a Tuareg guide who was willing to take me out into the desert and return for me three days later. I had never heard of a vision quest then, but that was what I was wanting to do. My dream was to be alone out there for a few days, far from all trace of humanity, and discover who it was that really inhabited this body. As familiar as my moods and my preoccupations were to me, I was aware at that time in my life that there was a depth to human existence about which I had only the vaguest notion.

We rode out just as the sun was rising and continued until early afternoon. We stopped only for Said to dismount and make his prostrations and pray, and once to let the camels nibble on a bush of thick leaves and thorns. For hours we crossed a plain strewn with rocks and gullies. Mountains, some as high as ten thousand feet, ringed the horizon. They were part of the Hoggar range, the most ancient rocks in the Sahara, the only land above water when (in the Paleozoic era) the Sahara had been a vast lake. This was not the land of rolling dunes that I had imagined. I knew that only 20 percent of the Sahara is occupied by dunes, while rocky plains account for half of the desert, but childhood images are tenacious. The plain was more desolate, more sobering, than the Sahara of my imagination: yet more vibrant too, orange and red everywhere, with streaks of black and purple shadow.

When we passed by two slabs of rock that were leaning against each other to form an open-ended cave, Said dismounted and untied a goatskin of water from the camel's flank. This was it, then. Three days under two rocks in a sweltering plain. With a word of farewell and a faint smile of bemusement, Said rode off with our camels back along the ancient riverbed that we had been following for the previous hour. As I watched him go, it occurred to me that I had never before put myself so trustingly, or perhaps unthinkingly, into another person's hands.

He disappeared over a slight rise and I turned to contemplate my surroundings. No wind, no trace of movement, no sound; everything just where it had been for centuries, so it seemed, illuminated by an unfiltered glare; yet the heat, muted by the altitude of a few thousand feet, was bearable, even in high summer. Gooseflesh ran along my arm. I laid my bedroll between the rocks, heard my breathing, felt the air pass an electricity through me. Never had I been so tangibly aware of my own existence. I wanted to sing out, but the immensity of space took all sound away from me. The rest of that day I sat beneath the rock in awe, with a sheer animal joy, not just at the world I had come to but at the marvel of my own living and breathing.

Within a day, it was all rather different. The drama and excitement of acting out a cherished dream had evaporated. No longer was I playing the lead in some movie. There I was alone in the midst of this desolate landscape, awoken in the morning at the first glimmer of light by swarming hordes of buzzing flies, churning out the same ordinary thoughts as I did back in London. Their triviality, my own mundanity, stood out starkly in the unswerving stare of the desert sun. I found myself beginning to laugh, not in self-depreciation but in genuine amusement. I was no great ascetic, no latter-day Charles de Foucauld or Carlo Carretto. There was nobody special waiting to be revealed beneath my humdrum exterior, no reserved destiny or Damascus experience about to proclaim itself on the desert stage. No, beneath the ticktock of my hopes and fears, past and futures, there was nothing much to speak of at all, simply a sense of clear and empty space, rather like the desert itself.

I soon discovered I was not the first to stay in the vicinity of these rocks. Halfway up the outside surface of my shelter, someone had etched a swirl of rings into the rock. On another rock, a few hundred yards away, there was clear outline of a giraffe, with all detail of its shading, and on another had been carved some cattle, with long horns gracefully intertwining as if they were in some kind of ritual dance. The presence of the ancient ones survives here still, even here, where no one passes now except for the occasional nomad and dreaming foreigner.

The Sahara is the greatest open-air museum in the world of prehistoric rock art. Where I stood was once a land of flowing rivers and tropical wildlife. Elephant and hippo used to roam this way; oak, olive, elm, and willow grew on the Hoggar Mountains. These etchings before me were the accomplishments of men who had lived here, perhaps under the very rocks that were sheltering me, some five thousand years ago. Lake Chad, far to the south, is the only large body of water left from a time when great rivers poured through the Sahara to feed dozens of lakes across North and West Africa. This desert, which seems as if it must have been since the dawn of creation, is just a few thousand years old. A million years ago people known as the Pebble Culture lived throughout the Sahara; their sharpened stones, the first tools, can still be found on the desert floor.

At night, my back against the prehistoric network of rings, I would watch the stars, stars that I had never seen, a whole constellation—Andromeda—I had only ever heard the name of. How much easier it must be to travel the desert at night, with such a compass overhead, the cooler air easing the way, an undiluted purity feeding the mind.

On my last day alone I walked out far from my rock into the empty expanse. At one moment I stopped and looked back over the way I had come. I seemed to have walked no distance at all. There was a wind that day, and my footsteps had already been filled by the shifting sand. There was no evidence whatsoever of the effort I had made to come this far. Suddenly, there in the uncompromising light, I was stripped of all self-preoccupation and artifice. I became aware of the deep insignificance of the personal story that I had imagined to be my identity. I knew now with a quiet certainty that the events of my life and the interpretations I had given them would pass like those footsteps in the sand. Standing there, a speck on a vast canvas, I felt returned to proportion: true, authentic, and unashamedly small, without even a story to tell.

When Said appeared on the morning agreed, it felt so ordinary it was as if nothing had happened. And in a way, nothing had. Bobbing up and down on that camel to Tam, I felt profoundly at peace with the world and myself. No ecstasy, no revelation, just the sense of being at home. I asked Said to take me to the Little Brothers, and he dismounted outside a house indistinguishable from any others in the tiny back street.

The door was opened by a Frenchman in overalls. Frère Michel ushered me into a small room where two or three other men were sitting on the wooden floor. They were about to eat their evening meal. White bowls were before them; they invited me to take one for myself from a small table and to join them. One of the men was a visitor from another community of Little Brothers, in Mali. The rest lived together in the house and worked in the town. Frère Michel, a Parisian in her mid-forties with a fine, chiseled face and clear blue eyes, was working as a mechanic. Another was a baker. Their life on the outside was like that of any other worker in the town, except they attended Mass daily and prayed together each evening.

The Little Brothers are not a contemplative community, or a

missionary or a charitable one. Their inspiration is the figure of Christ in Nazareth, the incarnation of love in the midst of daily life. They are invisible. They run no schools or hospitals, give no alms, preach no sermons, wear no habit. They seek out the poorest, the most socially neglected communities in the world, take on their burdens alongside them, and live out their lives in the practice of seeing the other in themselves and in the all-embracing love of Christ. There are perhaps two thousand of them around the world.

We said little that evening in Tam; mostly there was just the clink of spoon against bowl. They asked me if I had been to Assakrem. I had never heard of the place. It was the highest mountain in the Hoggar, they told me, some two days' camel ride away. Charles de Foucauld had built a retreat hut there, and a small chapel. Two brothers lived there all year round.

"God speaks on Assakrem," said Frère Michel in a matter-of-fact way. "It is so removed from the world there that it is difficult not to hear what one needs to hear."

"Strip your prayers, simplify, de-intellectualize. Reach God not through understanding but through love." These were the first instruction that Carretto, newly arrived in the desert, had received from his novice master. The Little Brothers were in training to be people of no importance, what Zen Buddhists call "the man of no rank." I understood now why the desert was their church and why they sought out the loneliest mountain there for their place of retreat.

A few days later, returned to my everyday world, insulated by glass and concrete, by cities and streets and cars and planes, by ongoing relations with others, I found it not quite so easy to remember what was obvious in the desert: that all the bustle, the urges to action, the plans and projects, veil a deeper, more lasting stream. Easy to forget, too, that nature bears an awesome majesty, terrible and mighty, that her wild places reflect our own untamed and primal ground. All the homage, the prayers, the love songs, the devotions to nature that have been sung on the wind for millennia are almost beyond our hearing now. For our ancestors, the voice or the vision of God would strike into the heart with a bolt of lightning, surge out of the desert, or speak on a mountaintop far above the tame and peopled valleys.

The voice of spirit cries out now in the wilderness of cities, and increasing numbers of people are hearing it, yet whenever I return to nature's empty wilder-ground, I am given a new breath and vision that restores me to my essential humanity.

I returned to the desert several times since my first journey there, through the years, too, the name of Assakrem lingered on, symbol of something not quite finished there in that forgotten corner of the Sahara. I would wonder occasionally—on a bus journey, in the subway, walking down a busy street—what unusual attraction this Hoggar mountain had held for Charles de Foucauld and why, with all the spectacular country around them the Little Brothers would speak of Assakrem in such reverential tones.

Finally, fifteen years later, in 1990, I returned to Tam to take my original journey on to what, in my imagination, had become its final stage. Journeys are like that; they start out as imaginings, generated from a word heard here or an image seen there, then they take on a vitality of their own that may bear fruit just once, or even several times in a life. They can mature in a day, sometimes over years; but when they are ripe, conditions often oblige and bring them to the light of day. This time I flew to Djanet, a couple of hundred miles to the east of Tam.

Djanet is a tiny outpost in the southeast corner of Algeria, far from any paved road; far, indeed, from anything and anywhere at all. I wanted to take the long route to Tam, so that I could absorb the variety of desert landscape. I hired a local Tuareg team, one of whom walked with me, the others following us each day in a Land Rover with provisions. For the first couple of days we walked in a huge canyon that split open a range of red cliffs that soared straight up from the desert floor. Birds circled overhead, and I saw the tracks of hare, snake, and rabbit. On a rock lay a lizard eighteen inches long, a streak of iridescent blue. Old tree trunks shot out shoots of new life among twisted dead branches, and seed pods as large as small coconuts hung open from thorny bushes with tiny flowers emphatic as eyebright.

Beyond the cliffs was an empty plain, eerie and littered with black stones, like the aftermath of some volcanic eruption. Then, in the distance, loomed a mountain plateau, the Tassili-n-Ajjer, which means "mountain of rivers." Deep ravines and gorges were cut into its side, witness to the water that had once poured from the mountain. Olive trees, figs, dates, lime, and elm once grew there in profusion. This massive table of rock is the home of tens of thousands of prehistoric rock paintings and engravings. They must have lived in the land of plenty, those early artists, among all the animals of the present-day African savanna.

To walk with Mohammed, the Tuareg, was like traveling with an antelope. He moved over the rock and the sand like air, his long *jelaba* flowing gracefully behind him, his face covered in the traditional veil that protected him not only from the elements but from the danger of evil spirits entering him through the mouth and nose. In the evenings, by the fire, he would tell me how his people had safeguarded the passage of caravans through the desert for centuries; how they were a noble warrior race who disdained mundane work; and how, more recently, the national governments had been moving them into settlements. He told me how they loved to eat couscous with grasshoppers, sand mice, and a big firefly called *dobb*, which according to him contained forty precious medicaments. One evening just before sunset we had stopped for the night when he pointed to a sticklike object standing up out of the sand a hundred yards away.

"That snake is very clever." He laughed. "He is standing up like that so a bird will come and rest on him, thinking he is a stick."

Traditionally, the only activities worthy of a Tuareg were war and raiding. When a family reached a water hole, the women would erect the tents, and slaves would tend the animals and fetch water. They would stay till the water or the pasture ran out, and then move on. Their policing of the caravans—of slaves, gold, and salt—was more in the character of a protection racket. Travelers had to pay to ensure a safe passage through their territories. The last great caravan, from the north down to Timbuktu, was in 1937; since then the influence of the car has steadily eroded the Tuareg way of life. It takes 240 camels to carry the same load as one truck. The Tuareg are a mix of Berber, Libyan, and Greek blood, a unique culture with their own language, oral tradition, medieval tournaments, and festivals. Some of them earn a living now guiding groups and individuals like me, though with the political troubles in Algiers, visitors are few and far between.

Mohammed and I wandered on past the Tassili to a pale-yellow land beyond, where the horizon was broken only by sporadic outbursts of rock, dropped from nowhere and thrown together in untidy heaps. After a day of walking along an old riverbed, we passed across deepening sand through a forest of tall rock needles, to the largest dunes in the area. Nothing could have prepared me for this. The colors struck me in the chest; the desert floor was pale yellow, but then the dunes were bright orange, with a sudden shift in tone here and there the higher they rose. Occasionally there would be a neatly defined band of white between the tones of orange, and all of this against a sky so densely blue I felt I could plunge my arm into it. The shapes were designed by the wind: mountains of sand with twirling edges just like the soft ice cream that twists out of an ice cream machine, each dune with its own sharp crest that wound up to a point. The whole spectacle was unearthly, yet the Sahara takes up more of the earth than the whole of Europe. What, I found myself wondering, is more foreign to the earth: the desert, or the teeming cities of the world?

How simple it would be to disappear without a trace here. The Tuareg find their way by the stars and with the aid of signs—the color of the sand, the shape of a dune, a rock, a tuft of grass. In the early colonial days, two Tuareg guides drew a map of the whole southern Sahara for their French masters with bags of wet sand. One caravan that could have used that map set out for Timbuktu in 1805. Two thousand men and a thousand camels were never seen again. In 1933, Captain Lancaster tried to beat the flight record for London to the Cape. He reached Reggane, where he stopped for fuel, and the local French watched him take off. He was never heard of again. It was only in 1962 that his remains were found, by Titus Polidari, on a mission seventy kilometers west of Reggane.

Lancaster had made a forced landing and had survived eight days waiting for help. His journal of those days, less the binding, which he had ripped off to make a fire, was tied to the fuselage. On the eighth day wrote, "No wind. Dawn is breaking on the eighth day. It is still cool. I have no more water. I am waiting patiently. Please come soon...I had a fever last night."

On my last day before driving on to Tamanrasset we walked in the Ténéré, another world to the land of the dunes. We had spent the previous night in the lee of a red rock, the last of several we had passed the previous day. When I awoke, I stared out from the shore of the cliff onto an endless sea of sand that was utterly becalmed; not a ripple, not a rock, no relief of any kind to break the mirrorlike surface.

After a few hours of walking on the plain, I was jolted with the same realization I had had all those years before when I had walked out from my rock in the Hoggar Mountains: it was obvious I was going nowhere. This land was so much vaster than my stride that any idea I may have had of getting somewhere seemed ridiculous. Having no reference points also obliged my attention to stay where I was, with this step. I realized on the Ténéré how our sense of self is so intricately dependent on the other, even if the other is no more than a contour in the land. Without even a contour for reference, Roger Housden himself seemed to slip away for a while, leaving little but the sensation of being alive—not as this identity or that, just aliveness itself.

We arrived in Tamanrasset in the early evening, and it was light enough to see that the town had undergone a transformation since I had last been there. There were avenues on the outskirts, a large army base, streets of concrete buildings. Tam was now the main administrative center for southern Algeria, and the population had grown from five thousand in 1975 to almost sixty thousand in 1990, including many refugees from the various troubled countries farther south. The old town was as I remembered it, however, and I checked into the colonial caravanserai with the cell-like adobe rooms.

Despite its expansion, Tam was still a slow southern town with an easy pace. In the morning I strolled out to the little square and sat with a coffee, watching the world go by.

Not much went by—a few Tuareg, an Arab keen to change money, a boy who would have liked to sell me a Tuareg dagger, a man selling oranges. But everyone had a word to say. The selling seeming more of an excuse to gossip. Then a European woman, in her early sixties perhaps, with a warm open face and clear blue eyes, came out of a shop and made to get on her bicycle. I asked her if she knew where I could find the Little Brothers. "Will a Little Sister do?" she replied in French.

She came over and joined me. Her name was Sister Madeleine, and she had first come to the Sahara in 1959 as a nursery teacher: She had met the Little Sisters in Tam at Easter of that year, had joined them and had been in different communities in the desert ever since. After the Second Vatican Council, they stopped wearing the habit and dropped much of the rule, living instead more from the inspiration of Foucauld, a simple life of being with others in the ordinary world. Even so, they still spent two hours daily in solitary prayer and an hour in "adoration" together. Sister Madeleine lived with one other sister in some rooms near their church.

That evening I went to their church to join them for Mass. It was a tiny adobe building with a sand floor, empty except for a square stone block that served as an altar, and lit by a narrow shaft of light from one small window. Outside was a small courtyard with an acacia tree and a well. Three sisters and four brothers came to the service and two Africans. One of the brothers was Michel, whom I had first seen all those years ago. His features as clear as ever, he was graying now, as I was myself.

That church was like a desert cave, and it reminded me that I was in the Sahara to restore my vision. I intended to go to Assakrem and stay there for a week on my own. Michel told me that a brother was going there in a couple of days and that he could arrange for me to share his Jeep.

The next day was a Sunday, and when I arrived at the church to speak to Sister Madeleine, thirty or so black men were listening to a man from Nigeria preaching in the courtyard. "Don't you know that God's foolishness in greater than Man's wisdom?" he was crying out. "Didn't the walls of Jericho fall at the sound of a trumpet? Isn't that foolish? And you, you all want to leave Tam, you want to find your dreams in Europe, and it seems an impossible task. No money, no passport, no visa, and you want to go to Europe. Yet I tell you God will provide, and He will provide in a way that you will least expect. You must trust in His foolishness, brothers, and His foolishness will see you through."

It was an impassioned speech, and the longing eyes and cries of "Yes, yes!" from the congregation saddened me. I was being witness to a part of the world stage that I never knew existed.

"So many fine young men in search of a real life," sighed Madeleine as we sat on her step and looked on. "Thousands of them have poured into Tam in the last few years from all over Africa. They live in makeshift refugee camps on the edge of town. Their own countries—Zaire, Mali, Niger, Nigeria, Ghana offer them nothing. The only option for them is to eke out a living on their family land, if they have any, and that is precarious in the extreme. Their countries are all on the verge of bankruptcy; there is often no higher education; AIDS is rife; the social structures are breaking down. The young don't want to follow the traditional ways of life anymore. Their eyes are fixed on the consumer society of the West. They imagine it to be a paradise there. They risk losing even the clothes they are wearing at the hands of Tuareg bandits on the border with Niger, and most of them arrive here with nothing at all. They cannot go forward up the road to Algiers, and they cannot go back, because there is nothing to go back to. The only ones with some money are the Nigerians, who have brought in the drug trade and sell their wives in prostitution."

How strange, I thought, as I watched their faces; they dream of the West and I dream of the Sahara. Most people I know in Europe have money and all the consumer trappings, but they are in search of a real life just as these men are. I had come here, to the Sahara, because I, too, wanted to feel the real life that once again seemed to have slipped away from me.

That evening two Spaniards were eating dinner at the caravanserai. One, Abel, was a lecturer in fine arts at Madrid University. Every vacation he traveled to a different part of the Sahara photographing the prehistoric engravings and paintings. Back in Madrid, he digitalized the photos for posterity, with the intention of making the first complete record of all the Saharan art. He traveled everywhere on a 500 cc motorbike, using aeronautical water maps.

"I used to travel on a 500 cc Honda," he told us over coffee, "but I learned my lesson when I skidded and the machine fell on me. I was trapped for two days. I nearly died. I eventually managed to dig my way out, wearing my nails to the bone. 'When you don't know what to do,' my father used to tell me 'find the animal in you.' I had to walk 120 kilometers before finding help. Now I only take what I can repair myself. I drink two liters of water daily, and find much of my food on the way. There's no other choice. Most of these drawings are way off in the middle of nowhere. The Tuareg taught me how to hunt. I catch lizard, snakes, and hare. Snake is delicious if you cut a hand's breadth from each end. I catch hare using hooks and a circle of guitar string."

Juan was much quieter. A mechanic by trade, he loved to travel in the Sahara as soon as he had saved enough money. He wrote and published his own books of poetry. He was from Sorija, the town in northern Spain where Antonio Machado, one of the great Spanish poets of the twentieth century, had lived much of his life. Juan loved Machado and told me the whole town revered him as a saint. Every time he came to the desert, Juan brought toys that he would give away to the local children. The desert always attracts romantics, adventurers, those with their eyes on the stars.

As I crossed the courtyard on the way to my room that night I passed a man who was washing the dishes in a fat aluminum tub. He was singing his heart out. Our eyes met and I stopped to exchange a word. He was from Zaire, he told me. He had left with his brother just before all exit visas were stopped. He had been studying biochemistry at university when all the schools and universities were closed by order of the president because they had been the scene of riots. They were still closed three years later, and the only people who could get jobs were those connected to the president's family. The president of Zaire, he told me, was one of the richest people in the world and had helped to fund the last campaign of President Bush. The people of Zaire were destitute, and he had come here in the hope of getting to Europe to find work and send money home.

"I know I will get there." He beamed. "I have so many dreams. I trust in God. He would not give me talent to waste in washing dishes. I know that so much is possible, but first I must earn the money to get to Italy. That is the easiest place to get to from Algiers. There are boats which will take you for a price, and the Italians, you know, they don't care so much about visas and all the official things."

Such life in his eyes, such hope in his voice. Our hands clasped, and we wished each other luck. I lay awake a long time that night, thinking of these African men, their dreams and longings like those of so many people around the world. It was fitting, somehow, that the desert, this empty and neutral land, should be the limbo where we all tussled with our devils and angels. Yet I felt an anguish for these men on the road in search of a life. Surely so much aspiration couldn't have grown merely to be whittled away here in the sand? I knew the answer to my own question, and that was what was keeping me awake. In the middle of the Sahara, where I least expected it, I was face to face with a global predicament. There is nowhere to hide now from the face of suffering. I wanted to help, run out into the yard and give him my money. But the worst thing was, I knew it wouldn't help: he would be back in the same situation a week or two later, when the money ran out. I myself was powerless to affect the situation. I had to stare the reality of it in the eye, and if my heart broke, so be it. This is our world, and I am as responsible for it as anyone else.

I met the Little Brother the next morning with bleary eyes. I clambered into his Jeep and we set off for the Hoggar along a track through the shanties on the outskirts of town. By late morning we were grinding our way up a narrow stone path that wound through gray cliffs and slopes of black scree. By the afternoon we had reached the rest house below Assakrem, a desolate stone building that served as a way station for travelers. With our provisions on our back, we started out along the footpath that looped up to the tabletop summit.

A low building with a courtyard came into view, just in the lee of the highest outcrop of rocks. A Little Brother appeared, greeted me quietly, and ushered me in to the courtyard to sign the visitors' book. "Your hut is across the top and on the other edge," he said. "There is a tank of water, but I hope you have brought everything else you need. There is one other retreatant here at the moment, a priest from Lille. But I don't expect you will bump into each other."

I thanked him and continued on up to the top. One square building faced the way we had come. It was the retreat hut that Charles de Foucauld had built all those years ago. A little way off was a small chapel, next to a tiny meteorological station that Foucald had also built. The rest, a desolate expanse of black stones overlooking the most eerie and dramatic land I had ever seen. Off in the distance, across brown-and-black valleys, pillars of red rock rose up on the horizon: ridges twisted into sleeping giants; huge boulders strewn at random by the force of some ancient volcanic eruption; mountains in the shape of cones, saddlebacks, tabletops. Dust hung in the valley air below; an old riverbed snaked its way off to the east.

I followed the track that had been pointed out to me and came on a low hut on the far side of the tabletop. I stood on the plateau just above it, gazing at its walls of volcanic stone, its corrugated iron roof, its view over hundreds of miles, then made my way down into its little courtyard. The hut was divided into two parts, each with its own outside door: tiny living quarters, with a bed, a camping stove, a table; and a chapel that was bare except for a stone slab of an altar adorned with a miniature picture of Christ and an animal skin on the floor.

My head was feeling light already from the altitude; when the wind died for a moment, the only sound I could hear was the pulse in my ears. When have I ever felt so completely alone? Only when

I was last here, somewhere down on the plain, fifteen years ago. I sat on the courtyard wall and gazed across the valley. Heavy clouds hung trails of vapor over the nearest crests, while on the horizon the mountain waves were shrouded in dust. I sat there till dusk and watched a crack of gold slit open the gray in the west. Two birds danced along the courtyard wall, then flew off into the void. A faint flurry of pink, and the day was done. The dun color of earth pervaded sky and land. I peered out over the fading view. "This is my religion," I said out loud. That night the wind rattled my cage from every quarter. The door creaked resolutely through the night, the iron roof flapped, two birds began courting some time before dawn, mice scampered around beneath my bed. I awoke with a head thick from the altitude, a mouth furry from lack of water. I got up to wash, and there over the sink was a plaque with the words *Jesus, Master of the Impossible*.

Outside, a pale light filtered through clouds, the black stones and eerie peaks looking more somber than the day before. I was beginning to discover already that they wear you down, the wind, the rocks, the altitude. Try to think straight in a wind that whips through your coat from one direction, then stops suddenly, only to start up again from another side, and this at an altitude that had your head crashing before you are even awake in the morning. Nothing to look at but rocks for hours on end, volcanic ones with a magnetic field that turns the mind one notch away from it customary bearing. No green, no life, no relief from the burning ground. Nothing moves, nothing but thoughts in the head, and even those on a short lead that brings them quickly round to the beginning again. Meditation, which I had expected to practice regularly in such a perfect setting, proved to be more difficult than I had ever known.

That first day or two, I held many conversations with myself; sometimes I talked to myself aloud. I surprised myself by noticing how I was already missing the bustle of town; I wondered about writing a novel to bring the plight of the Africans to public attention. What was I doing here, up here, "above it all," on some godforsaken mountain far from the world and its troubles? Everything came up from down below those first few days, the anger, the impatience, the torpor, the lack of direction or purpose, the lusting after voluptuous images.

For the first few days I stayed outside in the wind and the light, now up, now down, a slave to the buffets of mood and body. On the third afternoon I was sitting with my eyes on a small icon of Christ Pantocrator that was pinned to the wall of my cell. Suddenly I got up and, for the first time, opened the door of my chapel. It was dark in there, and the humidity soothed me. I sat on the animal skin on the floor. Something softened inside, let go.

Over the days that followed, my internal conversations began to give way to silence. To begin with, I had tried not to recognize my own boredom and depression; I had pushed them away with reading and writing. Now, as the days passed, there seemed less to be afraid of. Even when I was doing nothing, which was most of the time now, there was no sense of boredom to run from. I had taken to sitting in the chapel darkness three or four times a day; just sitting there, the wind in the roof always. I see now why wind is the breath of life. Everything stirs in its presence; without it, this is a land of death, burned to cinders long ago by some prehistoric volcanic eruption. There was a taste of death on my own tongue, too. My house of cards seemed to be tumbling down.

In that chapel I began to see the sense, and also the beauty, in those old Christian terms "chastening," "being made straight." Like a bent piece of wood straightened with steam or an iron being made true in the fire. This mountain was knocking the stuffing out of me, returning me to an original mettle. The heart is opened, I was reminded again, by the awareness of one's self feeling a genuine sympathy for the Christian doctrine of original sin. Beneath all the perversions that have turned it into a weapon of oppression for almost two millennia, I could begin to grasp a deep and profound teaching that my own prejudice had blinded me to since childhood.

I knew on that mountain that my own nature—all human nature—contains a built-in fault line that severs me from authentic living. I had no choice but to see it—there was no healing balm, no soothing beauty to divert my attention. The beauty of the Hoggar was hard-edged; it reduced everything to essentials, to whitened bone. Another old word, I remembered, also much misused, was "repentance." The original Greek was *metanoia,* which means "change of mind." There was no blame or guilt attached to my fault line, but seeing it and accepting the fact were enough to turn the heart in another direction. By the end of that week on Assakrem, I was starting the day with an offering in the chapel. I offered my own divisions to that One—call it God, the Presence, the Self, the Beloved—who was more real, more true, than the contents of my own mind, and without whom I was nothing.

> If we value the great poem of Christianity, we cannot reject one meaning of Christ's incarnation, that while God's relationship to humans may not change, humans' relationship to God must, as Christ's did, even on the cross, ranging from the certainty with which he promises the thieves on their crosses that they will see paradise together, to the mournful cry to God in the question "Why have you forsaken me?" experiencing in death both despair and hope.
> —Patricia Storace,
> *Dinner with Persephone*

I came down the mountain in the company of the priest from Lille, whom I had not seen at all during the time I was there. I never saw anyone that week, except a shadow once on the rocks in my courtyard, whose origins I never discovered. The priest had been up there for forty days and looked like he had just come back from a weekend picnic, all jolly and jovial, and keen to find some fresh toothpaste. He was between lives, having been a school chaplain in Lille for ten years and now about to spend a year in America.

The first person I met on my return to Tam was Juan. He was sitting in the garden of the caravanserai reading his beloved

Machado. He read me one in Spanish, which I barely grasped the meaning of, and then asked me about my time on Assakrem. In answer to this question, I remembered an English translation of a verse of Machado that had meant a lot to me once. "This is how it was," I said. And I recited the lines:

> I thought the fire was out
> I stirred the ashes
> And I burnt my fingers.

In the morning, before leaving, I saw the washer boy from Zaire again. "Will you please do me one favor?" he asked. "My cousin left Zaire at he same time as me, and he managed to get to England. I know he goes to the church of the Jehovah's Witnesses in a place called Wembley, near London. I have heard that through my family. He has been there two years already. Please will you find him and tell him I am here, at this address? I know he will help me. He will be so glad to hear from me. His name is Emmanuel."

I promised to do what I could. The following Sunday, back in London, I drove up to Wembley to find the church of the Jehovah's Witnesses. I got there early, before the morning service, and told the man at the door whom I was looking for. "He comes most Sundays," said the warden. "If you sit in this room I will bring him to you when he arrives." After half an hour the service was about to begin, and no one had come to the room. I got up and stood by the glass door at the back of the congregation. The singing had just begun when a man in a brown suit hurried in. The warden whispered in his ear and pointed in my direction. We went outside and I introduced myself, telling him about my encounter with his cousin.

He was dumbfounded, more uneasy than happy. "I am glad he is safe, but what am I to do? I am a mechanic here. I earn just enough to live in one room, and I am not even sure they will let me stay. My visa is only temporary, and I'm trying to do everything right to get a permanent one."

"Here is his address and phone number," I answered. "At least get in touch with him."

"But what can I do?"

"I don't know what you can do. I don't know what anyone can do. I'm here to give you the message. Perhaps the only thing we can both do is to hold him in our heart. Take him with you into the church. But here is his address."

The cousin took the piece of paper with the name of the caravanserai on it and folded it away in his pocket. We shook hands, he went into the church, I went outside. I stood there for a moment in the gray London street and breathed in a deep breath of dank morning air; then I saw the washer boy from Zaire in his hotel courtyard, whistling under the desert sun.

Roger Housden has led sacred journeys in India and the Sahara, and was a therapist at the Bristol Cancer Center, a freelance journalist, a public relations and management consultant, and a teacher of the Alexander Technique. As founder of the Open Gate, a holistic workshop and conference program in England, he was responsible for bringing innovative voices in American Buddhism and Christianity, psychology, and philosophy to a European audience. He is now a full-time writer and photographer, and is the author of numerous books, including Travels Through Sacred India, Fire in the Heart: Everyday Life as Spiritual Practice, *and* Sacred Journeys in a Modern World, *from which this story was excerpted.*

* * *

The Road to Bethlehem

Palestine has changed a great deal since this journey
in the early 1930s, but you can still walk
in the footsteps of Jesus.

THE ROAD WAS LIKE ANY OTHER ROAD IN PALESTINE. THE SKY WAS a hot lid above it. The snapping of grasshoppers in the olive groves was a steady rhythm in the heat.

The road was white with the dust of powdered limestone, a floury dust which the heels of the donkeys kicked up in clouds; but the soft feet of the camels hardly moved it, as they passed silent as shadows. White stone walls lay on either side, and behind them the stony terraces, planted with olive trees lifted themselves in sharp white ridges against the darkness of the sky. Little brown lizards with the watchful heads of frogs lived in the chinks of the stones. They would come out to lie in the sun, still as the stones, except for a quick beating in their throats. Sometimes I could go to within a yard of them and would be just about to touch them with an olive twig, when, swift as whiplash flicked out of the dust, they would be gone.

The heat was a nervous tension enclosing the world. All sounds were an invasion, except that of the grasshoppers, which was the palpitating voice of the heat. A shepherd boy piped somewhere on the hill, playing a maddening little tune without beginning or end, a little stumbling progress up and down a scale, like the ghost of a waterfall. And the white road led on under the sun.

It was, as I have said, just like any other road in Palestine. But there was one thing that marked it out from all other roads in the world. It was the road to Bethlehem.

As I walked on, I thought that travel in Palestine is different from travel in any other part of the world because Palestine exists already in our imagination before we start out. From our earliest years it begins to form in our minds side by side with fairyland, so that it is often difficult to tell where one begins and the other ends. Therefore the Palestine of reality is always in conflict with the imaginary Palestine, so violently at times that many people cannot relinquish this Palestine of the imagination without a feeling of bereavement. That is why some people go away disillusioned from the Holy Land. They are unable, or unwilling, to reconcile the real with the ideal.

Any truthful account of travel in Palestine must mention this conflict. Every day you hear travelers say, as they visit some place: "I never imagined it quite like that," or "I have always thought of it in a different way."

And as I went on to Bethlehem I remembered a place hushed in snow where shepherds wrapped in thick cloaks watched their flocks under the frosty stars. There was a little shelter in this place in which beasts stamped in their stalls and blew the fog of their breath into the cold air. On the straw near the mangers, sitting in exquisite detachment, was a Mother with a gold circle about her head and a little Child. The stars shone coldly, and through the air came a sound of far-off bells.

I know perfectly well that this picture was edged with gilt. It was my own private little vision of Bethlehem, something that has been with me all my life, something made up in my mind from Christmas cards sent to me when I was a child, from pictures that I loved before I could read, something formed by the piety and reverence which cold northern land has cast round the story of the Nativity. Every Christian nation had translated the story of Christ into its own idiom and cradled Him in its own barns. The great medieval painters have, each man in his own way, painted in the national background of his own country and his own time. And we who come from Europe to Palestine come from an enchanted country to the bare rocks and crags of reality.

I walked along in the airless heat, sorry to say farewell to this little picture of mine; and the heat of the white road to Bethlehem quivered like fire over the limestone walls and beat like the breath of a furnace upon the grey little olive trees and shone through the greenness of the uncurling fig leaves.

I came to a place where a few trees made a pool of shade on the dust of the road. And under the trees was an old well with a stone basin beside it, so that shepherds and camel-men could pour out water for their beasts.

This well, like so many things in this land, has several names. Some call it Mary's Well, because of an old story that the Holy Family, traveling the five and a half miles between Bethlehem and Jerusalem, once rested there and drank its waters. It is also called the Well of the Star. The legend is that the Wise Men on their way to Bethlehem lost the Star and, coming to this well to slake their thirst, found it again shining in the water.

Bethlehem today remains a center for pilgrims and travelers of all stripes, particularly at Christmas when the town virtually explodes with activity. Located ten kilometers south of Jerusalem, surrounded by vineyards, olive trees, and villages, Bethlehem has an almost entirely Christian population of nearly 22,000 people, including nearly all of the Palestinian Christian minority. After having changed rule several times in the last century, Bethlehem returned to Palestinian control in 1995. In addition to its historical and religious significance, Bethlehem is known for its friendly people, olive-wood hand carvings, beautiful embroidery, and mother-of-pearl jewelry.

—SO'R and JO'R

I went on past the Well of the Star. On the left, the earth suddenly fell into space. The terrific landslide fell away into the heat, and down below, far off, like land seen from an aeroplane, lay a brown-and-blue map of the Dead Sea and the Mountains of Moab. Ahead of me was Bethlehem, with slender cypress trees rising above the flat roofs, white buildings shining among the olive trees, and terraces falling away into a wall of heat. Beside the road, facing the view of Moab, was a stone seat. There was no shade above it and the stone was hot. A lizard streaked away into hiding as I rested there. There were words carved on the stone: "Thou shalt love the Lord with all thy heart, and with all thy soul, and thy neighbour as thyself." Beneath this summary of Christ's teaching was an inscription which stated that the seat was placed there in memory of William Holman Hunt by his wife, Edith.

Holman Hunt's picture *The Light of the World* was the most famous religious painting of the nineteenth century. It must be known to everyone. Holman Hunt painted it when he was twenty-seven years of age and at a time when, discouraged by the difficulty of selling his pictures, he was trying to make up his mind to forsake art and take up farming in the Colonies. This painting decided his life. The recognition it brought enabled him to realize his dearest ambition: to live in Palestine and paint biblical subjects in the country of Christ's birth. Of all the famous pictures painted by Holman Hunt in Palestine, perhaps the best known is *The Scapegoat*, a pitiful study of a poor, starving creature wandering in dreary solitude among the salt hills of the Dead Sea, bearing the sins of humanity upon its head.

I remember reading somewhere that Holman Hunt's favourite view was that from the road near Bethlehem, and I suppose this seat marks the place. No doubt the hot, forbidding vista of the Jordan Valley from this point first suggested to his mind the idea of *The Scapegoat*.

The sight of the parched valley and the barren, waterless Mountains of Moab made the hot road seem cooler. Down there, I thought, the Dead Sea would be warm to the touch. The palms would be standing in a burning stillness, and the water would have dried in the baked mud trenches that run between the banana trees.

It is not difficult to know why mystics have always gone into those terrible hills to find Truth. Such indifference to Mankind seems to promise a revelation of God; their unwillingness to quench the thirst of the body suggests that they might be willing to slake the thirst of the soul.

I went on, past the white-domed Tomb of Rachel, which is venerated by Christian, Jew and Moslem, and, just where the road branches off to Hebron, I looked over a stone wall and saw something which an archaeologist in Jerusalem had told me not to miss; the only surviving relic of Pontius Pilate. It is the ruin of an aqueduct which ran from the Pools of Solomon to the Temple area. It was an engineering work which involved Pilate in a financial scandal.

Pilate was appointed procurator of Judea in A.D. 26 and remained in office for ten years. The custom of long-term governors was approved by Tiberius, who used to say with bitter cynicism that an enriched governor was better for a country than a new and still-rapacious one. Much more is known of Pilate's career in Palestine than is to be found in the Gospels. Josephus and Philo give long, but biased, accounts of his record.

He expressed an active dislike for the Jews and a bewildered contempt for their religious taboos. He regarded them as dangerous maniacs and instigators of every kind of sedition. He had the plain, blunt soldier's loathing for the political intrigue by which he was surrounded, and he possessed the worldly man's dislike for the fanaticism which he met at every step. He lost his temper quickly and frequently ordered his troops to attack the Jews; but, reading the history of his time, one wonders what else he could have done. Roman tolerance was always interpreted as weakness.

His first act did not endear him to the Judeans. It was a custom with the Romans, who always observed the greatest respect for the religious beliefs of their subject peoples, never to permit troops to march into Jerusalem with the image of the Emperor on the legionary standards. These were always unscrewed and put away out of deference to the Mosaic injunction against graven images. Pilate, however, when moving troops up to Jerusalem,

marched them into the city under cover of darkness with the eagle
and the imperial image on the tops of the standards.

When the Jews awakened in the morning and saw this, the city
was in an uproar. Deputations surrounded his palace for five days,
begging him to remove the images. He threatened that unless the
agitators went away he would order a massacre. On the sixth day
he was forced to meet the deputations, who cried that they would
willingly die rather than suffer the violation of their laws. Pilate
was beaten and had to order the removal of the eagles.

Another and an even more serious conflict was that of the
aqueduct whose remains still lie beside the Bethlehem road. In
order to bring water from Solomon's Pools to the Temple (although his enemies said that the water was really intended for
military purposes in the event of an insurrection), Pilate raided
the enormous funds known as the Corban, lying in the Temple
treasury. The appropriation of this money created violent opposi-
tion. The storm broke when Pilate came up to Jerusalem from his
headquarters at Caesarea, probably during the annual Passover pilgrimage, when he was always present with extra troops in case of
trouble. This time Pilate sent troops disguised as Jewish pilgrims
among the crowds. These troops, at a signal, attacked the Jews and
quelled the disturbance. If this episode occurred at Passover time,
there seems to be an echo of it in Saint Luke, who mentions the
"Galileans whose blood Pilate mingled with their sacrifices."
Should this supposition be correct, a remarkable possibility is
dependent on it. The Galileans whom Pilate slew were not subject to him: they were the subjects of Herod Antipas. Now, when
Pilate handed Jesus, the Galilean, over to Herod, we learn from
Saint Luke "and the same day Herod and Pilate were made friends
together: for before they were at enmity between themselves."

If it is possible that Pilate sent Jesus as a peace offering to the
ruler of Galilee in return for the Galileans he had attacked on a previous occasion, then the strange thought occurs that the building of
this aqueduct—the cause of the original enmity between Pilate and
Herod—was a contributory factor in the crucifixion of Jesus....

I climbed over the wall and inspected this extraordinary relic.

Few people know that it exists and, unless someone takes care of it, the remaining water pipes, or rather stones, will be carried away and used for building material. In fact the head of the Magi's well farther back along the Jerusalem road is one of these stones. The aqueduct runs at the edge of the boundary wall and disappears from sight beneath a house. It is formed of huge blocks of stone with a central hole drilled in them, and so arranged that each stone fitted with a neck firmly into the next, making a solid rock channel for the water.

If the theory I have advanced is reasonable, this line of stones is one of the strangest and most significant relics in the world. In any case, a few of them deserve a place in Jerusalem's magnificent new museum.

I went on toward Bethlehem thinking of Pilate and of the odium that has been cast on his name. The trial of Jesus gives us a full-length portrait of the Roman: haughty, blunt, weak enough to be blackmailed, but distinguished from [those around him] by a sense of justice. He did try to save Jesus. He tried again and again with a growing sense of exasperation and hopelessness…. The cry went up: "If thou release this man, thou are not Caesar's friend!" It was blackmail. And it sealed the fate of Jesus.

Pilate's attitude changed when that cry went up. He had good reason to visualize an influential embassy visiting Rome behind his back and plotting against him. "The Governor of Judea," they would say, "has set free a man who calls himself King. He is not Caesar's friend."

Pilate owed everything to Tiberius. One word from the Emperor and he fell from power, perhaps into exile and disgrace. Pilate knew, and the Jews knew, that there is nothing easier to poison than the mind of an autocrat.

So Pilate, too weak and too worldly to challenge the voice of the blackmailer, was once more beaten by the Jews. As a last gesture of disapproval he called for water and washed his hands.

He survived in office for another six years: until, in fact, he made a serious error in judgment which those who lay in wait for him used in order to procure his recall. A certain impostor appeared in Samaria and summoned the Samaritans to the top of Mount Gerizim, promising to reveal to them the sacred vessels which he said Moses had buried there. An armed crowd gathered at the village called Tirabatha. Pilate, who was always on the look-out for armed rebellion, misjudged the seriousness of the assembly and sent troops to disperse it, which they did with great slaughter. The Samaritans appealed to Vitellius, the Legate of Syria and Pilate's superior, who, finding that Pilate was in error, had no other choice than to send him to Rome to answer the charges made against him. While he was on his way to Rome, Tiberius died, and the inquiry into Pilate's conduct was apparently forgotten in the confusion of the new reign. So Pilate disappears from history to emerge again in legend. It was related in very early times that, falling into disgrace under Caligula, Pilate committed suicide. But there is no historical justification for this story.

In the apocryphal gospels, *The Acts of Pilate* and the *Gospel of Peter*, which were written centuries after Pilate's death, he is shown in a favourable light and is assured of divine forgiveness.

Legend, however, shows him, like Judas, pursued by demons of remorse and despair. It was said that his body was flung into the Tiber, but evil spirits so terrified the neighbourhood that it was taken up and conveyed to Vienne, in the south of France, where it was flung into the Rhone. There the same thing happened. The body was therefore taken up a third time and carried to Lausanne, in Switzerland, where it was walled up in a deep pit surrounded by mountains. Another story says that Pilate's corpse was eventually flung into a dark lake on the mountain still known as Pilatus, and it is recorded that people traveling by night in those desolate parts have been horrified to see a white figure walk from the lake and go through the motion of washing its hands.

The white houses cluster on the hill like a group of startled nuns. They stand on the edge of the road and gaze down into a pit of heat. Where the stripped terraces end and the bare rock begins, the last olive trees seem to be struggling desperately to run back up the stony terraces away from the heat and the sterility of the rock. The white houses watch them with open mouths that are doors, and startled eyes that are windows. And the hot sunlight beats down from the blue sky.

Above the flat white roofs rise the bell-towers of convents and orphanages and monasteries. There is always a bell ringing in the heat. If it is not the bell of the Salesian Fathers, it may be the bell of the Sisters of St. Vincent de Paul. At the bottom of the road that leads up to this white hill-town is a notice-board which absurdly pins this region to reality: "Bethlehem Municipal Boundary," it says. "Drive slowly."

The traveler, approaching Bethlehem with his mind on Saint Luke and Boticelli, pauses in surprise before this board because it has never before occurred to him that Bethlehem could be confined by municipal boundaries. It seems to him, at first, almost sacrilege that Bethlehem should possess a mayor and a municipality. Then, when he ceases to feel and begins to think, it occurs to him that the Mayor of Bethlehem is a wonderful symbol. He is a sign of an almost terrifying continuity of human life. His predecessors in office extend back before the time of Christ into the days of the Old Testament, and probably into dim, distant regions of legend. Bethlehem is typical of the strange immutability of these Palestinian towns. Wave after wave of conquest has swept over them without, apparently, making much difference to them. Bethlehem has known the Jews, the Romans, the Arabs, the Crusaders, the Saracens, and the Turks. They have all erected their notice-boards on the boundaries. And now there is one in English at the bottom of the hill asking you to "Drive slowly."

I once read a story, I think it was written by H. G. Wells, in which someone discovered a door in a very ordinary wall which led into the Garden of the Hesperides. The memory of it came to me in Bethlehem when I encountered a door in a massive wall. It was so low that even a dwarf would have to bend his head in order to pass through it. On the other side of it was the Church of the Nativity. They say in Bethlehem that all the doors into this church were walled up long ago, except this one, which was made low in order to prevent the infidel from riding into the building on horseback and slaying the worshippers.

But no sooner had I bent my head and stepped across than I straightened up—in Rome! It was the Rome of Constantine the Great, or, perhaps I should say, New Rome. It was the biggest surprise I had had in Palestine. I expected the usual ornate church, the dark, burdened altars, the confused stairs and passages of a reconstructed building, and here I was in a cold, austere Roman basilica. Massive Corinthian pillars made of some dull red stone upheld the roof and divided the church into a nave and aisles. I was in the church that Constantine the Great built long ago as a sign that he had become a Christian. Surely one of the marvels of Palestine is the fact that this church should have survived the dangers that have swept the other buildings of its time to dust? Here it is, the earliest Christian church in use today, and more or less as it left the hands of its builders. On the walls are the remains of dim gold mosaics.

I looked up to the roof. Is there, I wondered, anything left of the English oaks with which Edward IV reconstructed the roof of the Church of the Nativity? He cut down oaks and sent tons of lead for this purpose, which the Republic of Venice transported to Jaffa. There the Franciscans took charge of the pious gift and conveyed it to Bethlehem. I believe the lead was melted down by the Turks in the seventeenth century and used as bullets against the very Republic that had conveyed it to Palestine; but somewhere, perhaps, high up above the Roman nave, may linger a fragment of oak from the forests of fifteenth-century England.

The church is built above a cave which is recognized as the birthplace of Jesus Christ two centuries before Rome became a Christian state. The grotto must have been sacred to Christians in the time of Hadrian. In order to defame it, as he tried to defame Golgotha, he built over it a temple to Adonis. Constantine pulled down this temple and built this present church in its place. There seems to me something so touchingly formal about it, as if the Roman Empire did not yet quite understand this new faith, but was making a first, puzzled genuflection in its direction. One feels that these pillars are really the pillars of a temple to Jupiter.

A service was in progress. I thought the choir was filled with nuns, but they were ordinary Bethlehem women wearing the tall veiled headdress of the town. Beneath the high altar is the cave which tradition claims as the spot where Christ was born. It is entered by flights of steps on each side of the choir. On the way down I had to press myself against the dark little staircase as two Greek monks, black of eye and beard, came up in a cloud of incense.

Fifty-three silver lamps hardly lighten the gloom of the underground cavern. It is a small cave about fourteen yards long and four yards wide. Its walls are covered with tapestry that reeks of stale incense. If you draw this tapestry aside, you see that the walls are the rough, smoke-blackened walls of a cave. Gold, silver, and tinsel ornaments gleam in the pale glow of the fifty-three lamps.

I thought I was alone in the cavern until someone moved in the darkness, and I noticed the policeman who is always on duty to prevent disputes between the Greek and the Armenian priests. This church, like the Church of the Holy Sepulchre, suffers from divided ownership. It is in the hands of the Latins, the Greeks, and the Armenians.

So jealous are the various churches of their rights that even the sweeping of the dust is sometimes a dangerous task, and there is a column in which are three nails, one on which the Latins may hang a picture, one on which the Greeks may do so, and a neutral nail on which no sect may hang anything.

In the floor there is a star, and round it a Latin inscription which says: "Here Jesus Christ was born of the Virgin Mary." The removal of this star years ago led to a quarrel between France and Russia which blazed into the Crimean War.

Such truths may seem terrible; but this, alas, is an imperfect world. It is therefore necessary, as you stand in the Church of the Nativity, or in the Holy Sepulchre, to try and forget the frailties of men and to look beyond them to the truth and the beauty which they seem to obscure.

As I stood in this dark, pungent cavern I forgot, I am afraid, all the clever and learned things written about the Nativity by German professors, and I seemed to hear English voices singing under a frosty sky:

> O come, all ye faithful,
> Joyful and triumphant,
> O come ye, O come ye to Bethlehem.

How different is this dark little cave under a church from the manger and the stable of one's imagination! As a child, I thought of it as a thatched English barn with wooden troughs for oats and hay, and a great pile of fodder on which the Wise Men knelt to adore "the new-born Child." Down the long avenues of memory I seemed to hear the waits singing in the white hush of Christmas night:

> While shepherds watched their flocks by night,
> All seated on the ground,
> The Angel of the Lord came down,
> And glory shone around.

There was a rhythmic chinking sound on the dark stairs. A Greek priest, with a black beard curled like that on an Assyrian king, came slowly into the cavern swinging a censer. The incense rolled out in clouds and hung about in the candle flames. He censed the altar and the star. Then, in the most matter-of-fact way, he genuflected and went up into the light of the church.

Beneath the church is a warren of underground passages. In one of them, a dark rock chamber, Saint Jerome conducted a number of his keen controversies and translated the Vulgate.

But I found my way back to the cavern where the incense drifted in the lamp flames. The grotto was full of little children, silently standing two by two on the stairs. They came forward, knelt down and quickly kissed the stone near the star. Their little faces were very grave in the candlelight. Some of them closed their eyes tightly and whispered a prayer.

No sooner had the last of them gone, then I heard the chink-

chink of the censer; and into the gloom of the Grotto of the
Nativity came again a Greek priest like an Assyrian king.

There are a number of old houses in Bethlehem built over caves
in the limestone rock. These caves are exactly the same as the sacred grotto under the high altar of the Church of the Nativity, and
they are probably as ancient. No one who has seen these houses
can doubt that Jesus was born in one of them, and not in the stable of European tradition.

I suppose the idea that Christ was born in a stable was suggested
by Saint Luke's use of the word "manger." To the Western mind
this word presupposes a stable or a barn, or some outbuilding separate from the house and used as a shelter for animals. But there is
nothing in Saint Luke to justify this.

These primitive houses in Bethlehem gave me an entirely new
idea of the scene of the Nativity. They are one-room houses built
over caves. Whether these caves are natural or artificial I do not
know: they are level with the road, but the room above them is
reached by a flight of stone steps, perhaps fifteen or twenty. The
caves are used to this day as stables for the animals, which enter
from the road level. There are, in most of them, a stone trough, or
manger, cut from the rock, and iron rings to which the animals are
tied during the night.

The family occupies the upper chamber, separated only by the
thickness of the rock floor from the cave in which the animals sleep.

Now, if Joseph and Mary had visited the "inn" at Bethlehem
and found it full, there would have been no stable for them to go
to, because the "inns," or *khans*, in the time of Christ were merely
open spaces surrounded by a high wall and a colonnade under
whose arches were rooms for the travellers. The animals were not
stabled in the European sense, but were gathered together in the
centre of the enclosure. The Greek word *katalyma* used by St.
Luke, and translated a "inn," would be more exactly rendered as
"guest chamber."

Therefore I believe we must imagine the Nativity to have
taken place in one of these old cave-houses of Bethlehem. The

guest–chamber, or upper room, which it was the Jewish custom to offer to travelling Jews, was evidently already occupied, and therefore the host did his best by offering to the Holy Family shelter of the downstairs room, or cave.

It is interesting in this connection to remember that the earliest tradition in the church was that Jesus was born not in a stable or an inn, but in a cave. Justin Martyr, who was born about A.D. 100, repeats a tradition current in his time that, as Joseph had no place in which to lodge in Bethlehem, he discovered a cave nearby. But even before Justin's time it seems that the cave below the Church of the Nativity was venerated as the scene of Christ's birth. It is not unreasonable to assume that the caverns below this church were once above ground and formed the bottom stories, or basements, of inhabited houses.

Saint Matthew, describing the birth of Jesus, says:

> "And when they were come into the *house*, they saw the young Child with Mary his mother; and fell down, and worshipped him."

One of the houses which I visited might have remained unchanged since the time of Christ. The man was attending to the animals, two donkeys and a foal, which were tied up to the rock in the cave. In the room above the woman was sifting some small grain, like millet, through a sieve. From time to time she talked to her husband as he busied himself in the room beneath.

The living-room was, like most rooms in the East, bare of furniture. In a corner of it were the matting beds rolled up and tucked away out of sight.

The thought came to me that the nearest approach to the kind of building in which Christ was born is probably a Connemara cabin. I remember once going to a wake in a little white cabin rather like these Bethlehem houses, except that it was all on one floor. The living-room was separated from the animals' quarters by a pole and a curtain of sacking. The noise of beasts stamping came clearly to us as we sat round the turf fire. I remember thinking at the time that perhaps the Nativity took place in the same humble surroundings.

H. V. Morton was born in 1892 and died in 1979 in Cape Town, South Africa. He was the author of many wonderful books, including A Traveller to Italy, In Search of Ireland, *and* In the Steps of the Master, *from which this story was excerpted.*

JEAN SHINODA BOLEN, M.D.

✶ ✶ ✶

Pilgrimage to Glastonbury

The ancients were up to more
than we'll ever know.

MRS. DETIGER'S INVITATION HAD BEEN EMPHATIC: "YOU MUST GO to Glastonbury." Her certainty, not to mention the timing of her letter, contributed to my feeling that this was no ordinary invitation. For she could not have know that this was a destination that I myself had been drawn to by a dream that I had had many years earlier, a place that had captivated my imagination since reading *The Mists of Avalon*. In this novel, Glastonbury was the place where one crossed through the mists to Avalon, the last realm of the Goddess where women were priestesses, healers, and visionaries.

Glastonbury is actually a small town in Somerset, in the western part of England. The town surrounds a forty-acre rectangle, on which still exist a few impressive ruins of Glastonbury Abbey, once the greatest church in England. The most notable feature is an unusual hill with a tower on its top, on the outskirts of the town. This is Glastonbury Tor, which rises 518 feet above sea level.

Glastonbury is surrounded by a wide expanse of low-lying fields. From the Tor, one sees a gentle landscape with soft contours and cultivated greenness. From afar, the Tor rises sharply above the fields out of a cluster of hills, giving it the air of an island. The flat region that extends westward toward the Bristol Channel and the sea was once covered with water. Boats would have docked alongside what are now hills; traces of a wharf have been found at Wearyall Hill.

Wearyall Hill is so named, according to the Christian contributions to Glastonbury legend, because this is where Joseph of Arimathea and his companions from the Holy Land came ashore, weary all from the long journey. On disembarking, Joseph, who in the New Testament provided the tomb for the crucified Jesus, purportedly drove his staff into the ground, where it miraculously came to life as a tree. This tree, called the Holy Thorn, blossomed every Christmas. While this tree was destroyed, its descendants in Glastonbury still bloom during late December and early January. A sprig of the Holy Thorn's winter blossom is even now sent annually to the reigning English sovereign. The Holy Thorn is unique among English trees, resembling most closely a tree that grows in or near the Holy Land.

Glastonbury is a Celtic, Arthurian, Christian, and esoteric legend and history. Geoffrey Ashe's books (especially *Avalonian Quest*) provide the most useful perspective on the many claims made about Glastonbury: that it was venerated as the holiest place in Britain before Christianity and was the site of the first Christian community; that Joseph of Arimathea came there with the Holy Grail from the Last Supper, which was afterward lost; that the Tor and hill that cradles Glastonbury was once the Isle of Avalon, where Arthur was taken wounded after his last battle; that it is one of the great energy centers of the Western world.

And now here I was on my way to Glastonbury, this place that had been in the back of my mind for more than twenty years, ever since I had had the following dream:

> I was going down a dimly lit, narrow, secret spiral stairway
> that led beneath a cathedral to a hidden room. The room
> was airy and spacious and filled with light. In it was the
> body of a knight or a king in armor. He had been dead for
> centuries and yet looked as if he had in life (like Snow
> White did after she took a bite of the poisoned apple). He

wore a ring with a large oval green or bluish stone, which
was now given to me to wear. Then I was in the basement
of a very large department store. It was as if I had gone
through the wall of the room under the cathedral and
emerged into this bustling, ordinary place. I was wearing
the ring but had turned the stone so that it was hidden
inside my cupped hand where only I could see it. Only a
plain band showed outwardly.

This was a significant dream in which I discovered that an
Arthurian knight or king was hidden below the church floor. He
was symbol of masculine authority, spirituality, strength, courage,
and honor, and for me to have received and worn his ring on my
right ring finger meant that I was to be true to or carry what he
represented into the world. Yet because the stone would be immediately noticed and give away something that I was to keep secret, I had to turn the ring so that the stone was hidden from view.

When I recounted the dream to my Jungian analyst, he asked
me if I had ever heard of Glastonbury Abbey (which I had not). I
imagine that he knew that the remains thought to be King Arthur
had been found beneath the abbey grounds He also mentioned a
book that he had come across many years before called *The Gate
of Remembrance*. Both Glastonbury and the book title stayed with
me over the years, as do things that carry a sense of mystery. At the
time of the dream I tried to locate the book and could find no
trace of its existence.

I have been reminded of this dream many times over the years
and have had several related dreams as well. Here is another dream
from the same period:

I am in a medieval building made of stone, with a cloister
and an inner court area. I go into a small room off the
cloister, where the wall pivots open—like a secret wall in a
mystery film—and I am now outdoors, in a Sunday-at-the-
park setting, with lots of picnicking people who have no
way of knowing that just a moment before I was in a
different world.

It's no wonder that *The Mists of Avalon* would intrigue me, for my own dreams pointed to the possibility of crossing from one reality to another. Also, considering that I could dream of an Arthurian knight and of wearing his ring out into the world, it's not surprising that it was like entering a dream landscape that was imbued with legends and stories, including the claim that this is a place where the veil is thinner.

To get to Glastonbury, we drove west from Heathrow Airport on a highway that took us past Stonehenge. Several smaller roads later and we were on the Shepton Mallet Road, a narrow and not particularly straight road bordered by hedgerows, and fences. The road took us through fields in which sheep grazed and through part of the disputed Glastonbury Zodiac, whose proponents declare that Glastonbury lies within a Zodiac Circle roughly ten miles across, the figures of which are formed by features in the landscape that are supposedly in the same relative positions as the constellations in the sky.

Suddenly the road changed—it could have been a shift in angle or elevation, or a gap in the hedgerow—and there was Glastonbury Tor! I say this with an exclamation point, because that is the impact; it is something to behold. The Tor is a mountain that is really only a hill, except that calling it a hill would not do it justice. It was lushly green and apparently terraced, with a sentinel tower on its summit. Since it was late May, there were apple trees in bloom near its base and in the fields nearby. From the initial vantage point, the Tor looked triangular in shape, like a pyramid. Then, as the road took us past it, its outline changed, as the angle of one slope elongated.

From any angle, the Tor emanates power and mystery. There is something unnatural and sculptural about its shape, with its spiral terraces that appear to wind around its sides and the tower on the top that looks like a Stonehenge-sized megalith. The tower is the only remaining part of the Saint Michael's Church that once dominated the Tor. An uncommon earthquake collapsed the church and left only the tower standing.

In England, places that were once sacred to the Goddess were taken over by Christians in one of two ways: by building churches named for Saint Michael, as on the Tor, or chapels in honor of Mary. Saint Michael is usually portrayed stamping upon a serpent, which was a symbol of the Goddess, and one that also expresses the telluric energy currents or ley lines (as they are called in England) that "snake" under the ground at sacred sites. In China, these lines are know as *lung-mei*, the paths of the dragon; to this day in modern Hong Kong, Chinese geomancers are consulted about these dragon currents before buildings are constructed.

Areas where the energy is strongest became sacred sites or, in current idiom, power points. The images that are associated with this energy are archetypally similar, whether you're in Western Europe or China. The snake and the Chinese dragon and the serpent all have undulating bodies and power. But whereas in a culture that respected the Earth, the dragon was thought of as benevolent, in Judeo-Christian cultures where the Earth (and goddesses and women) had to be tamed and subjugated, dragons, snakes, and serpents were to be feared—stamped out by Saint Michael, driven out by Saint Patrick, or killed by Saint George.

It amused me to think that the earthquake that knocked down Saint Michael's Abbey from the Tor might have been an expression of an offended Mother Earth Goddess who refused to be downtrodden. Saint Michael prevailed, however, for the Saint Michael's Abbey that was once on the Tor is one of many that still stand, located on a ley line that runs down the spine of southwest England to the island rock of Saint Michael's Mound near Land's End, Cornwall.

The second way of usurping goddess sites was by building chapels or cathedrals in honor of Mary on them. As a feminine expression of divinity, Mary is archetypally the mother goddess. In all but name, this is how she is worshiped at Chartres, for example. For regardless of discriminating points made by theologians, the man or woman who prays to Mary is speaking to the same compassionate goddess whose names were, among others, Demeter, Isis, Tara, or Kuan Yin, goddesses who, like Mary, understood suffering. Demeter's daughter Persephone was abducted into the underworld and Isis's husband Osiris was torn to pieces. Like Mary's crucified son, both Persephone and Osiris were resurrected. When Mary chapels are built on old goddess sites, they are, in effect, reconsecrated and renamed, places where it can be said that the Goddess continues to be honored.

The road took us past Glastonbury Tor toward the town, to Chalice Hill House where we would stay. On arriving, I found that Geoffrey Ashe, author and expert on the history and legends of the area, was waiting, a meeting that Mrs. Detiger had arranged. He took us up to where we could get a panoramic view of the area and discern in the landscape the figure of a reclining woman. Later Barri Devigne, a lifelong Arthurian scholar, took us to Cadbury, the probable site of Camelot. On the way, he stopped to point out specific features of the Glastonbury Zodiac. To look at the landscape and see what they were seeing was like looking at the constellations in the nighttime sky; the landmarks are easy to make out, as are the stars when someone locates them for us, but not so obvious are the figures of which they are a part. At Glastonbury, the landscape evokes imagination, inviting people to see beyond ordinary reality.

My first morning in Glastonbury, I arose early and took a walk by myself from Chalice Hill House past apple trees in bloom and up the slopes of the Tor. At that hour, I was the only person there. The spiral terraces, which look so well defined from afar and are supposed to number seven, were not easy to follow once I began to climb. As I had walked the labyrinth at Chartres Cathedral, now I wanted to walk the Tor. And as I made my way on these spirals up to the top, the experience felt puzzling and somehow wrong.

When one views the Tor from afar, the tower commands attention and seems to be the destination toward which spiraling paths go. On the Tor itself, however—as I subjectively sensed the place and let images arise in reaction to being there, which I had done at Chartres Cathedral—I had several impressions. The tower now felt like an imposed structure, an artifact that did not belong. Instead, it felt to me that power resided in this uterine-shaped mountain itself. And rather than having an impulse to go up to the summit, I felt that there should have been a tunnel going into the mountain from below.

These thoughts, I later found, turned out to be age-old conjectures that others have shared about the Tor: Might it have a hollow place within it? Might the Tor have an entrance to the underworld? Geoffrey Ashe writes, "To this day there is a stubborn local legend that the Tor has a chamber inside it. Usually the chamber is said to be below the summit, perhaps a considerable distance below. People are alleged to have found a way in and come out mad."

In Celtic mythology, the otherworld, underground realm is Annwn, a faerie realm. This realm has been associated with Glastonbury Tor. In Annwn, there was a magical cauldron of plenty that unceasingly provided wonderful nourishment. This cauldron was either the same as or interchangeable with the magical cauldron of rebirth and regeneration, in which the dead could be recreated, made new, and reborn. I see the cauldron and the Grail as symbolically related, for in some versions of the Grail story, the Grail is a vessel that provides whatever food the person desires. Also, as a symbol of Jesus and the Last Supper, the Grail is connected with his death and resurrection and the promise of eternal life. His three days in the tomb would correspond to being in the underworld in the cauldron of rebirth and regeneration.

Tunnels and hollow underground places are images that are universally connected with Mother Earth as womb and tomb, with the Goddess who gives us life and takes us back in death. The Earth certainly functions as a cauldron of regeneration: everything dies and goes into either the earth or the earth's atmosphere and is recycled and regenerated into new life. Mother Earth is also the cauldron of plenty, out of which comes everything needed to nourish life.

The uterine-shaped Glastonbury Tor evokes thoughts about the underworld and hidden spaces underground.

Walking the Tor, images and feelings arose in me that correspond to myths and legends long held about the place. On this first visit to Glastonbury, I was unaware of these stories about the Tor. I wonder now: Is there an underground realm there, or does the shape of the Tor conjure up the image? What is it about the Tor, anyway? For it seems that whether in the depth of the earth or in the depth of our psyches, images connected to the otherworld and to the Goddess come into the consciousness of visitor and native alike.

For me, walking the Tor and forming impressions that turned out to be part of legend and conjecture fit with what has been said about Glastonbury: it is indeed a place where the veil between the worlds is thinner. Here images came into my mind that related to beliefs held about the Tor, and my body seemed to sense that I was not following an ancient ritual path, when I assumed that there was a spiral path to the summit. Not only did it "feel wrong," it also isn't possible to walk such a path without occasionally having to scramble from one level to another.

> I'm increasingly uncomfortable with current images of God found in books and workshops that mix popular psychology with a theology wholly devoted to self-realization. They seem to reverse the first questions of the catechism I studied as a child, declaring that "the chief end of God is to glorify men and women, and to enjoy them forever." I really don't want a God who is solicitous of my every need, fawning for my attention, eager for nothing in the world so much as the fulfillment of my self-potential. One of the scourges of our age is that all our deities are house-broken and eminently companionable.
>
> —Belden C. Lane, *The Solace of Fierce Landscapes: Exploring Desert and Mountain Spirituality*

After much study and walking the Tor, Geoffrey Ashe concluded that there is a path and that it is in the shape of a Cretan labyrinth. At Glastonbury as at Chartres the labyrinth is present. This one is a three-dimensional, simpler version, whose path follows the pattern of a Cretan labyrinth, which is the most common shape for a labyrinth. Such labyrinths are found carved into the rock of caves in many parts of the world, I thus was walking on a three-dimensional version of the more elegant and symmetrical two-dimensional labyrinth at Chartres, and at both sites, the labyrinth evoked an image of the womb. I saw the Tor as uterine-shaped and the labyrinth at Chartres positioned where the uterus would be in a body of the cathedral.

If these impressions were true, then, in the language of *The Mists of Avalon*, they would be examples of the gift of Sight—a way of knowing that may come naturally to many or most women, as do spatial abilities for many or most men. In any case, intuitive or extrasensory ways of knowing are not given much credit in our culture.

I think a good parallel can be found in the experience of house hunting. On walking into empty houses readied for sale, or even into a particular room of a house, we often seem to *sense* whether memories here are happy, sad, or even dreadful. And sometime when we ask, our realtor provides some information that makes it likely that our impression is correct. This falls into the parapsychological category of psychometry; it's what a psychic does when she picks up an object and describes the owner.

Psychometry and the possibility that there are morphic fields, as theoretical biologist Rupert Sheldrake has proposed, account for and explain how it might be possible for us to get to an archaeological, historic, or sacred site and get a true impression of what happened there in the past. Sheldrake describes morphic fields as a source of cumulative memory based upon experiences of a species in the past. The human morphic field is what we tap into and are resonating with and influenced by when we respond as members of the human race, doing what humans have done. From prehistoric to contemporary times, humans have held spiritual beliefs, observed rituals, had places of worship, and related to divinity. Whatever the particular practice or place, whatever spiritual or mystical experience humans have had is in some way contained within the morphic fields of our species, the contents of which span time and distance. Sheldrake's morphic resonance theory (as applied to humans) and Jung's concept of the collective unconscious are very similar ideas. Both theories account for collective memories, knowledge, behavior, or images that we did not acquire in our personal lives; both account for transpersonal, collective, archetypal experience.

Through meditation or dreams, while in a mystical or ecstatic state, a person who taps into the collective unconscious or a morphic field has gained access to transpersonal experience where time and distance are immaterial. Sheldrake's analogy is that our DNA is like a television receiver that enables us to pick up transmissions; we "tune into" programs in the morphic field. Jung's collective unconscious has much the same implication: archetypal images, associated feelings, and patterns of behavior are the contents of the collective unconscious (or the field), of which we are unaware until they are activated and brought into consciousness. Plato was describing another variation on this same theme when he said that there exists a pure form to which everything like it is related, such as a perfect triangle. Aristotle described every entity as having a soul

Psychic research has not succeeded in convincing the scientific community that the phenomena it claims do in fact exist, largely because it is still attempting to prove them. Psychic phenomena are seen as anomalies which must be justified in terms of our current worldview. The very terminology used by researchers in this field—words such as "paranormal" and "parapsychology"— emphasizes that these phenomena are not within the range of normal experience. What is actually needed is a reformulation of our ideas and experience of the normal. Many "psychic phenomena" occur to everyone every day and simply are not understood and classified. We are like people lost in a forest who starve because we are unable to recognize food when we see it.

—George Simon, "Some Epistemological Considerations in the Study of Non-Verbal Communication" and said that the body is contained in the soul, rather than the soul in the body. The soul, then would be a "field" that would influence and be influenced by the body. This idea has similarities to Sheldrake's theory that we resonate with the morphic field, influencing it and in turn being influenced by it.

That which we know gnostically may be knowledge received through tapping into a spiritual aspect of the morphic field. Taking the analogy of the television receiver further, the part of the psyche we are identified with or are in may determine the "channel" we tune into. This existence of an invisible "transmission" field suggests this possibility. If such is the case, then predictably, if we are in our soul or in touch with the Self (rather than identified with the ego or the persona or a complex), which is the inner attitude of the pilgrim, we will be open to receiving spiritual or soulful experiences.

Since morphic fields span time, they contain everything that has been important to human experience. History may forget, and there may be only faint traces of a matriarchal time when a Goddess was worshiped. But if morphic fields exist, images and rituals that have not been recalled for thousands of years will be accessible to people who turn spontaneous rituals to the Goddess done by contemporary women are not invented but remembered. Tapping into a morphic field at a sacred site, a pilgrim may receive intuitively a truer sense of what went on there than would a scholar with limited sources from later though still relatively ancient times. Researchers dismiss the use of intuition, especially by women, as critics of archaeologist Marija Gimbutas have done because she made intuitive speculations about the meaning of shards and artifacts found at goddess sites. If morphic fields exist, and if she tapped into one, her conclusions would be correct.

There is a grassroots women's spirituality movement that is worldwide yet unorganized: women are gathering together in small groups or are acting individually, observing seasons and important transitions, doing rituals, making altars, finding symbols that express important spiritual and psychological themes and feelings. There is very little tradition to follow, and so women follow intuition and do what feels spontaneously right. After four to six thousand years of patriarchy and patriarchal gods, in the passing of spiritual traditions in a mother-line from mother to daughter, awareness of priestesses, healers, wisewomen, female divinity, or a Mother Goddess are lost from memory. In the spontaneous arising of a women's spirituality movement, however, "re-membering" may be occurring. In sacred places, where the Goddess once was worshiped or venerated, women enact rituals. In circles, women celebrate the seasons. Might it be that women are resonating with a morphic field as they bring the Goddess back into human consciousness? Might contemporary ritual reflect what has gone on before and be adding to it?

Experiences of the Goddess come through individuals who birth reemerging goddess consciousness through their own particular creative expression. While this is occurring mostly in women, it is not exclusively women through whom the Goddess is coming. She is appearing in the dreams of both men and women. The sacredness of the Earth and the body is felt by some men who also lack words for what they sense in their bodies as holy and are moved to express in some private act of reverence, ritual, or creativity.

Jean Shinoda Bolen, M.D., is a Jungian analyst and professor of psychiatry at the University of California, San Francisco. She is the author of Goddesses in Everywoman, Gods in Everyman, The Tao of Psychology, Ring of Power, *and* Crossing to Avalon: A Woman's Midlife Pilgrimage, *from which this piece was excerpted.*

PART TWO

In the Pilgrim's Heart

KENT E. ST. JOHN

⋆ ⋆ ⋆

The Devil's Wind

You reap what you sow.

As I stepped out of the wine cellar and into the wind, a strong feeling of being pulled came over me. Up toward the cathedral, drawn by an unknown source. The empty streets were soon filled with a soul-clutching sound, the vibrations swirling around in the increasing wind. The vibrations soon turned into mournful yet melodic words. The only lights visible this cold late February night were focused on was the single-spired beauty of Strasbourg's Gothic cathedral and nothing else. The only sound was the lone voice, incomprehensible yet full of meaning. As a solitary figure in the cathedral square revealed itself, clad in dark cloak and fur topped hat, I realized the source of the unearthly sound. After listening in rapture for what seemed hours, the figure beckoned me closer. As I approached, the large bearded person smiled and offered me some of his meager refreshments, bread and water. The voice belonged to Emmanuel Michalski, and the words were Hebrew. It seems Emmanuel sings here at the cathedral to remind people of Sturthof/Natzweiler, the only Nazi concentration camp that was situated on French soil, and the 44,623 souls that passed through there.

"Why on such a cold windy night ?" I asked.

"Because of the devil, the cathedral, and the wind," he replied.

Seeing my incomprehension, Emmanuel told me of the legend. It is said that when the devil heard about the splendors of the new cathedral he decided to see for himself. The devil summoned the wind and rode on its back into Strasbourg. When he arrived and saw the magnificent building dedicated to God and light, and not to the powers of his darkness, the devil erupted with a great rage. As the devil rode the wind around and around the monumental edifice, his anger grew until he stormed off. Incensed, the devil decided to leave the great wind behind, hoping that it would become a disruptive force for those entering God's house of worship. Three centuries later, even on a summer's day, a cold brisk wind can be felt circling just around the cathedral. As pilgrims and tourists alike pull up their collars and wraps and enter one of France's most beautiful cathedrals, it is evident that the devil's wind has not deterred the human appreciation of works dedicated to light. Emmanuel Michalski has taken a different approach; he uses the devil's wind as a vehicle to spread words of hope, remembrance, and faith.

And so I decided to go to Sturthof/Natzweiler on my next trip to Alsace. A cold wet wind blew off the Vosges Mountains down into the valley, and my stomach was tied into a tight ball. When I arrived at the camp, my eyes strayed up to the mountains looking for something more serene, much like the prisoners may have. Ghostly patches of fog streamed passed the barbwire fence as I entered. Even knowing I would be leaving, a chill jolted my spine. This was to be my first visit into a world only glimpsed in movies and old newsreels. With all tours in French I was given support material in English. Sturthof's beginning followed the pattern that the camp of Mathausen in Austria did.

In 1940 prisoners built the camp in atrocious conditions, the objective being to kill off most during the work. Those who entered were given categories:

red for politicians
purple for religious believers

black for Gypsies and nonconformists
pink for homosexuals
green for common criminals
yellow stars for the Jewish.

The thought that family, friends, and loved ones fit every color and category caused a deep gut wrenching. Worse yet was the terrible thought that some would have been made human guinea pigs for the medical experiments by Sturthof's doctors-come-torturers. As I entered the National Necropolis with its 1,120 graves, the mist in my eyes blurred the names…the family, friends, and loved ones touched by Nazi cruelty. Wandering around the compound I came upon a sign that read, "Lanterre Des Morts." As I pulled out my French-English dictionary, a clutch at my elbow froze me. A small elderly gentleman asked *"Americain?"* *"Oui, je suis Americain,"* I answered. "I am Mr. Muller and I will tell you what the sign says," he said.

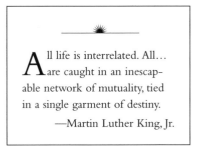

All life is interrelated. All… are caught in an inescapable network of mutuality, tied in a single garment of destiny.

—Martin Luther King, Jr.

Mr. Muller said the sign pointed out the field where the ashes of the cremated prisoners were spread. Suddenly a huge sob broke the silence between us and Mr. Muller's shoulders shook. I clasped the old gentlemen tightly, trying to comfort what I assumed was the haunted memory of family and friends who had passed through the camp. I led his frail body to a wooden bench as I felt all his control seep away.

After about an hour, Mr. Muller mumbled some words. I tried to comfort him by telling him those he lost at the camp would be honored by his visit. Suddenly his head dropped to his chest and another cry came from deep within the old man's body. It was then Mr. Muller gasped, "I was a guard here." At first a wave of nausea came over me like cold wind. I pulled back as if I had been struck by lightning. Then I sensed that I may have been one of the only people that this man had ever told that fact to. "What brought you back, Mr. Muller?" I asked. Mr. Muller, with red-rimmed eyes, told me about a cold February night when on a visit to Strasbourg he heard a mournful yet melodic voice that drew him to the cathedral. That voice belonged to Emmanuel Michalski, the very same voice that drew me in on a cold February night. It appears Emmanuel is indeed putting the "Devil's Wind" to good use, calling for a pilgrimage to look deep within.

Kent E. St. John is a contributing editor for Transitions Abroad *magazine and is working on a book of travel essays compiled after nine years as the owner of* Under the Palms Travels, *a company that organizes educational tours. He now listens to the wind.*

MICHAEL TOBIAS

✦ ✦ ✦

Naked on Mount Sinai

*Struggling for his life, the author's mind engages
in a fevered examination of history, theology,
and his own mortality.*

THE ROCK WAS EASILY 100 DEGREES IN THE MIDAFTERNOON SUN
of the Sinai. It was early summer, and I was naked, pinioned probably 700 vertical feet above Saint Catherine's Monastery. A gaggle
of amused monks had ventured out from their cool cloister to observe this newcomer's madness. I'd scrambled up the granite talus
earlier that morning, skipping between boulders beyond the camel
trail that was used by the local Tuarah nomads. They were the
Jebeliyeh, which means "mountaineers." These Bedouins had rendered themselves dependent on the monastery, laboring over many
centuries on behalf of the Greek Orthodox monks in return for
provisions. The long-haired Tuarah women were wrapped in red
cloth stitched with coins and pearls, their white veils sewn with
gold braid. They herded goats throughout these sultry mountains.
The Muslims—like the Jews and Christians—revere Mount Sinai,
Jebel Musa, also known as Horeb, the Holy Mountain of the Law.
A marble inscription in Arabic from the twelfth century, presumed
to have been copied from a much older original and located beside a gate in the monastery, refers to Mount Sinai as "the
Mountain of Dialogue."

Countless other pilgrims, beginning in antiquity, had preceded me, journeying from all over the world to reach Saint Catherine's Monastery and climb the holy mountain, but I'm sure few of them had ever forsaken the camel and goat trails or the facile 3,500 granite steps leading to the summit, in favor of this bulging head-wall on the west face, with its prominent dihedral of rebuff, where I found myself.

The down-sloping holds on the cliff were covered with a film of dust, making the boilerplate slabs treacherous to the touch. The gray quartzite surface was petrified, glazed like lunar palimpsest, battered by eons of wind, heat, and winter blizzard. I had moved rapidly up the lower corners, bottoming cracks, liebacks, and expanding flakes, all pieces of a puzzle inclining at a negotiable angle toward the nebulous base of the central pillar—in the middle of the face—upon whose toe-sized ledge I now stood perched. Directly overhead, a 20-foot overhang craned out and away. I could see nothing above but I knew that the 300-foot headwall eventually slackened into the low-angled summit crest. There was a chapel on top, and around the back, in the Valley of the Martyrs, a spring.

A gusting *hamsine* buffeted my body, which was burned from being so long out on the peninsula. The wind cornered and agitated me: Every move from here on was uncertain. I needed balance. The overhang frightened me. I would not have the strength to retrace my moves if something went wrong. There was no apparent way around it, and the prospect of down-climbing half the route was appalling. A view looking down is always more sheer than a view looking up. I didn't want to think about it. Thinking brings on doubt.

I reached for the crack, tucked my thumb into the crop of my palm, and expanded the flesh with a sensuous exertion inherent to the mysterious muscles of the hand. My toes were smeared into the jagged fissure that formed the vortex of the prow. I pulled up, jammed the toes higher, reached with a fist and plastered it into the ceiling above. My body started to fall outward. Damned gravity. I dangled free by my arms, a sure recipe for disaster. Within less than a minute I was pumped, exhausted, without a reserve flow of blood.

My brain was on fire, rebuking the enterprise. Without options, a redundancy of muscle, or an escape route, my adrenaline was telling me no. Already the fingers were getting wet at their first joints, moisture egressing from each wrinkle. Already the knees were beginning to shake, my breath faltering. A tear was welling in the recesses of an eye.

I backed down, straining with a big toe toward the little ledge, until there was contact. Then I dropped onto the stance, an alcove the size of a washrag. I leaned into the rock, protected from the sun, and began to ache inside. My heart was pounding. I couldn't go down. There was no choice. I would have to confront this nemesis one more time. It was one of the worst traps I'd ever gotten myself into. For years I'd known this would happen. It was bound to happen.

The monastery was far down below, out of view. I had several hours before dark would fall. Holding back panic, I felt confident that I could remain on the ledge for twenty or thirty minutes, sorting out my fear. I simply had to maintain calm, to shift from one toe to another every few minutes, to make no quick unconsidered jerks of the tendon, to keep my flank out of the twenty-knot wind until the idea of the moves was worked out in my head.

First jam, second jam, bring up the feet, use them, keep as much weight off the arms as possible. Don't stop moving. Let no desultory temptations swerve me from the singular flow of it. Move fast, fluently, reach in moderation, do not extend the arms rigidly. Keep them flexed, retractable, and fear not. Fear induces sweat and sweat kills. Become light—pure, unsullied light. Become spirit. The injunction was as subjective as it was Olympic or religious.

I waited, idly scanning the landscape, eyes flitting away, then tempted inward by the inextricable image of the gymnastic sequence that awaited me. My life hung in the balance.

All around me the rock was ribboned with charcoal-colored veins. Early visitors to the mountain had reasoned that these forested elocutions in the stone were evidence of the burning bush, the charred remains of fire following Moses's, then Elijah's, conversations with Yahweh.

I listened for the odd residual remark of Moses's arcane hours on this peak—ghostly grunts, Joseph's vigil, preternatural phonemes—stoking associative fancy in the wind.

By the slightest attunement, wish fulfillment, I soon detected whispers. Within minutes of this distraction, the whole cliff came alive with babbling. I could hear it. Not merely my own heart, but a steady din of vocables clucking, tongues darting, molecules materializing.

Far off to the south lay the Red Sea, Suez, the coast of Egypt. I could see it: a mirage of many layers, dozens of other mountains, the hint of a lone cloud shadowing an anonymous dead end of sand and dried riverbed. Somewhere in that labyrinth, simmering beneath the candescent heat, were canyons betraying time— canyons that had played host to first principles and passing tribes, to parables primeval and inscriptions of the afterlife.

This hegemony of Sinai, blanketed in light, was—in its entirety, at that moment of my visitation—an epiphany of God: the place of exile, vision, sanctification. I trembled on the brink of an alien communion, a climber's madness.

For months I'd studied the manuscripts and icons of Saint Catherine's Monastery, a collection unequaled in the world. At night, I had been sleeping in a perfectly sculpted cave above the sixth-century fortress, devouring dates and peanut butter and chocolate bars, imagining my predecessors, guzzling water from a five-gallon plastic jug, passing out under the stars. By day, I poured over the myriad papyruses, cobalt iconographies, clues to a fabulous treasure map. Everything pointed to a philosophy that beautifully coalesced with this dihedral on the headwall.

I shifted my weight onto my right foot so that I could just manage to balance precariously, leaning in. My arms, seeking renewed strength, hung limp by my sides. The sun was inching perilously close to the ridge on the opposite side of the Valley of Er-Raha. In another hour, coolness would descend. Gnats were assaulting my genitals. I was parched. Unwilling, as yet, to address my situation. Stalling for time.

When a voice quietly soughed. An inner voice..."*In all this there*

*is no suffering for him…. It shall be near me on the day of death, it ought
to wait on that yonder side as my extoller…. Is it misery? It is a turning
point of life!"* the sounder concluded.

The words—like a prayer—rose in me to combat the physical
crisis, which was their very purpose from inception, one has cause
to believe. Crazy as it may seem, I remembered the text, more or
less. As an inveterate archivist in my youth, I'd exhausted the accessible antiquities, grabbing translated hieroglyphs from the stacks as
if they were chocolate kisses. That this document—this ancient
poem—should have surfaced in my head at that moment was
nothing short of augury, salvation, I felt. With the far-distant coast
of eastern Egypt in my hazy purview, half-imagined, here was living proof of a connecting-in-mind, of ancient voices reaching
across time to effect magic.

The elocution, part mistral, part remembrance, was composed
by the Egyptian Middle Kingdom Twelfth Dynasty poet laureate,
Khety, son of Duauf. Four hundred and fifty years prior to the
Exodus of the Israelites, Khety's literary instincts exploded—mysteriously modern, emotive, full of robust shades and controversial
larvae. There was nothing dry or austere about his characters.
These were no hieroglyphic stiffs, but men who wept for their lost
women and children, put their faces Lear-like into the wind, and
speculated on the nature of the soul. Yet their conclusions and actions are entirely archaeological, which is to say, wholly untrace-
able. One might be able to detect where a man pissed four millennia ago in the Valley of the Tombs, but poetry is more elusive
than urine. I was baffled by the personality of these protagonists.
Their logic, with its towering pyramids, now-extinct gods, and
funerary secrets, seemed, if I was not mistaken, to hinge on poetic
conditionals that defy our surest abstractions even in today's mini-
malist times.

There is an enormous gap in thinking between Khety and the
era in which I find myself. There on the cliff, I felt the loss of
something crucial in the intervening 3,700 years, as if the original
instincts of our ancestors were correct, their motives, zeal, and
methods all connected, whereas mine were not. Beneath the many

desiccated edifices of Egypt lies a secret I began to sense—like some wraith that had entered my head, the very droplets of perspiration off my brow, atoms speaking to atoms, tears welling up within tears, a seeming inner revenant reformulating my own physical crisis.

The recovered text itself is a mere 154 lines. An additional page or two are missing. "*The Report About the Dispute of a Man with His Ba*." The word *ba* means soul, the *soul* of the seeker. The dialogue, which is the subject of the poem, is between the seeker and himself. Thus, the very introspection, projected out loud, represents an essentially expressionist, dramaturgical mode of self-consciousness written during the troubled, expansionist reign of Amenemhet I, whose expeditions for turquoise and power forced his troops into the hellish regions of the Sinai and Nubia. It was a period in which nearly all animals were considered gods—whether beetle or ape, crocodile, hawk, bull, or pig. The deities of Ra, Aton, and Osiris *were* animals whose communion of earth brought the sun and the moon, the waters of the Nile, the darkness of the underworld, into an accessible range of human inquiry.

So there I was: perched along the inch-sized abyss, tears in my eyes, and strange gutterals from the far-distant past reaching out to tickle me. I supposed it was time to die, that the implacable ether was swooping down to absorb one more asshole who had climbed too high, but that same skyline of oblivion wanted very much to jabber. The whole cliff came alive with garrulous chitchat, and I seemed to be the energy field on which this linguistic forum, some psychic soiree, intended to hold forth. I was already *suspended*; extending that ominous configuration to *disbelief* required no additional courage or commitment.

The concept of the *ba* inundated the moment, crept up the rock face like a helping hand. It was crazy of me to indulge this academic bent in myself just then, and I knew it, but the alternative was probably suicide. I needed to gather strength, to muster more blood in my muscles. I did not want to die without at least contemplating options in the afterlife. If it looks as if you're going to die out in the wilderness, alone, you have every right to compose

your thoughts, take your time, and give in to it on your own terms.
So I angulated on the nubbin of rock, my eyes closed, pressing my

cock and thighs and sun-
burned torso against the
sleek and speckled granite,
ruminating at high speed.

I knew that the Egyptians
had likened the image of this
ba to the enigmatic jabiru
bird. The man whose work
had acquainted me with this
bit of esoterica was one Hans
Goedicke, an Egyptologist
who had brilliantly pointed
out that trying to derive any
sense of spiritual attitudes
from this now extinct stork
(the jabiru) would be "like
deducing the Holy Ghost
from the dove."

So it was a stork, another
tempter of the heights, a
wanderer like me.

This *soul* was also granted
by Egyptians the symbolic

Since the only real geography
is consciousness, it is not
where we are but what we have
become that makes the difference. We do not exist in the
earthplane so much to transform
ourselves as to experience ourselves. Once we have discovered
our true nature and our true
worth, once we have slipped between the cracks of our own
perceptual preferences, we automatically transform for the experience…we become who we
really are.

—P. M. H. Atwater, Lh.D., *Future
Memory: How Those Who "See the
Future" Shed New Light on the
Workings of the Human Mind*

power of birth, freedom, and flight. For the seeker in Khety's yarn,
this bird even represented the possibilities for redemption in a
world of pain.

Who could ever forget the actual story line? The man, intent
on taking his own life, having seen his wife and children die, had
settled on a final voyage to the West for his "landing place." If the
ba would only agree, the two of them together could erect their
own pyramid to preserve his spirit.

The *ba* refused, unwilling to die, to let go of happier times or of
daylight. It reminded the seeker that pyramids were for dead men
who had become gods. In relating two parables that were intended

to persuade the seeker to embrace life, rather than death, the *ba* only succeeded in exacerbating the emotional instability of the man. Keep in mind that the man was talking to himself and presently declared that he was "flooded" with *ba* but inconsolable.

"To whom can I speak today?" he repeated sixteen times, mumbling on about crocodiles and peril. "Opinions are bygone," "the peaceful are miserable," "gentleness perishes, violence overcomes everybody," "there is not the heart of a man upon which one could rely," and "wrong roams the earth, it will not have end."

The man, convinced that death was his only option, compared the sweetness of it to the "smell of myrrh" and "lotuses," to a "rain-washed path," to "sitting under sails on a breezy day," "returning (to one's longed-for) home from an expedition," under a clearing sky.

In response to all of these impassioned sentiments, the *ba* held firm. In what must be described as a unique and stubborn contribution to the reverential idea of nature, the *ba* set forth a "solution," at once spellbinding and salutary. Remember that this was the spirit speaking, a soul aware of its powers after death, of an Egyptian quotient that took immortality to be a given. Nevertheless, this *ba* renounced eternity for the more refined pleasures of an earthly existence.

> [As for] that which my *ba* said to me: "Give up the complaints about the stalling of this companion, my brother, while you last upon the flame, in order to be adamant about life!"

> [Man:] "As you say! Like me here, after you rejected the West Please, but like also the West, and your limbs join the earth, I shall alight, after you are weary. Therefore, let us make a harbor for the occasion."

Given the monumental constructions of Egyptian immortality rites, the pyramids of Zoser and Khufu, the royal tombs at Tanis, the temple of Ramses III at Medinet Habu, and the Great Temple of Ramses II, to name only some of the most popular relics, it was all the more compelling to discern such renunciation in a *ba* whose very destiny—literary or otherwise—was death. Every Egyptian knew that his *ba* would become Osiris, god of the underworld, and his body a living ghost. Egyptian medical practice elevated death into a science that has never been equaled. The reverence for nature that Khety enunciated utterly dispensed with the grim, funerary particulars, striking out into new territory, refreshing, alive, original: a soul that preferred life over eternity—unheard of, but there it was.

These thoughts bolstered my waning luck and added purchase to my fading ankle strength.

"Be adamant about life...make a harbor for the occasion."

The monks must have given me up for dead by then, but the *ba* would not give up. My inner cogitations pursued this enchanted pertinacity, which surfaced like an exhortation from my own funeral, a persistent reincarnation, one of those hallucinogenic déjà vus of which alpine literature is apparently overrun. A second chance, in other words.

I realized that what set Khety's universe wonderfully apart from anything soon to follow, either in later Egyptian belles lettres or in subsequent European romance, certainly up until the charged landscapes of *Beowulf* was the *alternative* that was prescribed within this text. That Khety and his culture could even assert such an alternative is startling.

Nature worship by itself had a long history prior to Egypt, but like the cult of Osiris most of it focused on the moment of death. The many curious evocations rattled in my head. I changed positions. My hands were sweating profusely. I wiped them off on the ungiving rock. My chest was heavy.

"Keep talking," Mount Sinai seemed to insist.

I was talking myself down, a parlance of extrication. Nature had always been my comfort, its stone my pillow. I had risked my life before and walked away from it. Now my only choice was to surmount the obstacle. I thought to jam the fist and go for it.

I stared downward, calculating my fall.

When suddenly, just short of this final morbid premonition, came the memory of the 4,000-year-old epic of Gilgamesh and, with it, the first documented paradise mythology pertaining to the land of eternal life, Dilmun. I was reaching, searching frantically for some consolation or promise, a philosophical precursor that might make my dilemma go away.

"Dilmun!" I exclaimed, as if convinced of my travel plans.

In the epic, there was this fellow named Utnapishtim, portrayed as the one human ancestor who had achieved that perfect place, an Adam living in a reachable Shangri-la. Gilgamesh reached out to that realm, to become half-wild, half-man, the implication being that human beings might achieve immortality in this life. It was a theme to which the Bible and all of Eastern art and philosophy were headed. Was I?

Three hundred years later, in the work of the Egyptian Khety, that search for paradise turned inward, described itself with a psychoanalytic flavor that was ground breaking. The meager script's pictographic whimsy seems simple at a glance but in fact conceals a contagion of meaningful, heartrending ambiguities that perfectly resolved themselves. The resolution, and the poetic conceit that had so painstakingly allowed for it, would be lost to later generations. Instead, those ambiguities would act like nettles of remorse, working their way into the troubled texture of future philosophical systems, inflicting dichotomy, resorting to desperate moves, tyrannical impulses, the demise of the natural.

Granted, this was no time for finespun webs or opaque connections, nor was the proximity of death (my own) any guarantee of concision or clarity. One may grope with added frenzy, but it does not translate into certitude or literary facility. I know now, thanks to that cliff, that the traditional death in one's bed must be far more oriented toward fancy literary swan songs, clever one-liners, final so longs, and extreme unctions. Not the Sinai.

The laconic Khety had fashioned a delicate precedent, the ecological conscience, after which all future mind-versus-body and human-versus-nature dialectics must feel trivial and ill-advised. Nevertheless, the world of the dying was evenly divided, it seemed then, between those who prattled on about the whys and wherefores, poet manqués, and those who simply vanished without a trace, silent and complete, even expectant in the end. Only on a cliff ledge, high above the killing talus, could one actually debate the predicament, staring right at it.

It is believed that Emperor Valens abolished the monastic exemption from military service in Egypt because, by the late fourth century, a huge population had taken religious vows and desert refuge. That period, which followed a time of widespread Christian persecution, would be dubbed the Era of Retreat.

They came to this place, right there, several hundred feet below me, where a sustained battle of the spirit to triumph over the vulnerable body, and by inference over the natural world (a heart-rending simplicity), had commenced with those Genesis

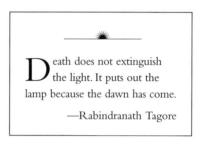

Death does not extinguish the light. It puts out the lamp because the dawn has come.

—Rabindranath Tagore

passages that blatantly forfeited the rights of nature for the allegedly greater needs of the spirit.

The Bible, and all subsequent commentary on the six days of creation, swathed the earth in a guilt-ridden symbology. Evil replaced joy; neurosis and separation were unleashed on the sexes: "Cursed is the ground because of you" (Genesis 3:17). The diversity of species was misconstrued as a form of retribution for Eve's original sin and subsequent fall from primordial grace.

And in Genesis 6:7, God even regretted having ever conceived of humanity in the first place and resolved to destroy us, along with all other creatures. If it hadn't been for Noah and his persuasive pleas on behalf of the innocent lamb and the gentle fawn, God's creation would have been the first myth in history to self-destruct. That the possibility even arose is astonishing. What would have happened in that case?

Haunted by lingering doubts of the kind stirred up throughout the Bible, multiple waves of hermits as well as artists would seek solace in this Sinai. A paroxysm of romance, of biblical exegesis, was coined in the transcendent moment of desert baptisms and

ascetic hours. It comes down to us as "wisdom" literature, the say-
ings of the Fathers. I was seduced in my teens.

I caught myself, shifted my weight to the other foot, rubbed
my hands against the rock, and shook out the jitters. The wind
had picked up even more. The roof above me was golden with the
alpenglow of a fast-descending sun. Soon the rock up which I had
to climb would be in shade, the holds harder to detect. Across the
partially shadowed valley, I could make out my cave. I wished
more than anything that I was there, safe, curled up in my sleeping bag beside a fire of tamarisk twigs, fraxinella plants, acacia
bushes, feasting on seedless dates. I would have loved a tofu salad
sandwich, lots of salt, cold mayonnaise, a slice of avocado, thin-
sliced ripe tomatoes. A far cry from the secretion of shield lice,
the indigenous Sinaitic species said to be responsible for the historical breadlike manna that sustained the Israelites during their
forty years of exodus.

Saint Matthew related how John the Baptist, clothed in camel's
hair and a leather girdle about his loins, ate locusts and wild honey
for his meat. Moses, Aaron, Elijah, Christ, David, Paul, John, and,
much later, Muhammad all pursued solitude in this desert. Where
they wandered, precisely, has been the subject of intense scrutiny
and debate for centuries. Mount Sinai may have been a 300-foot-
high peak near El Arîsh, hardly distinguishable from the surrounding dunes, or one of twelve other contenders scattered about the
Sinai and Arabian peninsulas. This particular peak (7,422 feet) of
granite, gneiss, and porphyry adjoining Mount Saint Catherine's
(8,520 feet), where the body of the Alexandrian saint was set down
following her martyrdom, came to be identified with the mountain of Deuteronomy. "The Lord came from Sinai," said Moses
(Deuteronomy 33:2) The Rabbis explain why Mount Sinai is
lower, slightly, than adjoining Mount Saint Catherine's: even God
is humble, they still say.

In A.D. 306, Saint Anthony the Great took up residence in a
mountain cave along the Red Sea near Clysma. Geological weath-
ering throughout this so-called Badi et-Tih plateau, and Wadi El-
Arîsh, provided suitable elevated caves for the stream of devoted

refugees that followed him. One of those followers happened to be Helena, Emperor Constantine's mother, who made a pilgrimage to the Holy Land. Her legions had apparently built a little chapel somewhere in the Sinai. The escapist tradition was growing.

Anthony moved on to an oasis known as Der Mar (later called Antonios) at the foot of a mountain near the Gulf of Aqaba, which was several days by camel from Mount Sinai. He was said to have climbed the peak. The scholar Jacques Lacarriere pointed out that the fact of both physical and spiritual ascent "is not a play on words, for the parallel between material ascent and spiritual elevation is maintained throughout *The Life of Anthony*.... When he had reached the height of meditation as well as the summit of the mountain he decided to stay for the rest of his days." I shuddered to think of it: there was unscrupulous, severe precedent for my demise.

Anthony died at the age of 105. I was only 20. The saint's life-long contest with evil and the myriad temptations to which he was prey would serve to propel a mass movement toward God, away from urban life, urban pleasure, social contact of all kinds. On the other hand, my useless death would pass as unconsequentially as a fart on a mountaintop.

The Temptations genre, such as Anthony himself must have experienced, became a favorite of Renaissance painters, who accented the legendary eccentricity and sadomasochism of the Sinai—and there was plenty of it. The loving message of Christ had been exported to a desert environ where the possibilities for empathy were limited to oneself; where loving thy neighbor had little applicability, which is not to belittle goats. Yet the psychology of this ascetic trend, I believed, had as much to do with an artistic impulse as it did with God. That's why I was on that cliff. Not just to climb, but to create an image out of myself; to be able to step back afterward, look to Mount Sinai's sheer cliffs, and know that I had become, for a few luminous hours, part of its ancient story.

That was it; that's where this condemned divagation had been leading to—art. The passions of Moses and Christ were *artistic* endeavors. Jews would not make images of Him or even repeat his

name, but they would make an art form out of life. Christ's growing band of followers expressed themselves more compulsively, as
artists. The four Gospels indulged, embroidered, enlarged a myth,
conveying the personality, hopes, injunctions, and dreams of a romantic character. The Nazarene was a rebel, penniless, in rags, his
background fraught with enticing contradictions—for example,
Mark tells us that Christ insisted that he was the son of Joseph and
Mary, *not* the Son of God. Until the age of twenty-nine, he might
well have been wandering the Tibetan plateau or the mountains of
Kashmir or climbing the peaks of Sinai. There was sufficient "evidence" to indicate as much. Along the road to Damascus, Paul's
vision of a risen, resurrected Christ, a hallucination on which the
whole success of Christianity hinged, furthered this literary apoth-
eosis. The identification of the cross with God, of the two thieves
crucified beside him, of countless other anecdotal parts of the
evolving parable, all testified to a collective quality of mind inherent to the epic in no less a manner than that of Gilgamesh and his
search for paradise, for the Kingdom of God. I viewed the Old and
New Testaments as Hollywood thrillers, adventure yarns.

By the time of Saint Anthony, Christ's person had become pure
poetry, the stuff of outrageous exploits, the distillation of his say-
ings, utter rhapsody. Followers of the Apostles spoke of *theosis-
photismos*, the making of a self-likeness to God, and of the sublime.
The implications were aesthetic ones. The artist/monk, probing
into the depths of nature, was thereby exposing himself to the possibility of God.

The *Hexaemeron* of Saint Basil (ca. 331–379) and the succeeding songs of Saint Ambrose (ca. 340–397) went on to state that nature blushed with balance, the sea kissing its beholder, the smallest
flower shouting out the Creator's name. One hears in such praise
Basil and Ambrose themselves blushing and kissing and shouting.
Speaking also of plants, Saint Augustine (354–430) would argue
that "their loveliness is their confession." One begins to smile, rec-
ognizing the weakness within rhapsody—weakness for earth. No
matter how hard the ascetics tried to forsake their body, the body
of earth, they could not refrain from nature-bound analogy. One

might even concede the Walt Whitman in a Saint Augustine, that is, until the second book of Augustine's own *Confessions* (ca. 399): "His happiness was due to the intoxication which causes the world to forget you, its Creator, and to love the things you have created instead of loving you, because the world is drunk with the invisible wine of its own perverted, earthbound will." It is not surprising that the world of the wine-drinking Bacchus (Dionysus) was ultimately scorned by Anthony in favor of Platonic spirituality.

In Augustine's own time, beauty, everywhere manifest in the harshness of the desert, was only beautiful in that it reflected the goodness of God, as it had for Plato and Plotinus. The ascetic's response to nature was pathologically contradictory: poetry and pain, hubris and humility. All of the agonies of the world, concentrated in a worry bead, flushed through the heart, made into a burden, suffered in solitude, always in anticipation of sweet victory. Nothing was what it seemed. Every act concealed a motive. Every motive proclaimed love but willingly incurred injury to itself. What kind of beauty was this? What kind of sickness?

The most comprehensive library of such asceticism was to be found in the more than thirty-four hundred manuscripts—in eleven languages—of Saint Catherine's Monastery, the books I'd come to study before being distracted by the tantalyzing granite all around the monastery.

The collection of icons was equally alluring. The painters of the icons had dramatic, physical subject matter to grapple with. Their visions of the surrounding mountains and desert took for a starting point the perception of the monk, tied torturously to some discipline or stake. Nature had become a testing ground for willpower and artistic perseverance. That myth and art became reciprocal, fed on one another, was clear from the record of activity at Saint Catherine's Monastery.

Consider the *aesthetic climate* goading the religious zealots. By the late fourth century, these monastic communities were larger than the towns of Egypt and Palestine, numbering tens of thousands of monks and nuns inhabiting caves throughout the mountains and deserts.

Every monastery had its own master, usually hailed according to the degree of self-torment that he or she brought to bear. The moral sanction for such self-infliction derived from the suffering of Christ on the cross and from theologians who argued that asceticism was the highest form of purity and of natural knowledge (*physike gnosis*). Asceticism was an art form. Nature was its medium. God—and, by inference, every parable of a future paradise, God's launching pad—was its goal.

Admittedly, in my own reading of these sentiments and anecdotes I had somehow come to emulate the passion that drove, for example, the mystic Symeon Stylites (390–459). Here was a man who lived in a cave for forty days with leg irons holding him to the rock. He spent his summer vacations buried up to his head in the sand (surface temperature 179 degrees). How did this early Houdini type survive? Was he macho, a real saint, or merely a committed artist? I had to find out.

Symeon spent thirty-seven years atop a high pillar. Called the "most holy martyr in the air" by his followers, he initiated an aerial tradition of suspended cages and high cliff monasteries that persists to this day. I had paid tribute to this stranger in the desert, precursor, in my mind, of every Don Quixote, every dreamer who had fixated on some particular of nature to satisfy his inner destiny. Others would circumnavigate continents or forge routes to the poles. Symeon chose his eccentric method, placing himself up on the stage, like a rock star performing for the screaming minions.

There were others in the Sinai who took to the depths and to macrobiotic diets. A nun by the name of Alexandra immured herself into a tomb for ten years with a tiny aperture enabling her to receive meager provisions (the Order of Inclusi). Saint Jerome (ca. 340–420) spoke of one follower who spent his entire life in a cistern, consuming no more than five figs a day. Some lived in the desert like camels, eating only the scant clumps of grass between boulders. A fellow named Portian tortured himself by chewing salt. Some hermits were never seen without heavy stones tied to their testicles. It was stated by the biographer of Saint Marcarius of Alexandria that he once went to live in the mosquito marshes of

Scete for six months, returning to his brethren so disfigured from the bites he gladly received there that he was unrecognizable. The fourth-century Saint Mary of Egypt spent forty-seven years in the wilderness, naked. The renowned hermit Agathonicus, his raiment having disintegrated, was said to have warmed himself in winter by sleeping with a herd of gazelles. There was one ascetic in particular, dear to my heart, named Sisoes, who stood on a cliff ledge at night to keep himself from sleep, a new form of torture. This order was called the Aksemetae, and I appeared to be its final member.

What all of these no-frills ascetics had in common, aside from a dubious posterity in my own rambling memory of them, was a pathological eagerness to kill themselves slowly on behalf of God—and to do it in the wilderness. The equation was obvious: One look at the Sinai, with its tortured colors and windless furnace, its incessant midges and stinging nights, suggested all of the ingredients of penance. One would be hard-pressed to take such actions, say, at Cannes—even the Cannes of 1,600 years ago.

By the time of Felix Faber, a fifteenth-century European pilgrim to Mount Sinai, one of several thousand, the legends of these ascetics could be mixed. They included the legend of the women "with flowing beards, who passed their time in a fearsome kind of hunting, kept tigers instead of dogs, and bred panthers and lions, so that no one could set foot on that mountain for fear of these bloodthirsty females, who even sprang naked on armed men and threw them to the ground.

Many were the occasions when a disciple, searching for a revered ascetic, finally found the right cave in question, stepped up to the seated hermit, and touched his hand, only to witness the entire body collapse in a heap of dust. It was written, "Behold, my son, for ninety-five years I have been in this cave...I even ate dust...from hunger, I drank water from the sea...Frequently they (demons) dragged me from here to the base of the mountain until there was no skin or flesh on my limbs...Finally...I saw the realms of the Kingdom."

If such asceticism were not sufficient to arouse the interest of a wrathful god, there were other sources of abuse, namely, the

Saracens—those nomadic tribes inhabiting the lands between Egypt and Arabia. In 373, the monk Ammonius of Canopus witnessed the massacre of nearly forty monks in the area of Mount Sinai at the hands of these barbarians. The monks' limbs and heads were hacked off. Some were tortured for hours before they died. The Saracens were looking for gold, of which they found none.

To protect the monks against such assaults, the eastern Emperor Justinian I sent an expedition into the Sinai to erect a fortress. By 527, Saint Catherine's Monastery, or Tor Sina as it was called, was completed. Although it was Greek Orthodox, the Papacy in Rome maintained strict ties with the fraternity of monks. Pope Gregory the Great (590–604) yearned to leave Rome, with its tiring wines and pastas and prostitutes, and instead spent the rest of his sallow days in a granite cell at Saint Catherine's. Sadly for Pope Gregory, his duties apparently kept him in Rome. Nevertheless, on September 1, in the year 600, Pope Gregory wrote to the abbot of Saint Catherine's, Saint John Climacus, in which he likened the world to a stormy sea on which its human inhabitants were "castaways" adrift—all except for the ascetics of Sinai who were, he applied, standing safely on the shore, calm, living in peace. He beseeched Saint John to stretch out his hand to the Pope, who could not join him, with prayer.

Saint John was another one of the monks who acted on my youthful imagination with all the fury of early lust. John Climacus was himself sixteen when he first entered Saint Catherine's. Later, he went off alone into these surrounding deserts and for nineteen years meditated. He might have even lived in the same cave I had been inhabiting those many months. He was then called back to the monastery to become its abbot, and it was sometime thereafter that John composed his extraordinary little book, *The Ladder to Paradise*, a work of ethical psychiatry that would encourage countless iconographic interpretations over the coming centuries.

"And he dreamed, and behold a ladder set up on the earth, and the top of it reached to heaven: and behold the angels of God ascending and descending on it" (Genesis 28:12). The symbol of height was most easily achieved in the logic of a Jacob's ladder. Spiritual ascension had used this metaphorical vehicle even before the Bible. *The Egyptian Book of the Dead* had provisioned Ra's ascent into heaven upon a ladder, known as the Maquet, and engraved on numerous tombs throughout the Old and Middle Kingdoms. This "stairway to heaven" reappeared in the legends of the Arabic *hajj*, or pilgrimage, celebrated annually at the holy mountains of Arafah, as well as the *Mi'raj*, the name for Mohammad's ascent to heaven. Farther east, the *Kojiki* outlined countless Japanese mountain pilgrimages involving vertical stairways hewn from sheer cliffs. The architectural impulse was universal—at Meteora in Greece, Sigiriya and Anuradhapura in Sri Lanka, Palitana in India, Taktsang in Bhutan, and Hua Shan in China. I, too, was addicted to ladders.

Climacus's book was divided into thirty chapters, or rungs, as he labeled them. Each perilous step was accompanied by a formal religious task. Of the myriad illustrations, the most common image took the form of a diagonal ladder on which numerous monks were grappling heavenward. Christ or Saint Peter was leaning over the top rung to assist them in their final efforts. Some of the monks had typically lost their footing and were seen plummeting upside down into hell.

This was not exactly the later Blakean ladder in which Beatrice, long-robed and sexy, strolled happily into the Milky Way.

In one mid-eleventh-century miniature, a double ladder was configured, its painter apparently unable to accept the notion of climbing thirty narrow rungs in a single flight. In the Princeton Codex (dated to 1081), one finds the wearied face and an arm of a solitaire protruding from a small cave near the summit of Mount Sinai. He is lowering a basket down the cliff by a rope to obtain food from the lower monastery, which his extraordinary penance has bade him to leave. The book explicitly states that to ascend the ladder is to ascend Mount Sinai, which is equivalent to attaining enlightenment.

Broadly speaking, then, the virtuous renunciation of earthly possessions—and, axiomatically, of earth itself—led the ascetic higher and higher, rung by rung, until union with God (*enosis*) was assured. The monks were always portrayed as barefoot, their caves and ladders stationed ever higher into the atmosphere.

Hesychia, or quiet, was—like verticality—also considered crucial to this ascetic ordeal. All thoughts, even those of goodness, were banished, a single prayer repeated unremittingly ("Son of God, have mercy upon me"). One's breath was conserved ("The love of God has priority over our breathing"), and then, after years of half-bowed obeisance and austerities of every magnitude, was said to come the inexpressible rapture, described again and again by the Fathers, this reunion with God, the incorporeal within the corporeal, "the light of the vision."

In the coming centuries, these many visions would proliferate into dozens of monastic and artistic "styles." In the teachings of Saint Benedict (ca. 480–543), prayer was fused with work. The Benedictine Rule held sway over much of Europe until the early twelfth century. Ironically, toil undertaken humbly in God's service generated great wealth and worldliness, as the Vatican attests. The riches of Saint Peter's in Rome, however, could only simulate the impoverished, lyrical sublimity of Sinai. Between these two approaches to God—the Pope on one hand, a Saint Francis on the other—the history of Christianity continues to tease philosophers.

In the same way, earlier Greek and Roman thinkers had debated what truly constituted *natural* perfectibility—the cricket-infested free space of a Delphi, with its cliffs and ancient Gaian oracles, or the congested forums and towns of civilization.

Saint John wrote his treatise in the shadows of numerous 3,000-foot granite walls. The work attested to a jubilantly physical mechanism driving his spiritual theories, as it did for Saint Anthony. To this day, the dozen or so monks of Saint Catherine's Monastery regularly hike up the mountain. A curious end-note, Saint John's treatise was one of the very first books to be published in North America.

"He who makes the true ascent must ascend forever," wrote Saint Gregory of Nyssa (ca. 331–396). The words, like those of Khety and all of these other ascetic crazies of Sinai, sang to me.

It did not stop with the melodious whispers of antiquity. Standing on my imperiled ledge, I looked out and saw Vincent van Gogh, furiously addressing his easel out amid the teeming fields of Arles and Saint Remy, and the seventeenth-century poet Matsuo Bashō, composing his haiku in the rain-soaked cryptomeria forests of northern Japan. Artistic dark nights of the soul, moments of contact with that immanence that has always been and will always be, however one chooses to describe it. Khety—like the more familiar French painter and the Japanese poet—was more than satisfied with the world as it was. Plato and the Bible, Plontinus and Saint John Climacus each looked elsewhere for their comfort.

Where did someone like myself fit in?

I have never fit in.

Nor have I avoided damp stone cells in my life. Exchanging every intimacy with my *ba*, I have made it a point of climbing up ladders, not for torment, but for pleasure. Egypt and Greece have given me innumerable joys, reason for being, a syntax of experience that has been anything but ascetic. The past has become part of nature. I translate it, step into it, as into a cool brook.

I have haunted the cathedrals and basilicas of Europe, from Saint Mark's to Canterbury. Coming out of the daylight into a pew of softened oak and serene distraction, a moment's solitude in the cool nave, a descending fountain of sun-drenched motes from the towering apses, echoes and susurrant voices, the soothing Gregorian chant, vaulted spires, fragrant incense, quavering candles, the shuffling of a priest's sandals over stone—these signals of nature, of other cool brooks, have always recalled for me the atmospheric Sinai's of early Christendom. But with a twist: I have interpreted historical moments that now only linger in my thoughts, without quite the reality, like a perpetual, undifferentiated twilight. The obscurant names, their books and paradises, all those rusting icons disappear like so many fictions. What's left is the stream of nature, obedient to an inner calling, altogether willing, compliant, generous beyond any measure of appreciation that I might, in turn, show to it.

The sun had gone down. I stood clinging to the rock. The

voices had vanished. Egypt was no longer visible. I could do nothing in the dark but suffer. It was cold, my body was numb. I pirouetted in the moonlight, a few inches from the abyss, pressing my bare skin against the cliff, which still irradiated heat from the daylight hours. I prayed for deliverance. I did not want to die, no matter how historical or aesthetic or spiritual such death might be.

Sometime before dawn, I heard the distant ringing of the wooden *symandra* from down in the monastery and the peal of bells. Monks were getting up for prayer.

The sun rose across Arabia. The whole desert turned the color of roseate, then copper. Warmth returned to my fingers. It is said that Raphael once remarked to Leonardo, "I have noticed that when one paints one should think of nothing. Everything then comes better." I'd spent the whole late afternoon and night resisting this wisdom, frantically delving back in time, thinking out loud, trying to avoid my situation. Now I obeyed Raphael, putting absolutely everything out of my head.

I won't describe the actual moment—the plunge upward, the inelegant fray of skin beseeching granite—but within a short time I had surmounted that grotesque ceiling, my hands were bleeding, and I was giving thanks inside the small stone chapel on the windy summit of Mount Sinai.

Michael Tobias is the author of numerous books including The Mountain Spirit, After Eden, *and* World War III. *He directed the ten-part miniseries* Voice of the Planet *for TBS. This essay is from his book,* A Vision of Nature.

JAMES D. HOUSTON

⋆ ⋆ ⋆

Black Stones, Ancient Voices

You can visit the place where you were born of fire.

MO'OKINI IS OUT THERE BY ITSELF, A MOUND OF STONES ON A treeless point. There are no coco palms for shade, no white beaches, no condos overlooking a turquoise pool. The dirt road is iron-red. It leads you through two miles of cane field to a broad clearing and a long rectangle of lichen-spotted chunks of lava. Inside the high, sloping walls there are pathways and restored stone platforms open to the sky.

He'iau is the Hawaiian word for temple or shrine. This one is said to be among the most venerable and sacred of all Hawaiian places—the walled worship site itself, which is nearly the size of a soccer field, as well as the surrounding terrain. Members of the Mo'okini family have been the appointed guardians of this site for over fifteen hundred years. According to their genealogical chant, the *he'iau* dates back further than Taos Pueblo, further than the temples of the sun and moon at Teotihuacan.

It was first laid out in A.D. 480, under the direction of Kuamo'o Mo'okini, the high priest from whom all guardians have been descended, down to the present day. The walls were originally six feet high. About a thousand years ago the temple was enlarged by a priest from Samoa, named Pa'ao. The walls were raised to their present height of thirty feet, without the use of mortar, and a unique scalloped altar was added inside the enclosure. The family chant tells us that the new stones came from Pololu Valley, fourteen miles down the coast toward Hilo. They were moved in a single night. Between sunset and sunrise, some fifteen thousand men stood in a line and passed the stones by hand, from the deep valley to this windswept headland.

Before I visited the place, I had heard these stories. I had seen photos of the ancient stones where the birth of Hawai'i's great king, Kamehameha I, had been consecrated (he was born a thousand yards away). I had read about the long stewardship of the Mo'okini family. And I also knew that this *he'iau* was the first site in all of Hawai'i to be designated a National Historic Landmark, back in 1963. But what I did not know, could never have grasped from afar, or by reading, or by studying all the photographs, was the impact of the location.

Hawai'i, usually called the Big Island, is the largest island in the chain. Mo'okini occupies the very end of the island's northernmost point, a peninsula that juts like a thumb, pointing across the channel toward Maui. Standing there you have behind you the green and rugged slopes of the Kohala Range, and in front of you, Maui's high shield cone, Haleakalā, The House of the Sun. It is the world's largest dormant volcano. Viewed from the south, it is certainly as noble and blood stirring as Fuji or Mount Shasta, with the added benefit that it comes rising straight out of the sea.

The wind through that channel is constant and as mysterious as the silence of the craters that made the islands, while the waters are spectacularly blue, a moving, shifting, current-driven blue. The point is empty. The sea is moving. Twenty-five miles across the channel the old volcano, in early afternoon, makes a dark cone against the tropic sky.

It is the kind of place you have to react to. You have to mark the spot, or write about it in your journal. Standing there, it isn't hard to imagine the first human who stopped and gazed toward the next island in the constant wind and felt an urge to consecrate the moment, to send a voice across the water, make a song or make a chant or gather a few stones in a heap, as a way of saying, "I touched this place, and the place touched me."

Perhaps that first visitor tells others a story that includes something about the look and feel of the barren point, and this story conveys whatever it called out of him. Eventually someone else wants to see what he was talking about and comes and stands and adds a stone to the pile of stones or sends another call across the channel. And there is an agreement that, yes, the place has a kind of power, which is to say, it releases something in those who experience it. Nowadays we might name this reverence, or wonder, or awe.

I believe that such feelings can linger in the air and in the land, gathering, over time, in invisible layers. And after enough people have visited a spot, to stand, to pray, to sing, to fast, to chant, century upon century, its original impact has been layered and amplified until the ancestral atmosphere around a site like Mo'okini *he'iau* is so rich with what Hawaiians call *mana*, you can feel it like a coating on your skin.

The atmosphere seemed denser there, thick with its own history of reaching toward the higher power. Though I am not Hawaiian and can claim no authentic ties to the long traditions of the *he'iau*, I felt profoundly connected to the place. During the couple of hours I wandered inside and outside the rocky walls, I felt I was in a state of grace. Later, trying to explain this to myself, I began to think of sacredness as a kind of dialogue between the human spirit and certain designated places. These sites that call forth reverence and awe and humility and wonder, we make them sacred. It is a way of honoring those feelings in ourselves. And when we hear the songs the places sing, we are hearing our own most ancient voices.

I believe there is a place in each of us where the entire universe resides, and it includes those lava rocks at Mo'okini as well as the craters that produced them. On the day I visited that *he'iau* I had been living on the Big Island for nearly a month. Home of the world's most active volcanoes, it is a very lava-conscious realm. Lava rocks, large and small, are everywhere—in house foundations, in fences marking property lines, in the numerous temple remains, and in all the legends. When you're there you can touch rocks that no one dares to move, and you can touch some of the newest rocks on earth, just recently cooled. In this island world of living, moving stone, it occurred to me that we had all been lava once. And that those ties are never lost. They may be forgotten. But they are not lost.

During that month I had been eating produce grown right there—papayas, bananas, mangoes, cucumber, onions. As I was driving away, back along the two-mile track through the cane field, I asked myself, where do all these local fruits and vegetables get their nutrients? From the soil, I replied. And where does the soil come from? It too started out as lava belched up from Kīlauea and Mauna Loa and Mauna Kea, to be broken down by millennia of rain and wind. And am I then that much different from the shaggy ohia tree, which feeds off the rock and is the stubborn dancer anchored to the lava fields and old volcanic mountainsides? These nutrients taken from produce grown in soil that began as molten lava, they are now somewhere in my bloodstream, entering my cells. *Multiply that,* I told myself, *by 4 billion years or so, by all the recycled incarnations of all the bits of matter I'm composed of, and isn't there going to be a chorus of voices to be listened to, called forth, released?*

A month on the island had made it clear to me that I have some things in common with the stones first gathered there at Mo'okini *he'iau* fifteen hundred years ago. Though they may be forgotten, these ancient ties are never lost. In the presence of the stones they come whispering, the oldest voices, calling from within.

James D. Houston is the author of seven novels, including The Last Paradise, Continental Drift, *and* Love Life, *as well as the nonfiction books* Californians: Searching for the Golden State *and* In the Ring of Fire: A Pacific Basin Journey, *from which this story was excerpted. He lives with his wife, Jeanne Wakatsuki Houston, in Santa Cruz, California.*

ANN ARMBRECHT FORBES

* *
 *

Thin Places

As Virginia Woolf wrote in The Waves, *"There are moments when the walls of my mind grow thin; when nothing is unabsorbed."*

MY SKIN WAS LIKE WET TISSUE PAPER. IT PEELED OFF WITH MY socks, pulled off under the damp bandage. It came off between my toes, from the soles of my feet and the edges of my heels. The exposed new skin was raw and tender. There was too much of it to cover and nothing solid or dry to hold down a new bandage. I had never seen anything like it and had no idea what to do. I glanced up with despair and saw the women already lifting their bamboo baskets and filing barefoot into the early morning mist. Pain was preferable to abandonment. Wincing, I pulled on my last dry pair of socks and laced up my soggy boots. I stuffed my jacket into the top of my pack and followed in the direction of the women—day number two on our pilgrimage to Khembalung.

At night in their dreams, shamans and priests from Hedangna, a village in the upper Arun Valley of northeastern Nepal, are said to travel to a cold clear lake on the right shoulder of Khembalung. Witches travel to the ridge as well, but they bathe instead in a lake of blood. When they are done washing, the shamans, witches, and priests stretch out on the rocks, drying themselves in the moonlight and arguing over which of them is the most powerful. Khembalung refers to several places. It is Makalu, the fifth-highest mountain in the world and the home, so the villagers in Hedangna say, of Lord Shiva. Khembalung is also a *bhayul*, or hidden valley of Tibetan cosmology, a pure enchanted land set outside the destruction and corruption of time. Here, so the legends say, one will find refuge from the enemies of religion and will attain eternal youth, beauty, strength, and fertility.

These *bhayuls* are physical places hidden deep in the Himalayas and rendered inaccessible by the magic of the Tibetan *yogin* Padmasambhava. Years ago, so the story goes, in the paradisal kingdom of Galdan, Arya Avalokitesvara made a prophecy:

> *Emaho!* In the future, during the epoch of conflicts and
> disputes the land of snows, where live those who follow the
> way of the great compassion, will be conquered by the
> demons of ignorance. At that time all the followers of the
> Arya, to flee from the demons will take refuge in this place
> which has sprung up from the flowers offered by the most
> powerful of the gods…It is the castle of the divinities, is the
> place of the purest prayers, is the natural site of the Vajra. It
> is surrounded by rocks and snowy mountains, and is known
> as *mKhanpa lung*, the valley of Artemisia. Everyone who
> arrives there will go to the paradise of Akanisthah.

At the time when all temples are destroyed, Giacomella Orofino describes, when servants become masters, when "people sacrifice their own animals, drink blood, and eat flesh of their own fathers," those disciples of Padmasambhava who "display greatness of heart" will take out the guidebooks hidden thousands of years before and set out to "open" these hidden lands.

The journey to Khembalung crosses the physical landscape, passing by a lake, so the guidebook says, that "by day is like boiling blood and by night like burning fire," through a valley like "the outer curtain of a door," and beneath "a mountain of black slate like untied hair." But what the pilgrims see along the way depends on what they are capable of seeing. Some travelers encounter rocks and trees, snow and empty forest. Others travel over the same terrain and see mysterious landscapes shimmering with jewels, spacious deserts beneath strange skies, and towering mountains floating above clouds of light. The hidden valley itself bestows a spiritual blessing on all who arrive there. How the pilgrims experience that blessing again depends on what they are ready to experience. Most who enter the hidden lands of Khembalung will have a vision of a peaceful and fertile valley with room for a settlement of 500 people. These pilgrims will receive health and long life, fertility, and strength, and all of their desires will be fulfilled.

Though yogis trek beneath the same mountains and enter the same lush, green valley, they also undergo a spiritual transformation on their journey to Khembalung, a death and rebirth that allows them to transcend their usual state of consciousness and awaken to deeper levels of the mind. These pilgrims experience a flash of insight into the nature of reality, a vision that is fleeting, but one that strengthens and deepens their own spiritual journey. The secret journey to Khembalung is reserved only for those who have reached the highest level of spiritual fulfillment. Here, at its most profound level, the hidden valley corresponds to the body and mind of the pilgrim, to the realm where no distinctions are made between oneself and the outside world. Upon entering this innermost realm of the kingdom of Khembalung, the pilgrim acquires clarity of mind and openness of heart, the two qualities needed to attain the ultimate goal of enlightenment.

Few attempt to undertake this journey to the hidden lands. It is too dangerous, and they fear they will never return. But many make pilgrimages to the edges of these valleys, to the "gateways" (Tibetan *gnas sgo*) mentioned in the guidebooks and said to have been hidden by Padmasambhava. Two caves carved out of a granite cliff 1,000 feet above the high-altitude summer pastures of Yangle Meadow, a day's walk south of the base of Makalu, are said to be one of the gateways into the hidden valley of Khembalung. Whether they are or not, these caves are believed to be places where gods have been; they are sacred places and are one of the most important pilgrimage sites for Hindus and Buddhists throughout the upper Arun Valley.

Priests and shamans, lamas and yogis may be able to make the journey to Khembalung in their dreams or through intense spiritual practice. Everyone else must get here on foot. And so, at the height of the monsoon of 1992, I set out at dawn with twenty-five villagers from Hedangna on a pilgrimage made annually to the Khembalung caves during the August full moon. Most in our group were Yamphu Rai, the original inhabitants of Hedangna, strong wiry people who have spent their lives as subsistence farmers in this remote subtropical Himalayan village.

Yamphu rituals and spiritual beliefs are based on oral texts passed down from the ancestors through the priests and shamans who learn these traditions in their dreams. Although they know that the caves are connected to the hidden valleys of Tibetan cosmology, they consider themselves to be Hindu and refer to the site as Shiva's cave. Two Brahmans from a less remote village to the south also joined us. These men were tall and thin and not at all suited to the long, hard days of walking. One of them complained incessantly, saying the trail was too hard, the trip too difficult. Each time the Brahman complained, Jadu Prasad, one of the oldest Yamphu men in the group, who was on his sixth pilgrimage to Khembalung, would reply, "It wouldn't be a pilgrimage if it wasn't difficult." By the end of the trip we were all repeating, again and again, "It wouldn't be a pilgrimage if it wasn't difficult."

Yogis and lamas travel to hidden valleys in search of enlightenment; they hope to escape samsara and attain eternal bliss. The Yamphu were going to Khembalung to ask for a son, a daughter, a job, a good harvest. As an anthropologist living in their community, I hoped to learn more about their pilgrimages, about what they did and found myself mumbling repetitive chants, over and over, to keep myself moving across the rocky terrain.

I carried a down sleeping bag, a Thermarest, a toothbrush, a pack cover, a flashlight, a notebook, iodine, four pairs of socks, long underwear, a synchilla jacket, a camera, rice, and the boots on my feet. Everytime I unpacked and repacked, the women gathered around to comment on each item I had brought. They carried a handwoven woolen blanket, bamboo mat to keep out the rain, rice, some spices, and a pot. They were barefoot. They had small bundles of string and bits of cloth, a shawl, their finest clothing to wear on the day we climbed to the caves, and *raksi,* a type of wine made from millet. That was all.

Each morning we awoke in the dark. We walked all day along steep narrow trails, fording icy streams overflowing from the monsoon rains, and climbing from 5,000 feet in Hedangna over two 16,000-foot passes and up the Barun Valley. In five days, we covered the same distance I had covered in two weeks the previous spring while trekking with family. The villagers would stop only at dusk, when we had reached a cave large enough to hold all twenty-five of us. We ate one meal of rice a day, mixed with wild plants gathered along the trail. While hiking we snacked on roasted corn flour. Occasionally, we drank black tea.

By the third afternoon, we arrived at Yangle Meadow, the grazing lands at 13,000 feet below the Khembalung

Tired after long days of hiking to Muktinath and returning along the Kali Gandaki River, I had the good fortune one day to fall in behind Kesang, the younger of our two Sherpa helpers. Feet clad in crumbling sneakers, he walked with a lantern swinging from one hand, and at such an unvarying pace that we called him the "human metronome." I followed two feet behind him, and after an hour of unwittingly mirroring his rhythm, fell into timelessness. I lost all sense of physical discomfort, up became the same as down and was traversed at the same speed. I had nothing to do but enjoy the view, as though I was inside a well-muscled android.

—James O'Reilly, "Stairway to Heaven," *Travelers' Tales Nepal*

caves. We sat on the grassy floor of the narrow valley, flanked on either side by towering granite cliffs. Our words were swallowed by the roar of the Barun River, which carved its way through the center of the valley. Jadu Prasad pointed out some invisible trail going straight up the vertical rock face: the path to the caves. I sat silently.

A chill that had been with me the entire trip slowly crept up from my stomach. The two oldest women in the group, both in their seventies, looked at the cliff and then looked at me. "Don't go," they said. "Don't do it. The trail is too hard. Stay below and wait."

I know how to rock climb, I know what to be afraid of, and I shared their concern. "If these grandmothers can do it, of course you can," Jadu Prasad said. Having spent much of the past year trying to keep up with these same grandmothers while collecting firewood and stinging nettle in the jungles around Hedangna, I wasn't so sure. But the men promised we would all go together the next morning, and they would look out for me. If I could go with them, I agreed, I would give it a try. We lifted our loads and went in search of a dry cave for the night.

The next morning we again awoke in the dark. It was drizzling. It had rained all night, and I had slept fitfully, dreaming of slippery mud and slippery rocks. I again asked Jadu Prasad if he thought I could make it, and he again reassured me, so I went with the women to bathe. The women were used to doing things on their own; they were strong, and they assumed I was equally strong. I couldn't count on them for help on the trail. After a perfunctory bath in the icy water, I returned to an empty cave. I waited, thinking the men must have gone to bathe as well.

Finally, one man returned. He was surprised to see me, said the men had already left, and that he had just come back to get something he had forgotten. I grabbed my bag and scrambled after him. We walked silently and rapidly through the drizzle, turning off the main trail onto a narrow, overgrown path that climbed toward the cliff. We caught up with Jadu Prasad and the two Brahmans. They greeted us as we approached and told me that the trail was too slippery for my boots, that I should go barefoot; they then returned to their discussion of whether the two menstruating women should climb to the sacred caves. I was curious to hear what they had to say, but was distracted by the trail and, now, by my bare feet. Until now I had never thought of the cold. The soles of my feet were numb, so numb I didn't notice the stones underneath.

Soon the trail disappeared into the base of the rock. Those

ahead had been slowed by the climb, and the women coming from behind caught up with us. Hands gripping the rock, we slowly followed the others up the cliff. Along with our group of twenty-five from Hedangna, there were Bhotes (Tibetans) from the northern Arun Valley and Chetris (Hindus) from the south. Together, sixty or more people were making their way up the rock face.

In the West, we climb rocks with rope and protection. We wear soft rubber under our feet. We are on the rock, yet not on the rock. With these pilgrims I climbed to the Khembalung caves barefoot, with no rope. Perched on a tiny ledge, Jadu Prasad reached down to pull me over a difficult section. I clutched his hand as he hauled me up the cliff, not letting myself think about what he in turn was holding on to. At a particularly difficult part, one of the grandmothers looked at me with concern and suggested I go down. But then a man appeared with a twelve-foot piece of rope. He knelt above the difficult section and held the rope as I used it to climb up the crack.

Once, at a Quaker wedding I attended, the father of the groom talked about thin places, about places where one's nerve endings are bare. We take pilgrimages to thin places, to places where gods have made their mark on the land. As the legends of the hidden valleys make clear, these journeys are internal as much as they are external. How thin the place seems to us depends on who we are and where we come from; most important, it depends on what we bring and what we can relinquish in order to make our journey.

I often joined the women in the fields in Hedangna, helping with digging and planting and cutting and carrying, doing whatever I could to create something in common for us to share. Though I was slower and clumsier, they welcomed the free labor and perhaps the novelty of having me around. During breaks in the work, when we were gathered on a rock or under a tree, the women, old and young, would reach for my hands and rub their fingers slowly across my skin. They would turn over my hand and feel the palm, pulling the fingers up close to their eyes, and they would comment to each other on how smooth and white it was.

Then they would hold up their own hands and feet, which were tough and dark, next to mine and shake their heads. They lived by their hands, they would say, and I lived by my head.

The women in Hedangna want skin like mine. They want some padding in their lives, want to be able to stay inside for a while and let their bodies become smooth and white and soft. I went to Hedangna because I wanted skin like theirs. I wanted its thickness and its toughness, a toughness that seemed to be a sign of an internal strength, a thickening from the inside that allowed them to get by without a lot of external support. Their dark, callused skin enabled them to walk through their lives barefoot, enduring, not avoiding, the sharpness and the pain encountered along the way.

I was raised in a world where the answer to a problem or the solution to pain was always out there, around the next corner, in the next place or next job or next year. I was educated away from my home, taught to believe there was more to be gained by moving forward than by staying put. I came to Hedangna, a community where people still farm the land their ancestors cleared eleven generations ago, because I wanted to learn what it took to stay at home. I wondered what life was like without the leather and the plastic. I came to Hedangna because I wanted to relearn what it meant to live from the inside, with my hands and my feet and my heart—because I wanted to remember what their ways of living have never let them forget. And as I climbed the rock face to the Khembalung caves, I found myself entering one of the thinnest places I had ever been.

Two hours after leaving the valley floor, the trail leveled, and we began to climb the final section through thick clumps of juniper. Spiky roots and sharp stones under the juniper bushes made me aware of my bare feet, by now used to the cold. While climbing, we had only been able to see the rock immediately ahead and the valley dropping out below. As we came over the last incline, the most sacred site in the upper Arun Valley—the Khembalung caves—suddenly loomed before us: an immense amphitheater carved out of the cliff with a torrent of water pouring from an opening at the top of the cave. Buddhists say Padmasambhava meditated here on his way to Tibet. Hindus say Shiva bathed here on the evening before his wedding to Parvati. Now, snatches from the high-pitched chants of the Chetri pilgrims drifted down from the base of the amphitheater.

We approached the cave from below, first stopping at a smaller stone cairn to hang offerings of narrow thin bits of colored cotton cloth. Then, in single file, we walked through the waterfall. Those before me stood directly under the torrent and drenched themselves in the freezing water. It was still drizzling, and cold. Already chilled, I skirted the edges, hoping no one would notice, and followed the others up the last rocky stretch and into the cave.

The air inside was cold and dry and laced with the sweet smell of burning juniper. Red and green, blue and yellow prayer flags brought by the Bhotes and attached to long sticks rose out of a pile of stones in the center of the cave. Smaller bits of cloth were attached to sticks or rocks. String candles, clumps of wildflowers, red *tika* powder, coins, even a watch were placed haphazardly on the pile of stones beneath the prayer flags.

Until now, people had been quiet, focused on the trail and the destination. Once in the amphitheater, the atmosphere changed. There was work to be done, and everyone set out busily to do it. Two women pulled out clumps of string that they coiled into bundles, dipped in *ghee*, and lit as candles. One couple carefully placed a small tin trident below the prayer flags. A young man who had come on the pilgrimage to assist his mother sat off to the side, staring at the opening in the top of the cave through which the water flowed. There was no way people could have made this hole or the waterfall, he told me. It could only have been made by a god. That is why we had to give offerings. A middle-aged man who had moved to Hedangna from southern Nepal paused in his preparations to scan over the amphitheater. He had heard about this place for a long time, he told me, since he was young. Now that we are finally here," he said, "we have to take our time and make sure we do things right."

The time spent in the cave was not what I think of as spiritual.

There were too many people, too much commotion, too much concern about this piece of string, that piece of cloth. I was too preoccupied with how we were going to get back down the cliff. But the cave was awesome. Now the voices and din echoed off its high ceiling, but I imagined what it would be like to be there alone, with only the sound of the wind and the torrent of water spraying against the rock. Outside, the ground dropped out abruptly and steeply, and all I could see was the Barun River, silver and silent, winding its way through the distant and green meadows far below.

We finished at Shiva's cave, walked down a narrow path through the juniper, around the ridge to a smaller cave set in the rock face. For Hindus, this is the cave where she is said to have bathed. For Buddhists, this cave is where Padmasambhava and his consort, Yeshe Tsogyel, are said to have stayed on their way from India to Tibet. We took turns crawling into a space that would hold only three or four at a time. The air was pungent from the burning butter. Light from string butter candles set on the floor illuminated exposed chunks of quartz crystals along the inside of the cave. The rest of the cave was in shadows. Several red plastic bangles and a white cotton shirt sewn by a tailor in Hedangna had been placed amidst the usual bits of cloth and coins: offerings brought by a couple seeking a child.

Outside, more juniper was burned. One of the Brahmans chanted prayers for the well-being of our group; we tossed bits of uncooked rice into the juniper smoke, and the Brahman wiped the ashes on our foreheads as a blessing, a *tika*. We then began the descent. Not until we reached the dirt trail coming up from the valley floor, two hours later, did I begin to relax. I paused to pull my boots back on and followed the others back to the cave where we had spent the previous night. The women who had been unable to go to the sacred caves because they were menstruating sat by a smoldering, smoky fire. They added some wood to the coals to heat water for tea, and we snacked on roasted corn flour mixed with sugar. The two oldest women said they were too tired to continue north up the valley and that they would wait for us there. We packed our loads and set out once again.

The valley floor was brilliant green from the summer rains, and there was finally a bit of blue sky. The air on my bare feet that morning had dried the skin, and the raw parts felt less painful. With the climb to the caves over, I felt carefree for the first time in days. As we walked up the valley, one man speculated that the weather had turned because of the particularly strong dharma (spiritual practice) of someone in our group. The idea that sun and rain responded to our thoughts and actions reassured me somehow and made me feel less exposed in this vast landscape. We walked until early evening and spent that night in a huge open cave at 15,000 feet. The next morning we climbed the remaining few hours so that we could bathe in the headwaters of the Barun on the morning of the full moon.

The next evening, another cave, another long day walking in more misty rain. There had been confusion over a bag I had left behind with the grandmothers, who we discovered had decided to head home before us. One of the women reprimanded me for not taking responsibility for my own things. A man who had told me the previous day to leave the extra weight behind looked at me with disdain and said that he had told me he would carry the bag. I turned and walked off to the river's edge to fill my water bottle. It was dusk, and the sky was still overcast. I stood on the banks of the Barun River, alone, I thought about how hard I was trying—trying to walk fast enough, to say the right thing, to understand the right way—trying to get it right. In Hedangna, I had novels to read and a tiny room with a door I could shut, a door that, oddly enough, was what protected me from this stark realization of my solitude.

For the past five days, these barriers had been stripped away, and this sudden and complete exposure made me acutely aware of the gap between my world and the world of my companions. I stared at the cold gray rapids thundering through the cold gray fog. Why was I here, alone, in the middle of nowhere? Why did I keep going out on my own into the wind and the rain and the wet?

I inhaled the cold, moist air and searched the shadows beneath the Khembalung caves, searched the thick fir trees clinging to the edges of the valley floor. The mist moved swiftly and silently along the banks of the Barun. The silty river roared. Then the clouds suddenly opened and a shaft of light broke through the fog, turning the gray water silver, the black fir a deep green. An angular cliff appeared out of the clouds high overhead. The red-gray granite, softened by the yellow evening light, was framed by the heavy dark clouds. And then, just as suddenly, the fog closed in again, and night fell.

I took a deep breath and turned to walk back to the cave to help prepare dinner. In the cave, a younger woman came over to tell me that they were all with their families and neighbors, that for them it was as if they had never left home. She said that they had forgotten that it was different for me, that sometimes, she thought, I must feel lonely or homesick, and that she hoped I was O.K.

During the whole trip, I felt an ache in my chest, a longing that would not go away. I thought there must be a place, somewhere, where I could be held, here, no *here*, on the inside. If only I could get to that place, I was sure the yearning would disappear. Now I realize that this feeling of aloneness is not something that ever goes away. It is always there, underneath the words spoken, inside my boots. It's what comes up in thin places. It's what you feel when the skin peels off your feet.

Three months earlier at a cremation in Hedangna, as we watched the burned body float down the Arun River, the mother of the dead man held up her hand in front of me. It was cracked and dark. "We all feel love," she told me. "We all feel pain. We all bleed when we are cut. It is only the *mindhum* (oral tradition) that is different." The skin contains the blood, preventing it from spilling over; it creates the distinctions that enable us to live. But the skin can become too thick. It can keep us from seeing blood underneath, from sensing what Roberto Calasso calls the "connection of everything with everything, which alone gives meaning to life." It can keep us from experiencing the sacred.

We make pilgrimages to sacred places, but the places themselves are not inherently sacred. We enter the sacred when we let go of the fear of being exposed: Only when I gave up trying to hide what was inside did the boundaries between us begin to dissolve. And in the moment I felt most alone, I realized I was never alone. The sacred, as Calasso writes, is always there "waiting to wake us and be seen by us, like a tree waiting to greet our newly opened eyes." It is simply up to us to let ourselves see.

Having reached our destination, everyone was suddenly in a hurry to begin the trip home. Rice fields needed to be weeded, millet planted, houses looked after. We left early the following morning and walked twelve hours,

Panting as I climb to the top of a ridgeline, I can feel my pulse pounding in my head, as if entrained with my thoughts. My heart is breaking, and it is the yearning borne of too-great beauty that is the cleaver. I am met at the crest by sunlight, bursting through clouds in great coronal streamers. Irradiated with sunglow, I am struck by the truth of the assertion made most forcefully by the Sufis—that the broken heart was the gift supreme, because it generated the magnetic force which drew the Divine to you. So if you were smart, you wouldn't even want to have that wound healed by the usual consolations. The broken heart was like a beacon for the Absolute. It was *meant* to bleed.

—Moss Campion, "Decaf"

over a 15,000-foot scree pass, and then descended steeply past grazing yaks and shepherds' huts. We walked on after dark for an hour, searching for a place to spend the night. Finally, ten of us crowded into a small empty bamboo hut. I had a mat, so I kicked away the cow and goat dung, spread it out on the dank floor of the attached livestock shelter, and tried to sleep. We again woke before dawn and started walking hard and fast until we reached another shepherd's hut where we stopped to drink sour buttermilk. Since climbing to the caves, I had given up bandaging or even looking at my feet, but by this time, I was no longer the only one limping. The women leaned heavily on walking sticks and groaned with each step. We joked and laughed to keep our minds off the pain.

The trail continued to descend steeply. Yaks gave way to water buffalo and cows, and we began to meet shepherds from Hedangna. Finally, we could see the village, far down the ridge. We had been rushing, and now the women wanted to linger, to hold on to the remaining bits of time that were outside regular, routine time. We paused on top of the ridge to eat the last of our corn flour. One woman sighed and said she was so happy up here, in the meadows and the mountains, that she didn't want to go home. Two women separated the tiny wildflowers they had collected from the fields beyond Yangle Meadow to bring as gifts for friends who had had to stay home. Two others divided a bottle of water, taken from the headwaters of the Barun. The sun was beginning to set.

We began the last stretch, down and down. We came across leeches for the first time but were too tired to pull them off. An hour later we entered the edges of the village, in the dark. I was the only one with a torch and my batteries were dim, so our pace slowed to a crawl. The trail wound beneath thick clumps of bamboo towering over the stone and mud houses. People broke off from the group as we passed the narrow paths to their homes. Eventually, it was only the two oldest women and myself, walking down to the houses at the bottom of the village. We finally arrived, I dropped my pack and leaned it against the stone wall. Someone went inside to cook rice. The children gathered around, and I sat on the mud porch to unlace my boots. My socks were wet with blood. I carefully peeled them off so the air could begin the slow process of healing—and thickening—the exposed raw skin.

Ann Armbrecht Forbes teaches in the Environmental Studies Department at Dartmouth College and is the author of Settlements of Hope. *She is currently working on a book about her work in northeastern Nepal.*

TARA AUSTEN WEAVER

⭐ ⭐ ⭐

Shikoku Pilgrimage

*An island cycling journey serves up
an inner transformation.*

THE SLOW BOAT FOR SHIKOKU DEPARTS HIROSHIMA AT 8 A.M.
Early one cloudy, May morning, my cycling companion and I
carefully wheel our heavily loaded mountain bikes onto the lower
deck of the small, rusty ferry. Tent poles and sleeping mats sprout
from the sidebags of our bicycles, rain jackets are strapped to the
rear. Our plan is to spend ten days riding the salty ups and downs
of the Shikoku coastal route, a much-needed break from everyday
work and life in Japan.

Lying just off the eastern coast of the Japanese mainland, the island of Shikoku is only ten kilometers from the skyscrapers and
pulsating, technology-fueled nightlife of Osaka, but in all other
ways it is a universe apart. Dense foliage blankets the island's
mountains, shadowing thatch-roofed farmhouses and terraced rice
paddies. Groves of orange and loquat trees cascade down steep hillsides, and in weather-battered fishing villages clinging to the coast,
old men continue to eke out a meager existence from the sea.

Most visitors to Shikoku are pilgrims who come to walk the
eighty-eight-temple circuit founded in the 800s by Kobo Daishi,
who brought Shingon Buddhism from China to Japan. Pilgrims
circle the 1,400-kilometer course in hope of gaining inner peace

and karmic merit. Some leave their jobs and families to complete the two-month pilgrimage; others take a few days each year covering as much distance as possible in time stolen away from commitments and careers. This is Japan's most famous pilgrimage, drawing seekers for more than a thousand years.

> This [Shikoku] pilgrimage has no goal in the usual sense. No holy of holies to which one journeys and, after celebration in worship, returns home. This pilgrimage is essentially a circle: a circle has no beginning and no end. And so it is not at all important where one begins. What is important is that one go all the way around and return to one's starting point. One must close the circle.
>
> —Oliver Statler,
> *Japanese Pilgrimage*

Pilgrims are far from my mind this May morning. Boarding the ferry, I feel as if I am escaping. The spring has been hard. Recent staff transfers in the Japanese office where I work have thrust me into a job for which I am neither trained nor qualified. I try to *gaman*—to persevere— as is the Japanese way and work hard to make up for the deficiencies, but I am worn to the breaking point from feelings of constant failure and lack of sleep. Shortly before leaving for Shikoku, I received a letter from my best friend. Standing in the small, cramped entryway of my apartment, I hungrily read the letter and her words, so kind and comfortable, brought me to tears. What was I doing here, I wondered, so far from those I cared about?

Three years of living in Japan have caused all the edges of my life to blur. From the beginning I wanted to experience the country and culture as deeply as possible—to become part of it. I didn't want to leave Japan laden with photographs of quaint festivals, yet with no real understanding of the *why* behind the culture. If Japan is an enigma, as is often said, I wanted to get as close as possible to its enigmatic heart.

But in my attempt to become part of Japan, I seem to have lost part of myself. Three years of living here have given me the gift of insight into the Japanese way of doing things. By birth and up-bringing I instinctively understand the *gaijin* (Western) way, but I no longer know where I belong. I fall somewhere between the two extremes now, a place where there are no clear rules or boundaries. My manner of dress, body language, and sense of humor have all been toned-down in order to render them under-standable and acceptable to my Japanese colleagues and friends. The end result leaves me feeling like a pale, washed-out version of who I really am, or who I thought I was.

A week before the planned trip I came down with a *kase*—a virulent Japanese cold. Feverish and coughing up small pieces of what felt like my lung, I considered staying home to use this pre-cious time to rest and recuperate. I quickly rejected the idea. I needed to go, I needed to get away. The word "escape" crossed my mind; I am escaping to the island of Shikoku.

On the ferry the ocean air feels like a wake-up call. As our boat draws near, the island emerges out of the mist: emerald-green mountains rising from clear waters. The mountains are impossibly steep, like ancient scroll paintings of rocky cliffs studded with pine branches in an Asian art museum. I had always assumed the steep-ness an artistic device, and find myself overwhelmed by the reality.

The mountains become my challenge, a physical mirror of my inner struggles. The sidebags on my bike weigh heavily as I slowly pedal up near-vertical inclines. The hills never seem to end and each mountain pushes me farther than I comfortably want to go. I'm coughing badly and breathing is difficult. I consider turning around, going home, but the idea of reclimbing the mountains al-ready behind me is heartbreaking. I decide life must be lived in the forward direction, at whatever speed I am capable of.

While every incline tests me, the payoff is worth the struggle. To stop pushing, to simply coast down thrilling, spiraling hills from summit to sea, wind streaming past my face and tugging my hair out from beneath my helmet, is perhaps as close as I will ever get to the joy of natural flight. I feel like a child on a swing-set with the world rushing up to meet me. I shout out my joy to the empty green canyons, and it echoes back at me and all around.

I am riding back through time to a Japan unknown to the children of today living in cement apartment blocks in the urban sprawl. I cycle through misty, jungle-like ravines, past terraced rice paddies aflock with white cranes and hillsides covered with blooming orange trees, their heady perfume overwhelming the senses. At night we camp on deserted beaches, the sound of waves invading our dreams, and wake to the noise of villagers on their way to harvest seaweed from the rocky shore. I am struck by the beauty of this ancient life and reminded of why I was drawn to Japan, a world so unlike my own.

Sticking to the coast, we pedal our way through towns bypassed by the new highway. The tiny villages where we buy food are festooned with colorful carp banners hung to celebrate the upcoming Children's Day holiday. The bright, fish-shaped flags dance merrily on the ocean breeze, the only visible movement in many of these faded, sleeping towns. We ride past local festivals and through a blessing ceremony for a new house. The Shinto priest and members of the family throw pieces of celebratory *mochi* rice paste to the villagers assembled in the street below. Wrapped in brightly colored kitchen towels, the balls of *mochi* go sailing by on the spring breeze, only to be snatched up by the wrinkled hands of the practical *oba-chans*, the village grandmothers. Once the villagers see us, we are inundated by offers of these colorful parcels. Uncooked, the *mochi* tastes like glue and sticks to our teeth. We tell them it is delicious and they laugh, delighted.

The unlikely sight of two foreigners on bicycles livens up most places we pass through, and we become the center of attention whenever we stop. Where are we going? Where are we from? Where will we sleep tonight? We answer their questions, doing our best to wade through the unfamiliar local dialect, and in return they give us gifts of food for our travels. *O-settai,* they call them, gifts for the pilgrims. We receive so many oranges, the local specialty, that by the third day we are forcing them down and swearing off all citrus fruit for months to come.

The kindness of the local people is touching. One night it begins to rain and, when the locals in the public bathhouse where we've gone to bathe discover we are planning to camp, a playful competition erupts over who will take the foreigners home. Not wanting to impose, we ask the owner of the bathhouse if we might pitch our tent in the covered parking area after the baths are closed. Instead she takes us to a small shed built on the roof of the bathhouse. It is filled with *tatami* mats and evidence of a late-night card game, but it is dry and comfortable. In the morning we offer her money, but she refuses. Other pilgrims have stayed there before, she says.

The pilgrims are always with us. Carrying wooden walking sticks, and dressed in traditional white clothing and pointy straw hats, they plod along the pilgrimage course. We exchange greetings of *"Ganbatte"* (Do your best) when we pass them on our bikes. In ancient temples along the route, their chanting blends with the scent of burning incense and wafts by on the wind. What lives have they left behind them, I wonder, and what are they searching for?

Days spent on the bike leave me with time for thinking. Realizations dawn slowly, the result of hours of uninterrupted cycle meditation. While never a disciple, I too am searching. However, it is not karma I hope to gain. Through my travels and my life in Japan, I am searching for new horizons and challenges. I want to push myself beyond what is comfortable—both mentally and physically—in order to test my own spirit. I want to discover myself: my boundaries, my strengths, and my weaknesses. It is not the succeeding lifetimes that concern me; I want to fully experience the present and to discover new vistas, not only around me, but within me as well.

Shikoku is the answer I seek. Amidst early-morning climbs up steep ravines and adrenaline-filled, late-afternoon sprints along a rocky coastline, I find my stride. Recovered from my illness now, my body responds to the demands of biking, growing stronger each day. Sweat-stained and dirty with bike-chain grease and sore from days riding and nights sleeping on the ground, I am happier than I have been in months. The mountains—along the road and in my life—no longer seem overwhelming, and I am excited about the surprises that lie around the next curve. I begin to lose the feeling of being lost between two worlds. I am not lost; I am simply in a place I have never been before.

One morning late in the trip, I slip outside the tent to watch the sun rise. Sitting on a sandy beach, so like the beaches of my childhood, I look past the small, offshore islands cloaked in mist and across the ocean toward the country that is my home. Soon I will return to my job—and the small apartment that is home for the moment. My job will not have changed. I will still be faced with the challenge of balancing who I am with what is acceptable and appropriate in this traditional society. However, Shikoku has left me with a clarity of vision and a sense of self I had not known before. I am a bridge connecting two worlds—one, the world of my birth, and another, more ancient world I have sought to understand and come to love. I may always feel this conflict, this fear of losing what I was, but I am compensated by the process of learning another way of being. I will never fit entirely in either world, but I have the gift of being able to connect the two and find parts of myself in each.

The sun begins to break through the mist and glints off calm waters. I fill my hands with the sand of Shikoku and watch as the grains slip slowly through my fingers. As the early-morning sunlight warms me, I realize what I had thought of as an escape was really a search. The Japanese dawn begins to break in all its fiery brilliance, and I realize I too have been on a pilgrimage and, like the pilgrims of Shikoku, I have found the peace and knowledge I was looking for.

Born to traveler parents, Tara Austen Weaver crossed her first international border at five weeks of age and has been hooked on travel ever since. To date, she has lived in five countries on three continents, including four and a half years spent in the mountains of Japan. She now lives in the San Francisco Bay Area where she works, plays, and commutes by bicycle across the Golden Gate Bridge.

RUTH KAMNITZER

⋆ ⋆ ⋆

In the Dust of His Peacock's Feathers

On the road to Murugan, the author finds
the deity in the pilgrims as much as
in the shrine.

THE CHANT IS ENDLESS, ITS POWER ENORMOUS. IT FILLS MY EARS, my blood, carries me forward in this human wave that knows no containment. It is the India I have always dreamed existed. And now it has found me.

"Palani? It is nothing interesting madam. Just a small temple. They will just raise a flag at the top of the hill and everyone will go home. Nothing for tourists to see. Better you come Madurai, we have float festival, very nice." During the last month of cycling around Tamil Nadu, my friend Karen and I had passed many pilgrims dressed in green, on their way to see Murugan, they said, the errant son of Shiva, at his hilltop temple at Palani. But the man in the Madurai tourist office had just assured us, nothing to see. Well, we decided, we would, of course, visit the temple when we happened to pass through, but there was obviously no reason to rush.

Then biking along one day, we ran into a human wall that stretched for miles in either direction. These weren't just the pilgrims in green. This was everyone, and they were all going to Palani. And so now, of course, were we.

Only in India can you bike into a town where you know

absolutely no one, and ten minutes later have found a secure place to store all your belongings for the next week and be sitting down to a full feast while entertaining the steady stream of visitors who have come to pay their respects. In our case it was the owners of the local gas company who made us feel so welcome, and their hospitality was so effusive it seemed we'd never be able to leave for the mountain of food amassing on our plates. Eventually our hostess was satisfied that we had eaten all we possibly could, photographs were taken, hands pumped repeatedly in farewell, and addresses exchanged. We ceremonially removed our shoes, wiggled our toes, and set off, with the thousands of others, for the temple at Palani, just over a hundred kilometers away.

The black tar is scorching, and it doesn't take us long to realize why everyone else is waiting out the heat of the day at the side of the road. But Karen has already burned the bottom of her feet almost beyond repair, and excruciatingly painful blisters will plague her the entire walk. Families beckon us from the shade of tamarind trees, where they lie napping on their jute sacks, or eating lemon rice out of banana leaf packages. Other's softly sing the names of Murugan while fingering the beads that hang round their necks. We sit with them, and learn the story of Murugan.

Once upon a time Shiva, the great god responsible for the destruction and recreation of this world, was given a golden fruit. The fruit was not to be broken, but consumed in one bite. Being a chivalrous type of god, he gave it to his wife, Parvati, who in turn wanted to pass it on to their children. Shiva and Parvati have two sons—Ganesh, the popular elephant-headed god who adorns the gateways of so many temples, and Murugan. Not knowing to whom the fruit should be given, Shiva and Parvati announced a small contest: whichever son managed to go around the world first would win the golden fruit.

Murugan at once mounted his peacock and set off, determined to claim the prize. Ganesh however, being rather stout and not much one for speed, merely walked around his parents, saying, "You are my world." Needless to say, by the time Murugan returned home from his transglobal journey, the fruit was already in

Ganesh's belly. Outraged that he had been tricked out of his prize in such a manner he fled to the hill at Palani, where the temple now stands. It was there that we were going to see him.

As soon as the tarmac cools we begin to walk again. There are truly thousands of pilgrims. It is an indescribable feeling to be part of something this large, this powerful, this timeless. Rich or poor we all walk together, all barefoot, all carrying only a single small bag slung over the shoulder or balanced on the head. The men wear *lungis*, a simple cloth tied around the waist, and the women saris, many of them red and gold. Every color is a symbol in India, a way of pronouncing something about your identity, whether it is your marital status, your region or a pledge you have made with a god. Almost all the pilgrims wear a *mala*, a string of 108 beads, put on at the beginning of the journey to signify the pledge of the *padi-yatra* to make the journey barefoot. *Padi* means foot, *yatra* means pilgrim. This *mala* will be blessed by the temple priests.

We walk, on and on, until night falls, and we sleep, with countless others, at the side of the road, in fields, in the homes of villagers who have opened their doors to us, or in the courtyards of temples. In the morning we rise and walk again. Never before have I felt so strongly that past and present are not connected by any line, any string, but rather the past tumbles like a snowball down a hill, an avalanche crashes violently into us, so that its pieces are rearranged but essentially the same. History doesn't repeat itself, it just wears different clothing.

As the only two foreigners, Karen and I are the object of much curiosity.

"*Ingeporinga?*" Where do you come from? they ask in Tamil.

"Canada *poringa*," we answer.

"Kerala?" (A state to the west of Tamil Nadu.)

"No, Canada."

"Karnataka?"

"No, Canada. USA, Canada," we explain, holding our fists up to represent neighboring countries.

"USA. England," they answer, nodding slowly with a look of vague understanding. Another group approaches. "*Ingeporinga?*" It begins again. We estimate that we meet at least twenty people an hour, for at least ten hours of the day (there are some quieter times in the day). If they have all come in groups of twenty, in the four days the walk will take, we will have met, directly and indirectly, 16,000 people. The figure is astounding.

With each passing hour, our line gets wider, longer, stronger. A man walks by, balancing on his head a rooster on a red velvet cushion. It is a gift for Murugan. Another family leads their cow who wears a garland of yellow carnations. She will be blessed by the temple priests before returning home. Women balance brass pots on their heads containing water taken from their village wells and scented with flower petals. It too will be blessed at the temple. Many villagers carry *cavatis*, temple replicas carried on the shoulder. No one can adequately explain to us what they are, and we only see what they are used for when we reach the temple, but they are beautiful nonetheless. Tiny children walk, trotting along to keep up with their parents who can't be slowed in their enthusiasm. Occasionally they are whisked up and carried on the head to save time. I see a couple pushing two children on a bicycle. There are groups of children who tell us their parents will join them in a few days, and groups of adults who say they have left their village in the hands of their children.

Karen's blisters are very bad, and she grimaces in pain as they burst and the tender flesh is exposed to the stony gravel road. The pilgrims carry her along, one at each elbow, chanting endlessly to keep her mind off the pain. *Subrimanike...Aro garah... Muruganike...Aro garah...Palanike...Aro-garah...Aro-garah?... Aro-garah.* At first her voice is thin and reedy as she struggles against the pain, and then she gains power. She hobbles proudly, head erect, Murugan ahead. I admire her determination and faith.

Sometimes we are adopted by groups of twenty or more, entire villages. Often they are followed by hired pickup trucks, carrying extra supplies, food, cooks, and tired children. Those riding in the back will at times go barefoot, at times wear shoes, but will not wear the *mala*, a sign of the pledge of the *padi yatra*. We rest with them in the midday heat. Karen and I are fussed over in Tamil, constantly shifted to more advantageous locations in the shade of the truck, while the cooks prepare huge vats of vegetable curry and rice that we eat off banana leaves on the gravel. Then we crawl right under the truck, spread our tarpaulin sacks and sleep till the sun at last dips enough for the pavement to cool and then we walk again. Sometimes we are swept along with richer folk, and we eat with them in makeshift restaurants at the roadside, where *masala dosa, idly, utapam,* and other south Indian specialities are served to thousands. These restaurants are like factories, the waiters sweating with profusion as *dosas* fly with lightning speed, the pails of *dhal* soup emptied almost as quickly as they are filled. Everywhere we are greeted warmly. Always we feel we are among friends.

For four days, virtually twenty-four hours a day, we are surrounded by Indian people. We fall asleep to them fussing over us, exclaiming over our hairy arms, our strange skin, or admonishing us for not covering our heads completely. They pull up our sheet and tuck it in, so that we blend in more fully with the faceless sexless sleeping masses. For a few hours we escape our identity.

On the third night we sleep in a large communal camp. There are at least 3,000 of us in this field. Oversized speakers scream *bajans*, devotional songs, till past midnight. Miraculously, the noise, which even a week ago would have been unbearable, now does not even bother me in the slightest and I sleep soundly. At 3 A.M. everyone rises as if on cue, and four minutes later their sheets are folded away, saris smoothed down and they are off. Karen and I are left alone in the field, still rubbing the sleep out of our eyes. The road is quiet, the pilgrims walking steadily to try to make some time before the sun rises and turns the black tar into a hot griddle. By draping our scarves over our heads and shoulders and looking down when someone passes we are for a few hours at least, just two more pilgrims on their way to see Murugan.

As we near the temple, numerous paths melt together. The line grows longer, wider, and with each hour more certain. It has no beginning nor end, no definition, not a line but a vector that points from everywhere to Murugan. *Aro Dgarah...Aro-garah, subrimanike…aro-garah?…aro garah!* There must be ten, twenty, one hundred, two hundred thousand of us. No one knows.

On the third day the gypsies arrive by the eastern path. They have a vibrancy that stands out even here, looking exactly the way gypsies are supposed to look; the men with long dark curls escaping colorful bandanas and the women possessed of a mysterious beauty that belies their rags and dirt-smudged faces. Murugan is the errant son of Shiva and so too the god of those marginalized in Hindu society. Now these people of the road are on the road to Murugan and the energy is uncontrollable. They discover us and swarm like locusts and we are carried in their wake.

In the lead is a woman I imagine as the elephant matriarch. Her sari is worn like an afterthought, doing nothing to hide her huge breasts and ass that stick out a mile in either direction. Bangles cover her arms and heavy gold rings sparkle in her nose and ears. She seems about to topple as she limps, very quickly, down the road, her bandaged, bloody feet unable to keep up with her spirit. A beautiful young man, his gypsy eyes dark and smoky, his body lithe and soft, begins to beat a tambourine against his hip. The cry mounts, the songs begin. The woman explodes in dance down the road, and her poor bloodied feet have no choice but to follow. I have never seen an Indian woman dance with such ferocious abandon.

Eventually they stop off at a temple for a free meal, beg some money off us, and we part warmly, with much hand clasping and promises to meet again. I am sorry to see them go.

Coconut stalls now line the road. The machete thwacks as it hits the nut and slices away the fibrous shell until at last the sweet juice runs and the white flesh lies revealed. We drink three or four of these a day, endless sweet tea and innumerable glasses of water from questionable sources. Roadside clinics have now appeared, where doctors dispense free medicine and treat wounded feet, while nurses offer massages. My feet are now almost as bad as Karen's, and I double my appreciation of her stoicism. We hobble together, the lame leading the lame. *Aro…garah?…Aro-garah!*

People from Rameswaram on the southeastern tip of the subcontinent have begun to arrive. Some have spent seven days covering the 300 kilometers, and their pilgrim's bags are even dustier than ours. But no matter where we have come from, we are all going home, and greetings are as between siblings not strangers. And we too have innumerable friends among this crowd. There is a group of six friends in their early twenties. One of them has taken a vow of silence for the duration of the journey, and his friends take the opportunity to arrange his betrothal to me. He only smiles devilishly as the joke is renewed every time we pass each other, dates set, and invitations designed.

The reporters find us. Amazingly enough, among the tens of millions and all that we have seen, we are interesting to them. Ruth and Karen become Ruda and Gareem, laborers who have saved for four years to make this return visit to India. The battle between being honest and trying to make Indians understand that our reality isn't as glamorous as they sometimes believe, lost. Our picture appears the next day in four editions of south Indian newspapers, boosting our already elevated status to new heights.

On the last day of the walk, we meet up with a group of about forty from our village of origin, relatives of the gas company owners with whom we entrusted our bikes. Two of them we recognize. They have covered the 100 kilometers in forty-eight hours, stopping only for a few hours in the night. They have been on the lookout for us, and they greet us now like long-lost friends. Another relative lives five kilometers from the temple, and we are going there for dinner, unannounced but surely welcome.

When we arrive, a well-dressed woman in a beautiful sari opens the door and introductions begin as pilgrim bags pile high in the corner. It takes twenty minutes to trace the lineage back to a common point. While the poor woman is mobilizing the household to feed the masses, the phone rings—thirty-five more are expected within the hour. She is unperturbed. Due to their strategic location near such a holy site, she tells me they receive about a thousand guests a year. I try and picture my mother in the same position. Dinner is obviously going to take some time, so due to our honored status as foreign guests a child is dispatched to the market to buy us *dosas*, which we eat with the women in the kitchen.

Then, unexpectedly, we are on the road again.

It is quiet now, most of the people having settled down for the night. Those last five kilometers take almost two hours, with frequent stops to laugh and argue over who is in worse shape. We imagine the story we will tell, how we hobbled to Palani, arrived at the throne of the great god bent and broken.

At last we see the lights of the village. This is a real temple town, and Murugan's picture adorns every restaurant and guest house. The lights and overabundance of tinsel is momentarily disorientating. Somehow we've lost the line and can't find the dusty feet that will lead us to the free pilgrims' sleeping area. We approach a small tea shop and ask where we should sleep. He gives us a slightly confused look and gestures to the plethora of guest houses. No no, we insist, you know, the sleeping. A *baba*, holy man, passes by and stops. He is dressed in orange cloth and shiva beads lie thick on his neck. You know, where do we…go? He looks us over, his eyes pausing on disheveled clothing, bent backs, bowed knees, and blistered and bloody feet. He says something to the tea shop owner and I think I hear the words *padi yatra*—foot pilgrims. He motions us to follow, and we limp behind him as we wind our way past Murugan's house of cloth, Murugan's dry goods and wholesale, Murugan's best tea shop, and Murugan with a plate of steaming *dosa*s until finally we find ourselves at the gates of the main pilgrims' sleeping area.

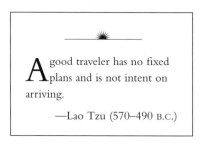

A good traveler has no fixed plans and is not intent on arriving.

—Lao Tzu (570–490 B.C.)

It has all the atmosphere of a Dehli train station. The whole place is the size of a football field. In the center sits a large raised concrete platform, its surface now covered in a mass of people packed head to toe like sardines. Overhead, from the rafters of the tin roof, burn naked fluorescent tubes dangling precariously on exposed wires. The surrounding ground is damp and muddy, and nearly every inch has been similarly claimed, tarpaulins and burlap sacks spread corner to corner. Even the bleachers on the far wall have been claimed for beds. Itinerant salesmen ply the crowds.

"*Chai, chai, sucameli chai.*" Huge aluminum kettles pour the local "tea"—a tasty sugarcane-and-millet brew—into plastic cups so thin they almost melt. *Dosas* fry in griddles over hot coals. "*Samosa, samosa, samosa, chai, chai, das rupee ah das rupee as.*" A wooden stand balanced on a head sells tin whistles, plastic airplanes, balm for tired feet. The blanket salesmen pitch their prices in an endless litany. We have been climbing slowly but steadily for the last few days and the air has a new chill. The whole place smells like a toilet.

From the far corner I hear the beat of a tambourine, and we hurriedly pick our way across the carpet of blankets and bodies.

Among the sleeping children and late night picnics is a circle of pilgrims, most dressed in dirty, white cotton cloths, many with their heads shaved. Someone beats a ratty old tambourine, and the rest chant and clap in a rhythmic swinging motion. The sound is a magnet, a vortex, Murugan's command, and before cognition even sets in I am sitting in the circle too, my hands clapping, my body swaying, everything else in my mind knocked out by this frequency. In the center of the circle is a woman. She is fairly old, her thinning hair pushed back in a sweaty tangle, and so thin I see every bone and tendon in her arms, yet her eyes burn, in torment or ecstasy I can't tell, or perhaps it is the ecstasy of torment. She writhes, as if fettered to the earth by a thousand elastic bands, the promise of a boundless freedom held just beyond her grasp, the chant, the incessant beat of our hands, urging her on. She writhes in dance that seems to have madness as its only conclusion. I have never seen anything like this. Wherever she is going we are the ones sending her. Is this human sacrifice? What does it satisfy in them, in me, to have her dance so intimately with madness?

I register events slowly, between my body's swaying, my hands clap. She will not fall off the edge. This is a dance, not a battle. Sometimes she falls too far and she is rescued. She tumbles in senseless convolutions, and she is smothered by knowing arms that guide her back to the world of the earth. Sometimes she loses her direction and our hands clap faster, buoying her up. Once she stops dancing altogether, stands swaying gently and signals to a well-dressed Indian girl in the crowd. The girl hurries forward and touches her forehead to the medium's feet, before rising to receive her words. I cannot understand them, but assume it to be advice and a blessing, as the girl nods vigorously, then bends to receive the medium's hands on her head. The ceremonies proceed until eventually the trance is lost altogether.

Another woman takes her place dancing. She is much younger, and her vitality less surprising. The tambourine begins with new enthusiasm, and she falls almost immediately into a trance. She kneels, her face raised to the sky, and her trance is so compulsive I see nothing but a whirling mass of angular limbs, the flash of her white sari, the shine on her head where it has recently been shaved. She is less controlled, more eager to embrace and devour whatever it is she sees. Suddenly CRACK she folds in two, and her head hits the hard trampled earth—surely a fracture I think but she only howls a laugh of complete insanity, her eyes wide with glee.

At length things quiet down and people begin to take an interest in us. But there is no need to struggle through the introductions—the *baba* across from us, bedecked in his orange Shiva robes, seems to know it all, and we listen to him recount our story in Tamil, picking out the key words like cycle, Rameswaram, *padi yatra*, Canada. It seems he saw us when we passed through the temple in Rameswaram on our bikes a month ago, and has heard about our pilgrimage by foot. We fall asleep to the distant screech of temple music, the cries of babies, the smell of urine, the fresh memory of the nights warm and happy in the knowledge that we also have a place in all this. We're the Canadians on bicycles.

The next morning I realize that everything we have seen so far, the four days of walking, the chants, the devotion, last night is only the beginning. Things only get madder.

Pilgrims are arriving by the thousands, and the wide two-kilometer road that rings the temple is fully packed by 7 A.M. The most auspicious day to pay respect to the half-meter-high idol will be tomorrow. We step out of the sleeping area and into the crowds.

I am swept up, the senses pulled in every direction. My eyes glimpse, but don't comprehend, the songs, the fever of devotion, the women whirling madly. Cymbals, drums, anklets of bells, Murugan's name a thousand times, we are almost there and it can't be contained any longer. Huge processions go by, and we fall into their song, our feet still bare following them as we dance down the temple road. A group of about twenty drummers passes followed by the holders of the *cavatis*, presents for Murugan, and in the front the dancers, goaded into trance. Karen is caught and I watch as her hands begin to tremble, her steps become feverish. An old Indian lady sees her too, and holds her hand in caution. She shifts from one foot to the other, like a nervous animal, straining to be let off the leash. She dances, her bloodied feet that made her grimace in pain a few moments earlier forgotten, and they fly as the Indian boys urge the drummers to faster, more dangerous rhythms. I am afraid. The old woman eases her back from the crowd, from the vortex. The procession keeps dancing and we fall back, Karen still trembling. The air is pungent with jasmine, incense, and humanity. The crowd becomes even more dense, and then we pass through the temple gates like a cork. Countless stairs lie ahead but the crowd does not pause. They have walked one, two, three hundred kilometers and the road has not ended yet. The strong don't aid the weak, they carry them. Murugan cannot wait. I see mothers grab their children, fly up the stairs two at a time, grandmothers virtually dragged by a nephew on either side, toddlers bouncing on their fathers' heads.

Yet we too climb, run on all fours. I see the faces around me and I think, how could so many people be wrong? For the first time in my life I seriously consider the possibility that God exists, not as a facet of ourselves but as a completely independent entity. And I am afraid, because if he does exist, if he is Murugan, he's not going to be very happy that I've remained skeptical for so long.

The temple is huge. We have reached the top of the stairs and stand in a huge courtyard, dotted with various places of worship that

surround the main shrine. People are going crazy everywhere. I don't
know where I am or what's coming next. There is shouting and the
crowd parts for a man, naked but for the simplest cloth, being rolled
across the filth of the courtyard floor. His hands are clasped above
his head, his eyes closed and when the hands of the group pause in
their turning of him he lies slumped in exhaustion. In the coming
days we will see that it is a fairly popular custom to be rolled around
the circumference of the temple, for both men and women. Watch
out, we will say to each other, there's a roller coming.

A man walks uphill, hooks in his back pulling a wooden *cavati*
on wheels. Another is even more grueling—he walks backwards,
the hooks piercing his nipples, in his cart a young boy tied to a
stick. Everywhere people are falling into trance, lashing at the
bounds of their bodies. Women dance and thrash, intoxicated with
this promise of freedom, in a manner I would never have expected
conservative Indian women to act in public. The man beside me,
carrying his child, falls into a heavy trance, suddenly lurching
madly. The child doesn't even seem to notice. Others rush up and
take the child from his arms as the drums begin, the chants start.
In the temple courtyard a small space is cleared. The now familiar
beat, that builds up so rhythmically, almost then completely breaks
down. Two men, a cloth tied around their waists, chests bare, are
goaded into trance. They face each other like wild animals whose
instinct for preservation has been demented by a long captivity.
One has his hands tied behind his back, his tongue forced out and
he is so wild I fear he will bite it off. The other man is given a
short spear, one end the spade of Murugan, the other a gleaming
point. They are released, circle each other, stamping in agitation,
and the man with the spear rushes and stabs it through the other's
tongue. They jump together in glee, ecstasy, and insanity.

"Excuse me madam," says the gentleman next to me in his im-
peccable *dhoti*, "You have camera?"

The next day we rise early. Today is the day, the fullest moon,
the biggest karmic bonus. The temple road is packed, fired with
expectation. We walk the two kilometers in a dense crowd.

Eventually we climb the stairs and enter the temple courtyard. There are three ways to see Murugan: You can shell out 1,000 rupees (about U.S. $30) and be ushered in within half an hour for a relatively peaceful visit, you can pay 100 rupees and wait for up to three hours before you file in with the others, or you can forego the concept of time altogether and sit patiently with the masses in a line already thousands long. We choose the 100-rupee option— you don't want to be too cheap when it comes to God, he's probably mad enough at me as it is, but he would be greedy if he thinks I've got 1,000 rupees to spare. The ticket booth has been swallowed and is only identifiable as the dense lump within this larger lump of people. A helpful man, also going for the 100-rupee option, offers to buy tickets for us. We each hand him the 100 rupees and an extra 20 to assure speedy passage. He emerges ten minutes later, unrecognizable in his degree of dishevelment. But he has the tickets.

By now we have Murugan fever almost as badly as everyone else. The 100-rupee line is already quite long and beginning to move, so Karen and I decide why not scale the four-meter-high, wire-mesh wall maintaining order and jump the queue a little. A couple of white girls, surely no one will mind. We scramble up the wire mesh and start down the other side. Men pound at our ankles, scream abuse, try and push us back over the other side—head first. I see the possibility for mob violence and quickly retreat. We go back and stand in the line, wait like everyone else. Murugan again.

Two hours later we shuffle into the main sanctuary. It is so crowded my nose is pressed up against the shirt of the man in front of me, and the air is a strange mixture of sweat and incense. The temple attendants keep us moving along at a steady pace, prodding when necessary. The inner sanctuary is dark, and the various statues difficult to make out. There is a small figure on my left, which sparkles a little more brightly than the others but almost too late it registers that this is Murugan, the all-powerful god I and a quarter million others have walked hundreds of kilometers to see. All of five seconds in his presence and it's over, we're back in the sunlight.

The festivities continue. Things are winding down now after the cusp of the moon. Every day the many shrines and courtyards on the hilltop reverberate with music as troupes from different villages perform for Murugan. Music that makes my heart bleed for its devotion, music that makes me cry for the richness of their lives, their love affair with God. Music that makes me wonder how I, in my twenty-six years, could have failed to sense a presence of such magnitude. Always they urge us to dance, and we often do, sometimes self-conscious at the scene we are creating, two white girls dancing to the music of so many young boys, and not wanting to draw attention away from the main event, sometimes feeling perfectly natural, as if we too are offering up what we have.

It goes on and on. Every day we think we are going to leave something else catches our attention.

Perhaps the most precious things I will take from the festival is a love of the Tamil people. I have never loved a culture as such, never even properly understood the word, but here I have seen a beauty that so harmoniously unifies every aspect of life.

The various peddlers, mostly women, who line the two-kilometer temple road, are our friends, our Tamil family. The pungent smells of their wares fill the road—fresh jasmine petals for the hair, carnation garlands, heady incense, and *vibutti*, the sacred temple ash. Others sell fruit. There's the sizzle of the *dosas* in the pan, stainless steel tins of spicy coconut chutney and the *subzi*, curried vegetables. There are knickknack stands that sell laminated photos of Murugan, garish wall hangings, *mala* beads, and other temple accessories. They are all our friends. Their attitude toward us takes some getting used to—they are incredibly invasive yet incredibly warm.

They can't stand to see us alone, physically do not seem able to tolerate it. If I ever venture outside the gate of our *dharmasala* (pilgrims' rest house) without Karen, I am mobbed. My extremely meager knowledge of Tamil does not seem to inhibit communication in any way. "Where is your friend? Why have you left her?" I try to explain that she will be along in a minute, I'm just going to take a wander down the road. It's not good enough, they say I shouldn't leave her alone and just go off by myself like that. Invariably I give up and go back inside, but later I discover that if I just explain that in exactly ten minutes I will meet her at the mango stall just there they visibly relax and let me go on my way. It's as if they just need to know that I know that we are together. Then it's O.K. But if they ever catch me just wandering around by myself and Karen is in the vicinity, all hell breaks loose. They don't even wait for an explanation, they just grab me by the arm and march at top speed till we find her and are reunited. It gets even funnier on the third day when a few other foreigners show up, some of them professional photographers in fancy cars. The Tamil women can't understand that we don't know each other, or that we don't necessarily want to stick together, so that I am continuously grabbed and marched up to strangers. I learn to accept it, and appreciate their concern. The other foreigners, however, think I'm mad.

The second problem is they don't like my hair. Karen doesn't have this problem, she generally is a bit better kept, but me, they can't understand. First thing is the morning as I sip my *chai*, not quite awake, they descend. My hair, it's terrible, will never do. Five at a time they fuss over me, my protesting hands slapped away. Tongues cluck disapproval, bobby pins are retrieved from their own probably lice-infested buns and my hair plastered down with spit. Even the toilet woman up at the temple gives me hell one day, her sign language was perfectly clear. I couldn't even get by her for a pee.

"You married?" she demands.

"No," I reply.

"Well, I don't wonder why, look at your clothes, look at your hair, and looks like you need a shave too," she said, her hand brushing my face. And this from a woman who cleans toilets.

Yet they have shared a sense of belonging with us that I have not found before, and I am honored that they accept us enough to treat us in such a manner. On our last night I go to see a singer on the temple sleeping area where we had spent our first night. The place is not as full now, but still there are hundreds of people, and much more garbage. It still smells like a toilet. The singer is an incredibly beautiful woman, her plumpness a sign of her good health. She plays a harmonium and is accompanied by a tabla player as she sings in Tamil.

But she doesn't just sing. She recites a poem, the story of a young girl in search of her destiny, and her voice moves so gently between narration and song that it seems the melody is born of the language. It moves, above the crying babies, the suckling infants, the smell of the urine and seems to infect everything with its song. Sitting there, I see that this is the Tamil's world, that behind everything you will find this ancient song. And I can't believe such beauty exists.

Ruth Kamnitzer always dreamed of exploring the world and spent most of her twenties doing so, with a predisposition towards bicycles and her own feet. She recently returned to university to work towards a career in environmental management and conservation. She currently lives in Edinburgh.

✳

My Father's House

Have you gone home yet?

THERE IT IS. MY HOUSE. A WHITE COLONIAL WITH DARK GREEN shutters, white pillars, and red-brick steps.

It's not my house anymore, but I lived there when I was a child, and I've always wanted to go back inside it again. So one Sunday afternoon in January, I make up my mind to do it.

I drive by the house three times before I have the courage to walk up the winding path to ring the bell.

A small, sweet-faced woman opens the door.

"I'm sorry to disturb you," I say. "But I grew up in this house. Could I come in and see it again? Just for a minute?"

She smiles. "Of course," she says, her accent European. "Please don't mind the mess. We just took the Christmas tree down."

I step through the vestibule into the center hall and catch my breath. I am a child again, safe inside with my mother and father in the 1930s. Safe from the frightening move to a new city when I was twelve, safe from my paralyzing shyness as an adolescent, safe from my embarrassment at having a retarded brother, safe from watching my youngest child become blind. I am here, safe from the future, seven years old again.

The woman introduces me to her husband and their three children who welcome me to their house.

I walk through the graceful archway into the living room and there, just to the right, is an upright piano in exactly the same place ours was. It's 1936 and I'm sitting on the piano bench with my father playing a Strauss waltz duet. He took piano lessons when I did, and he even played a duet with me in a recital for eight-year-old kids. Ten little children all starched and scrubbed and my handsome Scottish engineer father. I can see him now, curly dark hair, ruddy face giving me a hug as we finished *Die Fledermaus*. An old lady came up to him afterward and said, "Young man, you have a lot of courage." He loved it.

I had lost the memories of my father young and laughing. I hold a much darker image of him now. I only remember his silences, his frowns, his disappointment with his life. It must have been unbearable for him to find out that his only son—the little boy named after him—would always remain a child, dependent and helpless. He would never go to college, never marry, never have children. He would have to be taken care of all his life.

When Jackie was a year old, he was diagnosed as brain damaged with cerebral palsy because of a doctor's mistake at birth. My mother kept thinking he would be all right if only she could find the right specialist, the right teacher. So she drove to Boston on the bad roads of the thirties to Children's Hospital. She drove to Florida because the doctors said he needed sun. She persuaded the public school to take him in a class with the other children, but soon enough she had to face the fact that he couldn't keep up. She did this all alone, without my father.

My father withdrew deep inside himself. I never heard him cry, never heard him say anything about this deep hurt. When he was silent, I thought I had done something wrong. I loved him so and ached to please him. I remember running to hug him at the railroad station when he trudged up the stairs with the crowd of men who commuted to New York. But I was also afraid of him, of his anger. It felt like he didn't love me.

I know he did love me, but he was buttoned up, a closed New

Englander who couldn't say "I love you" easily. There wasn't a lot of hugging or touching going on in that house, but I do remember sitting on his lap while he read an alphabet book to me. "Here's your old friend A," he would say.

So it's a surprise to conjure up a picture of him now on the piano bench, sitting close to me, playing the "Blue Danube" waltz with me. I hated practicing scales and the Bach and Schumann I found boring, but the duets with him were like a banquet to a little girl starving for love.

The fireplace in the living room is hidden by a sofa now. My brother and I had our pictures taken in front of it every year. The walls of the living room are pale yellow instead of the soft green and white striped wallpaper my mother chose. Wall-to-wall carpeting hides the gleaming hardwood floors that were partly covered by an oriental rug in my parents' day. There is no grandfather clock for my father to wind on Sundays.

But there's my mother, young and pretty, sitting on the gold sofa pouring tea, laughing with a friend. She smells wonderful, like a bouquet of spring flowers. She wears small pearl earrings and a gold and pearl circle pin on her dress. She's happy and relaxed—an hour off from taking care of a retarded child. I never heard her complain.

I look out the back window. "Is the magnolia tree still there?" I ask.

"We had to cut it down last year," my host tells me.

That was my refuge, that tree. I used to climb up into it and lean against the trunk, magnolia blossoms all around me, writing stories about naughty children. They were my surrogates. I couldn't worry my mother—she had troubles enough. So I was always good, always smiling, biting my nails and letting my characters be the bad ones.

I walk across the hall into the dining room. It's huge. Big enough for dinner parties with my parents' friends. I thought they were incredibly glamorous and begged to stay up.

As I stand there in that large, bright room, the same chandelier over the table, remembering the china cabinet full of cut-glass bowls and Wedgwood plates, I can see my father again, the star of those parties. He was so smart, so funny, his humor wry and off-beat. But he could also skewer someone he thought had said something stupid—including me. He used to say, "You're just a little potato. You don't know what you're talking about." And I believed him. I thought he was always right so he must be right about this. I carried that around for a long time, thinking my opinion didn't count. I don't forgive him for that.

I move through another door into the kitchen. That can't be the same wallpaper with baskets and ivy curling around the breakfast nook where my father mixed a Scotch and soda every night and read the paper while my mother fixed dinner, can it? No, but it certainly looks like it. I loved being with my dad then. After a day in New York his white shirt was rumpled and masculine smelling. He would ask me what I did in school, and the words came tumbling out, "We made puppets and I'm going to be Mrs. Darling in the show." He wasn't really listening, but he smiled and said, "Well, well." Just a well well now and then was all I asked for.

"Would you like to see the upstairs?" my hostess asks me.

"Oh, yes," I say. "Please."

Up the stairs and into my bedroom. I don't see the boys' beds, the posters, the clothes strewn around the room. I see the three large windows looking out on the trees in our front yard, the white bedspread, the clean sheets, the warm blanket, my books. I am back in that blue-and-white room reading Sherlock Holmes under the covers with a flashlight. My mother, sweet and scolding, comes in and gently takes the book and the flashlight.

"Go to sleep," she says and kisses me. I would give anything to feel her soft hands touching me again.

Next to my room is my parents' room. I peek in the door and remember my mother's dressing table. It had a full-length mirror, two side mirrors and little drawers on the sides. Her delicate scent comes back to me again in a vivid flashback of combs and hair-pins and silver-backed brushes, nail polish and orange sticks, per-fume and boxes of Coty powder. I see her sitting at that table, beautiful, wearing a deep-purple velvet gown, ready to go out.

My father comes in dressed in a tuxedo and looks at her as if they had just met.

"Doesn't your mother look sharp?" he asks. I had forgotten until this moment the way he used to look at her with such pride and love. Most of the time I remember only his harsh words to her, his impatience with her. I haven't thought about him like this in years.

Still caught in that time zone, I walk into my brother's room. I taught him to read in this room. At least, that's the way I remember it. I was the bossy teacher with blackboard and chalk, he the often unwilling student. I wanted him to be all right, to be normal, to be like other brothers. When I ask him now if he remembers playing school, he looks at me shyly and says, "I'm not sure."

I wasn't as embarrassed by Jackie when we were children as I was when we moved away from this house and lived in Baltimore during the Second World War when my father did research on radar for Vannevar Bush in Washington and came home only on weekends. There, without my friends who were used to Jackie, I was a stranger. I was different because I had a retarded brother. I used to say, "Anyone who doesn't accept my brother can't be my friend," but I didn't mean it. I wanted their friendship desperately. I felt guilty because I was ashamed of my brother. I feel guilty to this day. My mother had sick headaches during those years when she lay in a dark room for hours with a cold cloth on her forehead.

She told me much later, when I was grown and had children of my own, that my father had fallen in love with another woman while he was in Washington. He wanted to marry her, but he was told he would lose his job if he left my mother and two children. So he broke off his affair and told my mother about it.

I hated him for this, for hurting my mother, until I sat by his bed when he was dying. He lay connected to a respirator for three months, waiting to die, wanting to die. As I sat there with him, I understood for the first time that he gave up a lot for us. It had never occurred to me before that he might really have loved that woman in Washington. I wondered if he ever saw her again. I wish I had asked him about her, but we didn't talk about things like that in our family. We never talked about anything. Why didn't I ever ask my father about his life?

Reluctantly I go downstairs and my hosts ask me to stay for coffee. Grateful to rest a little longer in this safe haven, I accept. Then something magical happens. The family's seventeen-year-old son goes to the piano and plays the third movement of Beethoven's "Apassionata" for me with great feeling and skill. It's as if my childhood has been set to music. I close my eyes and there's my father coming home from the golf course on Sunday, his cheeks sunburned, his eyes as blue as my own two daughters' eyes. He says, "Hi, toots," and when he kisses me his face is scratchy and warm.

When he played golf with his brother, my Uncle Arthur, they would joke about which one was the worst player and call each other Bill—neither one knew why. Sometimes when he was with his brother, my father would laugh so hard he had to wipe the tears away. It was such a rare sight to see him let go so completely that I longed to see him do it more often.

I wish I could see my father again. I'd ask him about being a Marine in World War I, about learning to ride a horse in Paoli, Pennsylvania, and going off to Haiti, where there wasn't even a war.

When the young man finishes playing, I tell him how moved I am, that he has given me a gift to take home with me. And I thank my hosts for giving me back my parents, young and beautiful and strong.

But more than that, I have found the father of my childhood— the strong, handsome, witty, perfect father I adored when I was a child. For a little while I had him back again in that house.

Mary McHugh is the author of Special Siblings: Growing Up with Someone with a Disability. *Some of the material in this essay originally appeared in her book. She also has written six other books, and has been published in* The New York Times, Good Housekeeping, Travel Holiday, *and in the Travelers' Tales collection*, A Mother's World: Journeys of the Heart.

TOM JOYCE

* * *

Mount Kailash, the Throne of Shiva

The center of the universe called to him.

CROSSING AN INTIMIDATING SPAN OF CANTILEVERED LOGS splayed twenty feet above the churning gray Karnali River, I pass a stone marker that informs me I am leaving the Kingdom of Nepal behind and entering the People's Rupublic of China. My feet touch down in occupied Tibet.

Meandering through the tiny border village of Zher, with its fieldstone huts and whitewashed *chörten* (conical domed monuments called *stupa* on the other side of the river) I enter an ochre and sienna wonderland where the Karnali evolves into the Mapcha Khabab, ("River Which Flows from the Mouth of the Peacock"). Stretching before me, like the sensuous folds of Tara's supine body[1], are the high desert plains of Central Asia.

Our entourage, led by Gary McCue, an American expat living in Kathmandu, has been six days on the trail from Simikot, a high mountain outpost with the only airstrip in far-western Nepal. We have been winding our way along an ancient salt trading route that

---

1. *Tara* ("She Who Helps Cross" in Sanskrit) is the female aspect of compassion, and the equivalent of the Chinese Kuan-yin, Japanese Kannon, or Tibetan Drolma.

follows the Humla Karnali River to the Himalayan watershed at Nara Lagna, a 15,000-foot pass. Our destination is a mythical mountain rising like a glittering pyramid of ice out of the arid Tibetan plateau, a mountain long considered to be the "Axis of the World" and revered by Hindus, Buddhists, Jains, and Bön-po as the most sacred place on Earth.

References to this mountain of legend first appeared in records from the Sumerian civilization of Bronze Age Mesopotamia and were echoed in the folklore of many ancient cultures. The Indian *Vishnu Purana* describes Mount Meru as the "Center of the Universe," encircled by the seven continents and seven oceans, a physical manifestation of the mandala (a geometric projection of universal consciousness). From Meru's summit, it was said that the sacred waters of the Ganges fall and divide into four great rivers. The epic *Mahabharata* describes this "King of Mountains" with lavish hyperbole:

---✳---

Tibetans call their country Bhöt (pronounced: *Pheu*), and their ancient, animistic religion is known as Bön. A practitioner is a Bön-po. The much later Tibetan Buddhism is a thing unto itself, consisting of Tantric ritual, Bön mysticism, and dharmic philosophy. It is usually distinguished as *Vajrayana* ["Vehicle of the Indestructable Diamond Thunderbolt"]. Hence the problem with literal translation.

—Tom Joyce

> There is an all-surpassing mountain that blazes
> like a pile of fire and
> Casts forth the splendor of the sun
> with its golden glowing peak—Mount Meru!

Although mythic in reputation, Meru was subsequently discovered to be geographically substantial. In the remote Zhang-Zhung kingdom of Western Tibet, a solitary peak called Gang Ti-sé by the shamanic Bön-po inhabiting the region fit the ancient descriptions of Meru with surprising accuracy. From a nearby watershed, the Indus, Sutlej, Brahmaputra, and Karnali rivers flow in torrents through the Himalaya, carrying life to the thirsty Indian subcontinent. Tibetan Buddhists who came to hold this place sacred named the peak Gang Rimpoche ("Precious Jewel of Snow"); Jains called it Ashtapada, but it is by a Hindi name that this 22,028-foot natural pyramid is best known: Kailash—the dwelling place of Shiva—wild primordial *yogin*, and Lord of the Dance.

In the mid-1970s, I had stumbled upon Sven Hedin's *Transhimalaya: Discoveries and Adventures in Tibet*, Lama Anagarika Govinda's *The Way of the White Clouds*, and Heinrich Harrer's *Seven Years in Tibet* in the musty stacks of the San Francisco Public Library. But most provocative among this peripatetic genre was an account by Herbert Tichy, an Austrian adventurer who set off from India in search of what Hedin had described as the "glittering pyramid of silver." In his 1938 book *Tibetan Adventure*, I encountered a picture that was to change the course of my life. Lying belly-down in the dust to conceal his camera, Tichy had photographed a group of Buddhist lamas in prayer before the sheer, ice-glazed face of an unclimbed holy mountain—more treacherous, from the look of it, than the infamous Eigerwand of Switzerland, yet more beautiful in its serene singularity than any natural monolith on Earth. Until the moment I fixated on this fading black-and-white image, I didn't know it was possible to fall in love with a piece of stone.

I felt utterly compelled to stand in the physical presence of Sven Hedin's silver pyramid; but that was quite impossible at the time. The Chinese People's Liberation Army (P.L.A.) had invaded Tibet in 1950, sealing it off from the outside world, and even though Richard Nixon's foreign policy had resulted in a strained diplomatic dialogue with Mao Tse-tung, Tibet had become more of a lost horizon than in James Hilton's day.

And why was I so obsessed with this "sacred mountain" anyway? Did I seriously think enlightenment was to be had by circling a piece of rock in the middle of nowhere? A recovered idealist, I got with the program, married, had children, started a business, got divorced—the whole catastrophe. Then, in the latter part of the

1980s, Tibet opened to limited travel, and the obsession was rekindled. I began to plot a course in that direction, convinced that the time had come to meet Shiva face to face.

I joined Gary, with whom I'd trekked previously, and our group of white, middle-class pilgrims in Kathmandu during the humid month of May. We chartered a twin-engine prop plane to drop us and our provisions in Simikot, situated in a green terraced valley surrounded by 18,000-foot nameless snow peaks, where lammergeiers play tag on the wind with kites. From there, it was all on foot.

During long days on the trail, I have managed to engage most of my fellow trekkers in conversation of a philosophical nature. After all, this is a pilgrimage, and stripped of our Western attire and attitudes, we are just another group of seekers approaching a mystery in the form of a mountain.

It's an eclectic group: Mahalia is a practitioner of Maulawi Sufism, Advaita Vedanta, Diamond Heart, and a few other things I've never heard of. Barbara, a student of the Karma-Kagyu school of Vajrayana, had worked with Mother Teresa in the slums of Calcutta. Michael, a schoolteacher and mountaineer from Seattle, spends his spare moments absorbing Mahayana ritual like a sponge too long deprived of moisture. Peter, and his fiancée, Leela, are just besotted with one another, and as mobile as I wished I could have been in my twenties. Edward, a practicing carpenter, has never been anywhere and decided to spend his fiftieth birthday in Tibet. Go figure.

As for me, I'm not a Buddhist. Nor, for that matter, am I a Christian, Hindu, Muslim, or Jew. If anything, I'm a heretic. It became clear to me at an early age that any "organized" religion will always choose to propagate structure at the expense of truth, because human beings create ritual to institutionalize what they don't really understand. And, although they often pay lip service to the concept, those in charge are rarely receptive to questioning authority—especially their own. I have twice been expelled from such institutions for vocalizing my unwelcomed questions.

Fortunately, heretics are no longer burned at the stake—in most places.

By midday we reach the village of Khochar (or Khojarnath, to Hindu pilgrims), where the whitewashed masonry is so bright with reflective sunlight that I cannot remove my glacier glasses. Here we meet our Tibetan guides.

Jampa, by sheer coincidence, was with Gary and me on a Kangshung Glacier trek in 1991. He is the product of school in Beijing, which can only mean that his parents were collaborators. There is no real education available for Tibetans who remained loyalists to the Fourteenth Dali Lama after his escape in 1959. The best job a young man can get is working for foreign tourists as a guide or driver. A woman's best bet is to marry one.

Our other guide, Rinchen, came up hard. His parents died in prison, and the young boy was taken under the wing of G.T. Sönam, who is as close as one comes to an entrepreneur in Tibet. Sönam specializes in the high-end tourist trade and is permitted to operate only because his profitable business lines Chinese pockets. We greet our amicable Tibetan hosts with the all-purpose phrase "*Tashi deley*," which seems to be the colloquial equivalent of "Yo" when addressing a Philadelphian.

Passing a field of newly formed mud bricks drying in the merciless sun, we traverse a *mani* wall[2] festooned with yak horns dusted in ochre, then penetrate a convoluted maze of alleys into the heart of a twelfth-century monastery complex under restoration. The central temple is awash with the faint glow of a thousand butter

---

2. A stacked wall of loose stones inscribed with the words *Om mani padme hum* in Devanagri script. It is said that these sounds echo the harmonic resonance that continuously creates all substance and life within the universe. Thus the mantra, whether chanted or carved, brings the faithful into harmony with the primal rhythm of the cosmos. But pedantic linguists insist on something more literal, like: "Hail to the Wish Fulfilling Jewel in the Lotus." Somehow, this falls short of the enormous significance the mantra communicates to Tibetans.

lamps flickering on the faces of three golden bodhisattvas—Jampeyang (wisdom), Chenrezik (compassion), and Chakna Dorje (power). But in other chambers we are shown nearly obliterated frescoes and mutilated statuary—relics of desecration by the P.L.A. One chapel has been used as a horse stable by the aesthetically barren "liberators."

As the afternoon shadows lengthen under a cloudless sky, we board Toyota Land Cruisers that will carry us to Purang, once known as Taklakot, the provincial capitol of the Ngari region. The dusty plateau is surprisingly hot during the day—even at an average elevation of 14,000 feet—and predictably cold at night. Our two-hour passage is flanked on one side by the 25,000-foot massif of Gurla Mandata, and on the other by the most astonishing mountain wall I have ever seen—the Zanskar Range to the south, merging on the western horizon with India's Byas Rikhi Himal, knife-edged peaks of eternal snow stretching as far as the imagination can project them.

Purang is a thoroughly wretched place, as are most towns where the Chinese have installed a military garrison. When we check in at the police station, our passports are confiscated and our bags searched—for what, we haven't a clue. And we are informed that the border crossing from Humla has been officially closed. Our group is apparently the last to be allowed through, which leaves us all feeling uncomfortably isolated.

To make the situation even more tenuous, the Beijing bureau-

> Arrested by the P.L.A. on the Tibet-Nepal border, my companions and I were led off to separate rooms for interrogation. The soldiers in charge of me confiscated everything remotely related to the Dalai Lama. It took a good deal of pantomime and a photograph of a little girl for me to convince them that the colorful drawings in my possession were not in fact Buddhist mandalas, but the work of my four-year-old daughter.
>
> —James O'Reilly, "Notes from the Roof of the World"

crats have barred our planned overland travel to Lhasa. The 43rd anniversary of the "Peaceful Liberation of Tibet," the Buddhist festival of Saga Dawa, and fourth anniversary of the Tiananmen Square massacre are all occurring in the next several weeks. Needless to say, troops are on full alert in Lhasa. But there is a silver lining to this dark cloud of political intrigue—we are permitted to proceed to Gang Rimpoche.

After our interview with the police, Mahalia and I go for a late-afternoon stroll through the dusty streets. We pass a young girl hustling customers into a Chinese restaurant, unemployed Tibetans shooting 8-ball with Chinese soldiers outside the disco, and truckloads of fur-clad pilgrims en route to Darchen. At the end of town we are greeted by a spectacular view of Gurla Mandata with a picturesque aqueduct traversing the hillside in the foreground. As I adjust the f-stop of my camera, a passing troop carrier screeches to a halt.

A green uniformed boy of twenty leaps from the cab, attempting to confiscate my film. I quickly back off, zipping the camera into my fanny pack, and fumble for my papers. The young soldier stabs his finger vehemently at the aqueduct and barks angry admonishments.

Upon further inspection of the hillside, I realize that there is more to the scene than had been immediately apparent. Above the stone aqueduct, built meticulously into the ochre landscape, an army gun emplacement is trained on the nearby Indian border. Naturally, it is forbidden to photograph such things. Mahalia and I grin and gesture effusively toward Gurla Mandata, extolling its magnificence in Pidgin English. Finally, the soldier decides we are just stupid tourists, spits a final caution, and climbs back into his truck, leaving both camera and film in my possession.

In the morning, we take the opportunity to wash our hair and clothes in the courtyard of the Purang Guest House—a grim synthesis of Gulag and the Bates Motel—as far from the latrine as we can possibly get. Refreshed, most of our group visits the cave temple of Gungpur, a *gompa* (a place in solitude) carved from a canyon wall just north of town.

Nearby, some of the local children engage us in a playful session of cross-cultural communication. One of the little girls, Agilamo, leads me by the hand up a trail to the mouth of a small cave dug into the crumbling walls of the cliff. There, she introduces me to an old man whose eyes are glazed over with cataracts, a common result of high-altitude exposure to ultraviolet light.

As he spins his copper prayer wheel, I speak to him in my own language, sensing somehow that he can comprehend the emotion in my voice. I tell him how I have just scaled the ladders at Gungpur, crossed a rickety catwalk to a tiny chapel excavated from the solid mountain wall, and knelt beside the 100,000 teachings— strips of hand-printed paper neatly bound and stacked into a compartmented alcove. There, before an effigy of Chenrezik, Buddha of Compassion, I feel my heart tear open.

I recalled the litany of atrocities: An estimated 1.2 million Tibetans dead as a result of China's invasion, occupation, mass-imprisonment, torture, and work gangs; 6,000 monasteries, temples, and chapels like this one destroyed; and a wholesale attempt to smash popular belief in the Buddha Dharma along with the theocracy that espoused it.

But just as I worked myself into a fine state of anger, I remembered that the pre-invasion government of Tibet was indeed a feudal, and sometimes oppressive state itself. And I remember that it was a Chinese man who wrote the *Tao Teh Ching*—arguably the single most profound collection of wisdom ever to appear on this planet.

Nothing is ever as black and white as our preconceptions, I admit to the old man. Experience opens our eyes to a most dazzling array of hues, and tones, and tints, and shades of truth. Perhaps the followers of Sakyamuni are paying a karmic debt. The wonders of Tibetan culture might never have been brought to Western attention had the Chinese not felt it necessary to liberate people who did not want or need their assistance. And, had Gyelwa Rimpoche[3]

---

3. Tenzin Gyatso, the Fourteenth Dalai Lama, is known to Tibetans as *Gyelwa Rimpoche. Dalai Lama* is actually a Mongolian title first given to the abbot of Drepung in the sixteenth century.

not gone into exile, we might never have been exposed to his remarkable compassion toward those oppressors. The dharma is indeed a curious unfoldment.

The old hermit considers the sound of what I have said, then
nods sagely and asks, "Gang Rimpoche?"

When I give an affirmative response, he smiles thoughtfully and
shows me his swollen ankles, indicating that he cannot make that
pilgrimage himself. He is too old, has been visited by too much
suffering. He seems to ask me if I will carry his greeting to the
Precious Jewel of Snow. I tell him that I will be honored to do so,
and his milky eyes drift into a peaceful silence. The old man re-
sumes spinning the wheel of dharma as if I never existed, and
Agilamo leads me back to the others.

On a ridge above Purang, about a kilometer to the north and
close to 15,000 feet above sea level, are the ruins of the great
Shepeling monastery. Once an enormous structure where thousands of monks studied and meditated upon the sutras, Shepeling
appears to have been deserted for at least half a millennium. In fact,
it was destroyed sometime after 1966, during one of the blackest
horror shows of recorded history—Mao Tse-tung's "Cultural
Revolution."

The great reformers of the People's Republic of China had no
use for a Buddhist theocracy. Tibet's ponderously complex art and
ritual represented ideas that were anathema to Mao's ideology, and
were therefore to be eradicated from the cultural fabric. Besides,
Tibet made a formidable military buffer zone between China and
India—and a great place to dump nuclear waste.

Shepeling is just one more forgotten desecration in a tidal wave
of annihilation—the dark side of nirvana. The P.L.A., undoubtedly
aided by Tibetan sympathizers, tore the roof off the earthenware
structure, leaving the harsh climate free to reclaim the elements
from which Shepeling had been constructed. No one remembers
how many monks were slaughtered there, or shuttled off to labor
camps for "re-education" in revolutionary values.

It is a place redolent with emotion, with ghosts howling in the incessant wind. As I wander through the crumbling ruins, the dying sun casts long shadows against ochre walls still showing faded pastel images of once-vibrant murals.

Then the psychic pictures of slaughter descend on me like a flock of raptors, and I cry out in anguish, "This isn't how it was supposed to happen!" But no. I realize, before the words have formed into a sentence that I am wrong…This is *exactly* how it was supposed to happen. It could never be any other way. This is the dharma.

As tears mingle with the red dust at my feet, I realize that my whole life, everything I have ever thought, or done, or planned, or avoided—every glorious and wretched moment—has been carefully designed to bring me to this place, and to this absurdly simple cognition: we don't begin to live until we face the absolute certainty of our own death. Knowing that this body will cease to be, changes everything. And, of course, it changes nothing at all.

Our dirty Land Cruisers lumber over the Gurla Pass, then descend to the Barkha

---

She tells me the story. She was in Dharamsala, some years ago, and there was a party down in the valley, below the main temple and the Dalai Lama's residence. A hippie party: "Lots of mushrooms in the omelette—if you get my meaning," and bottles of bonded Scotch. "Anyway, somewhat worse for wear, I drag myself outside the temple, and I do the sensible thing, despite my condition, which is to find a doorway and curl up in it. And the next thing I know, the door is opened and I fall through it, and there are two Indian soldiers, pointing their bayonets at me. And standing behind them is a monk in a red robe, and I think: I know you. He's laughing fit to burst at the sight of this stoned old woman in his temple. And he reaches into the folds of his robe and produces some sweets and a biscuit and gives them to me, with this wonderful smile on his face. That's what I'll always remember. That smile."

—Mick Brown,
The Spiritual Tourist

Plain where dust devils whirl like toothless cyclones across endless stretches of desert scrub. Off in the distance, I can see it. On the horizon, a white pyramid towers above the surrounding range of supplicant hills, a diamond glittering on the cusp between a lapis lazuli sky and the raw ochre of earth.

We are jostled on rutted tracks for fifty miles, bandannas covering our faces to stave off the unrelenting dust, until one of the vehicles gasps to a halt with a fouled fuel intake. As we mill about on the plain, Edward points to the east. Nearly camouflaged against the rusty hills, a herd of *kyang*, the rare Tibetan wild ass, graze on sparse vegetation. Finally, Rinchen signals that the repair has been made, and we climb back into the vehicles with a simultaneous groan.

In midafternoon, our caravan arrives at the pilgrims' encampment at Darchen, where we pitch our tents on concrete blocks above the garbage choked stream flowing through the bleak village and tent city surrounding it.

I can no longer contain myself. While the others nap and organize their duffels behind zipped flaps, I climb for ninety minutes to a 16,500-foot ridge, moving like a man possessed, pushing higher and higher, fighting a wrathful wind that presses me back with each step. Finally, after years of fantasy and impossible anticipation, pumped full of adrenaline from the strenuous ascent, I cast unobstructed eyes upon the Throne of Shiva.

Steadying myself against a *mani* stone cairn festooned with, skulls, flags, and wooden *pobas* (tea bowls), I drink in the last golden rays of light that bathe the surface of Gang Rimpoche. What existed only as mental image, a picture in a book, has finally become a solid reality—more perfectly breathtaking than can be fully absorbed in my oxygen-impaired state. Reveling like a drunk in the sharp, angular light and rarefied air, I am filled with a joy I could not have anticipated.

The wind on the ridge viciously swats my tripod and camera against the rocks as I set up to take a photograph, nearly knocking me over as well—doubtless, a *dakini* (female spirit of the mountains, a combination of siren and harpy) having her kicks. Even so,

I am possessed by the stunning sensuality of Kailash, and imagine a priapic Shiva making eternal love to his spiritual consort, Parvati, on the summit. This crystal wonder overwhelms me; the only words that can express my state are those already inscribed on the stones at my feet by others so enraptured.

The Mountain sings "*Om mani padme hum,*" and I resonate in the refrain.

After a nearly sleepless night of barking dogs and loud drunken pilgrims, we break camp at Darchen. While our entourage sets off on the prescribed route for the thirty-two-mile clockwise *parikrama*, or circumambulation of Kailash, Gary and I detour up the winding Selung Chu (Grey River Valley).

Among the rocks lining the rushing stream, I find the skull of a *bharal*, the Himalayan blue sheep, which is the preferred delicacy of *Uncia uncia*, the snow leopard. Whatever dispatched this animal has long gone, and the bone is bleached white. Good luck comes to one, I have heard, who prominently displays a *bharal* skull in his home. Although not particularly superstitious, I am cautious enough to hedge my bets. Cinching the brittle talisman to my rucksack, I continue up into the windy saddle between a cathedral-shaped butte called Nandi, after Shiva's bull, and the striated white buttress of Kailash.

A plume of snow avalanches from the long vertical cleft in the mountain's south face, known as the "Stairway to Heaven" long before Led Zeppelin was a gleam in the eye of the universe. It was carved, so the legend goes, by the sorcerer Naro Bönchung as he fell from Gang Ti-sé's summit after losing a magical duel with Milarepa, black magician turned Buddhist ascetic, reputedly the only human being ever to stand on the mountain's peak. But Milarepa did not climb to the summit; the tale is told that he flew—like one of the great soaring lammergeiers that float in endless meditation on the thermal currents.

By midafternoon we reach an overlook above the talus-filled amphitheater that marks the beginning of the *nangkor*, the inner circuit passing between the holy mountain's south face and the flank of Nandi. Entrance is forbidden to one who has not already made thirteen outer *koras* (clockwise circles). As it happens, I am way too tired to flout tradition.

Stripping off my gear, I sit down on a rock to contemplate the perfection of the geological architecture arrayed before me. Emotionally naked in the light of midday, I am beset again by the *dakinis*. These capricious sprites have a way of opening one's eyes to the illusion of reality. Or is it the reality of illusion? I seem to have lost my bearings. When—or if—I return from this journey, will I still be the man whose face I have seen in the mirror for the past forty-something years? Or someone else—someone I have not yet become?

On the slope where I sit, tiny cairns rise like Lilliputian temples over the studded hillside—"spirit houses," Gary explains. During the interval one spends in the *bardo*, the "gap" between one incarnation and another, according to Tibetan scripture, one needs a place to dwell in safety, for the *bardo* is full of the most abominable mental projections and irresistible temptations. We chuckle condescendingly at this myth—and then cautiously, ironically, reverently, we lay aside our civilized hubris and begin to build—constructing our spirit houses side by side on an icy piece of real estate facing the Stairway to Heaven.

The cold, desiccating, endless night has ended. A merciful sun finally crests the canyon walls and begins to warm the Lha Chu (God's River) valley. This is a barren, dusty world, over 15,000 feet in elevation, yet surprisingly beautiful in its utter starkness. Striated walls rise on either side of this sloping valley bisected by an icy silver ribbon of holy water. With food in our bellies, we set off to explore the Martian landscape.

At Chöku, a *gompa* directly above our campsite, pilgrims perform mini-koras of the structure, like slow-motion electrons whirling around a mud-brick nucleus. A separate shrine, called a *gönkhang*, is dedicated to Gangri Lhatsen, a "protector" of demonic appearance. But to our dismay, no women are allowed to enter this chapel. Spiritual chauvinism is apparently nondenominational.

A few of us continue up the defile to a cleft slashed into the wall of a mountain called Nyenri. Scrambling up the steep talus bleeding from that gash for a thousand feet, we are rewarded with the glorious sight of fluttering prayer flags marking a cave that sheltered Jetsun[4] Mila 900 years ago. A thin white cotton garment called a *repa* was all the mystic ever wore, even in the dead of winter. From his lofty aerie, Milarepa, as he is known in the West, commanded a view of Kailash to the north and Gurla Mandata to the south. His cave was constructed of tightly fit stones and a packed sod roof, but we suspect these were later improvements made to the site.

I descend into the saint's cave, and sit enraptured by particles of dust dancing on a single beam of light, floating ever upward toward a slit opening in the ceiling, then higher, toward the source of light itself. In this solitude of harsh contrasts, I am suddenly overcome with grief. Sobbing in darkness, I cannot remember what it is like to feel joy. I know that this body will inevitably return to dust, and, yes, I do fear the great unknown of death. But more than that, I fear for my children, for the harsh and violent world they will inherit.

When I finally emerge into the sunlight, I wonder if these thoughts came to Milarepa when he sat in the darkness, besieged by his own demons. Even saints must have their doubts.

Back in my tent, I lay on a thermal pad, bathed in the yellow glow of sun penetrating the nylon fabric. My gear lies in a pile on my duffel, a chaotic arrangement of colors, and textures, and materials. The reflection in my mirrored glasses reminds me, cruelly, that I am no longer a young man. The gray in my beard, the deepening lines in my face, the eyes that look sad and lost bear witness to my journey toward death.

A *drögpa* (nomad) pauses before the unzipped tent flap. This young, rather homely girl bends before the golden dome to look at the alien within. Her bright smile reaches out to me from a

---

4. *Jetsun*: an honorific title applied to revered teachers in Tibet.

dirty, red-brown face. "*Tashi deley,*" she intones, almost as a song, and I find myself returning her greeting, and smile.

Then suddenly, I am here, *only* here—in this instant, this now. The waters of "God's River" flow just beyond my vision, and my life has just begun. Observing this young nomad, I know that my children are safe, and healthy, and happy. I can see them playing with joyous abandon in the reflection of her dark eyes.

Rising at the entrance to the Lha Chu canyon, Darpoche looms like a garish Druidic Maypole. Each year, during the full moon of May, the huge wooden mast is lowered, new multichromatic prayer flags are strung, and the shaft is raised again to the deep trumpeting of horns, and the mesmerizing chant of lamas. There is a frenzy of activity as pilgrims on foot, on horseback, and piled into the backs of open trucks, make numerous *koras* around the perimeter inscribed by the pole's anchors.

Prostrators, sporting protective leather aprons over their loose-fitting *chubas*, make torturous circuits in the red dust. *Drögpas* open liters of Chinese beer, cook *momos* (little meat-filled dumplings), and celebrate in wild, drunken groups. Khampas, rose-brown people from the east, bedecked in daggers, silver jewelry, and colorful woolen raiment, braid flaming red tassels into their raven hair, and sell their wares out of white tents adorned with blue Tantric symbols. Such is the carnival atmosphere of Saga Dawa.

But, on a flat escarpment overlooking the frenetic celebration at Darpoche, we stumble upon a very different venue. At this "sky burial" site, the Roljolpa, lamas specially trained for the task of cutting up human corpses (presumably after the former inhabitant has been escorted through the *bardo*), roll the bits of flesh in *tsampa* (barley flour) and feed them to Egyptian griffon vultures all too happy to accommodate the recycling. It is the perfect synthesis of ecology and religion, in a land where firewood is exceedingly scarce—the point at which the food chain loops back upon itself and spirit is freed from imprisonment in *maya*—the "illusion" we call the physical world.

But no one has died today, and in the spirit of Saga Dawa, a group of Chödpa lamas beat drums, ring bells, chant, and confer blessings upon those who request their ministrations. Celebrants bring articles of clothing to leave on the flat rock, where cleavers, knives, and *tsampa* residue are everywhere in evidence. Some of the more devout pilgrims pull out a tooth and leave it on the rock, spitting blood into the dirt to remind them of their mortality.

Amid this pastiche of hypnotic chanting, primary colors, and frenzied spirituality, Gary introduces me to a flesh-and-blood *dakini*. Wearing a leather motorcycle jacket and a Khampa's fox fur cap, Raphaéla has brown eyes that sparkle in the intense sunlight, framed by a filigree of smiling creases. Her face is that of a former fashion model, sunburned and devoid of makeup, but beautiful nonetheless. She speaks Tibetan as fluently as her native French, and a man knows instantly that it would be insane to fall in love with her. There is a predatory seductiveness in her eyes, and a sense that she would devour me if I gave her half a chance.

"Do you have something to put on my lips?" Raphaéla asks with her sophisticated Parisian accent. I take deep breaths and hand her my Chapstick.

Raphaéla is an accomplished photographer who wields her well-worn Nikon like a pro. But it is her real estate holdings in Paris, she admits, that allow her to travel Asia in search of…well, whatever it is she's searching for.

As we snap pictures of each other like Japanese tourists, Raphaéla asks me quite seriously, "Are you doing the dharma?" I don't know quite how to answer. I am not a Buddhist, but I also realize that has nothing whatsoever to do with her question.

"What else *can* I do?" I finally reply.

"*Ah, très bon!*" She likes the answer, rewarding me with a perfect white smile, which I capture forever on film.

To me, the dharma is a process of peeling fine layers of cloudy intellectual and mystical membrane from the onion of truth. Somewhere at the center of this klugey human construct of hope and faith and good intentions is the reality that awakened Siddhārtha Gautama. He did not arise from beneath that pipal tree with a complex, ritualized cosmology, but rather with a simple observation of what is—and what isn't. Siddhārtha was not a Buddhist either; he was a heretic.

It is said that a *parikrama* of Kailash washes away the sins of a lifetime. Heaven knows, I have a lot of scrubbing to do.

I walk in solitude through the desolate Lha Chu canyon. With each step, my heels rub raw against boot leather as I painfully inspect a life stripped of illusion. By the time Gang Rimpoche's awesome north face peers over a shoulder of purple rock, I feel purged of excuses, emptied of alibis. Sitting down to eat lunch with my fellow pilgrims, I am possessed of a hunger that seems as vast as the great valley that stretches before us to the *gompa* at Drira Phuk (Cave of the Female Yak's Horn).

A few of us climb still higher along a scree-choked stream that empties from the Gangjam glacier. Beyond, blue seracs rise like frozen waveforms from the mottled ice, their shadows stretched into rippling daggers by the waning afternoon light. Beneath the sheer north wall, we begin to sink up to our crotches in the sun-softened glacial snow. Above me, Kailash rises in a 4,000-foot vertical thrust of ice-glazed rock. Michael and his brother Peter are accomplished mountaineers, but they gaze up at this monolith with open mouths. "Holy shit!" Michael exclaims softly, a nervous laugh underscored with reverence, "I don't see a good route on that wall."

Kailash remains one of the very few legendary mountains on this planet left unclimbed—not because of its altitude, nor its technical difficulty, but because of the complete awe in which the mountain is held by those fortunate enough to stand in its radiance. And now that I am standing here, my heart bursting, I realize that this is not just a mountain filling the expanse of my vision. It represents everything I do not yet understand, reified into impenetrable stone. Perfection, whispers Gang Rimpoche, is observing that which is, and feeling neither the need, nor the desire, to make it otherwise.

Michael and I build a cairn on a rocky promontory at 17,500

feet, securing a prayer flag beneath the capstone. I notice two figures appear at the edge of the glacier, trudging through the snow
in our direction. The pair of *drögpas* reach our little monument,
spot the flags, and immediately prostrate in prayer. I throw Peter an
ironic smile, suddenly remembering the words of Saint Francis of
Assisi: *Lord, make me an instrument of thy peace.*

As the Tibetans pay homage at our makeshift altar, Gary and
Edward reach the high point. We celebrate the carpenter's tenacity
with the last of our Pashupati biscuits.

After a few words with the *drögpas*, Gary cautions, "There are
most likely streams running below the snow up here, and that means
crevasses. I think we should call it a day and get back to camp."

Although I realize that we're rapidly losing sunlight, I am suddenly obsessed with touching the Throne of Shiva. Its siren song
beckons and I feel powerless to resist.

"It's not that far," I yell like a sugar-hyped child, bounding
through deep snow toward the dark, looming wall. "Come on, we
can make it to the face. We can touch it!"

But Gary knows better. He has seen too often how altitude can
obliterate reason. Our leader calls my name forcefully, and I stop in
midstride—as if on a psychic tether—then turn in the direction of
his deep, steady voice. "It's time to surrender that male ego!"

I look up at Shiva, bereft of words. So close, so goddamn close!
But Gary has exposed me; he knows I demand divine verification
just like my namesake, the doubting apostle Thomas. And we both
know that is a fool's game.

I sink into serene submission, content just to have reached this
spot, to exist in this moment. There is nothing to prove. It is perfect, just as it is. Parvati nods her approval, and I place my fingertips together in salute before descending to where it is safe for humans to live.

When sunrise turns Kailash primrose, I walk in chilled intoxication to the *gompa* at Driru Phuk. Climbing to the flat roof, I calcu-
late the spot where Herbert Tichy must have lain on his belly sixty
years ago, pointing his Leica rangefinder at the lamas paying

homage to Gang Rimpoche. And for just a moment, I experience the exhilaration he must have felt, and understand why he threw caution to the wind in order to snap the shutter. Although Tichy never achieved fame during his seventy-five years of exploration, his serendipitous photograph utterly changed the course of my life. How many lives might I touch with the image I am about to make?

I raise my camera to frame the shot. The mountain is golden, the sky a royal blue. My polarizer cuts the glare; I press the shutter release and…nothing.

My battery is dead. The *dakinis* always have the last laugh.

Before we cross Drolma La, the highest point on the *parikrama* (18,200 feet by Gary's altimeter), we are invited to share *pok*—a doughy mixture of roasted barley nuts, *tsampa*, and butter tea— with a group of *anis*, Buddhist nuns. I never cease to be amazed by the generosity of these people. Possessing so little, they are willing to share everything.

As I climb the steep, snowbound incline to the pass, my fingers caress a cool, flat object inside my Gortex pocket. Three years ago, it beckoned to me like forbidden fruit on Chakpori Hill, former site of the Medical College in Lhasa. It was so small, and there were so many of them, just lying around in the dirt. Surely, I thought, no one would miss this one.

The *mani* stone was kept on my office desk in San Francisco, occasionally eliciting a curious inquiry from a friend or client. I learned later that it is considered the worst possible luck to take a prayer offering as a souvenir. But, because of its location, the stone managed to survive the 1991 firestorm in the Oakland Hills that destroyed everything else I owned. And so I made a vow to return it to the cairn from which it had been taken when I returned to Lhasa—not because I'm superstitious, mind you, but because Murphy's Law is not likely to be repealed.

However, my restitutionary plans were changed by some Chinese bureaucrat barring our way to Lhasa. Then a bizarre thought occurred to me: perhaps the one who had carved this stone, like the old man with the cataracts at Gungpur, had not been able to make the pilgrimage to Gang Rimpoche. Might not the universe have made me the unwitting instrument of a circuitous destiny, the serendipitous porter of that incapacitated pilgrim's offering to the destination for which it had been intended all along?

Hey, why not?

Finally reaching the flag-draped boulder that marks the icy summit of the pass—named for Drolma, the forgiver of all sins—I wrap my indestructible *mani* stone in a yellow square of cotton printed with the Wind Horse, granter of all wishes. I wedge it into a niche, sheltered from the fierce wind, and stand back to admire the stone's new setting. I feel as if I and its maker had run an unconscious relay to place this symbol of eternal being at the Axis of the World—where it can touch, and be touched by, the thousands of pilgrims who will eventually make the rigorous journey.

In that instant, I recall Edward Lorenz's suggestion that something as seemingly insignificant as the fluttering of a butterfly's wings has the potential to affect global weather patterns. If the physicist's assertion is true, then at some quantum level, connection is all there is. Mutual Arising, as Sakyamuni put it.

> Our group continues the journey around Kailash, toward the highest pass. Ahead and behind us, a thousand other pilgrims continue, traveling from Tarboche in small groups. We climb in the company of wizened elders, barefoot women, young and old priests, cripples, delicate girls, militant-looking youths, and our strong Sherpas and porters. The pass blazes with thousands of prayer flags in brilliant primary colors. Pilgrims tie flags to the big rocks. They daub yak butter on the huge boulder at the summit. They attach ceremonial scarves, money, beads, and safety pins. They scatter rice and coins. Our group crests the pass. Some barely pause before hurrying down the other side in search of oxygen.
>
> —Joan Zimmerman
> "A Mountain, a Flag Pole, a Test of Sin"

*

Due south of Mount Kailash, the twin lakes of Rakhsas Tal and Manasarovar (Langka Tsho and Mapam Yumtsho in Tibetan) emblazon a natural yin/yang symbol on the geography. Rakhsas Tal is the dark sapphire repository of female energy, and its water is reputed to be poisonous—an intriguingly misogynistic, but apocryphal myth. Manasarovar, on the other hand, holds male energy, and it is claimed that full-submersion in its icy depths ensures enlightenment for Hindus; a mere drink promises the same for less intrepid Buddhists, who feel that dunking one's body would only befoul the precious water. Buddhists generally settle for a sip and a splash over the head—hence the name of the local *gompa*: Trugo, which, as near as anyone can figure, means "Holy Head Washing Gate."

We are camped near the *gompa* on a shingle of soft sand beside Manasarovar, the setting sun turning the surrounding hills to gold, and the wind-rippled surface of the lake to purple. With exuberance, we crack open liters of Chinese beer to celebrate the conclusion of our *kora*. Tomorrow, we will enjoy not only a day of holy head washing, but also the Zen of laundering our filthy clothes.

At 15,000 feet, the temperature of Manasarovar dissuades most of our group from seeking the enlightenment assured by full immersion. But Michael and I have decided that we are not about to let this once-in-a-lifetime chance go by.

With the solemnity of naughty children, we strip off our fleece clothing and wade into the frigid lake for a quick plunge beneath the surface. This frosty baptism elicits screams of exhilarated shock, and lunatic laughter. Waist deep in holy water, I scoop up a handful of Manasarovar and swallow a draught to replenish my depleted male energy. Ah, if only enlightenment were so easily attained.

That afternoon, I sit with Barbara near the edge of the placid lake, lazily watching the sun drift like a golden veil across Manasarovar to the distant glistening snow cone of Kailash.

"Do you think it's male or female?" she asks. "The mountain, I mean."

"Both," I reply. "The north face is definitely phallic, but that slit on the south face…"

"You're right," Barbara concedes with laughter. "It's a *yoni!*" She places her Walkman headset over my ears and plays a twelfth-century Gregorian chant written by the mystical prodigy Hildegard von Bingen. Backed by an angelic choral, Parvati sings me to sleep.

The overland return to Simikot has presented a logistical nightmare for Gary. Still unable to give us just cause for this interdiction, the local officials have posted border guards at Zher, not only to insure that no one else enters, but also to make certain we leave the way we came. Gary sent two Sherpas hoofing back to Simikot, where they wired Kathmandu for supplies and new trekking permits, rounded up local porters, and marched them northward to meet us on the Nepal side of the Karnali River.

To my delight, Raphaéla rolls into Purang with a group from the German Alpine Club, led by Bruno, an *übermensch* who wears an ornate Khampa warrior's belt and struts like a Luftwaffe pilot. Obviously, he is smitten by her; just as obviously, she is using him to get a ride to Shigatse, where she needs to extend her visa. *Dakinis* are like that.

Covered with grit and dust from the road, Raphaéla and I eat yak cheese and *momos* on the filthy steps of the Purang guest house, flirting with each other as if we were in a chic bistro on Boulevard Saint Germaine. When our passports are returned and our vehicles ready, she passes me a slip of paper with her European telephone number.

"I will be in Tibet until autumn," she says, "studying with the young Karmapa. Then maybe back home for a while. If you are ever near St. Cloud," Raphaéla adds provocatively, "fax me."

We embrace and I wish her well.

Arriving in Zher at twilight, we set up camp at the edge of the sleepy village, and bid farewell to Jampa and Rinchen. As our guides place white *katas* (ceremonial scarves) around our necks, I wonder what awaits them back in Lhasa. Life there is a tenuous proposition for Tibetans, now minorities in their own home. A wrong word, or a suspicious action could cause one to disappear into the black bowels of Dhrapchi prison—a *bardo* through which anyone would fear to pass.

I feel sadly relieved to be leaving this country. Oppression hangs in the air like the dark cloud of a nuclear winter, but one does not appreciate its full weight until out from beneath it. Without a doubt, feudal Tibet had its drawbacks, but crushing the human spirit seems a high price to pay for land reform and redistribution of wealth.

In the morning, we greet Sherpa Dendi and the porters who will lug our gear back down the Karnali gorge. Armed border guards check our passports far too carefully, then escort us to the river's edge. One young soldier roughly taps the *bharal* skull strapped to my rucksack and laughs contemptuously as I descend toward the Karnali River crossing.

The arrogant, coal-eyed boys with guns enrage me. Gary smiles knowingly before I say something that we all will regret. "It's not worth it. Keep walking."

I remember that they really are boys who, given a choice, would prefer to be somewhere other than the Tibetan border waiting for the appearance of an errant trekker, or an unlikely invasion of Indian troops. What purpose does it serve to be angry at these pawns of Beijing's octogenarian bureaucracy? True compassion cannot be conditional. It's easy to care about the oppressed, but very difficult to love the oppressor.

I suppose integrity is, after all, a lifelong pursuit, and the world a constant reminder of my vast imperfection. I think of Raphaéla's incisive question, and her lusty laugh reminds me that if I am not doing the dharma—it will be doing me.

Tom Joyce is a writer, photographer, and graphic designer who lives in the San Francisco area. He is currently working on a documentary film project called The Heretic's Pilgrimage.

✦ ✦ ✦

Falling Out with Superman

Disenchantment can be a good thing.

I STUMBLED UPON FRIEDRICH NIETZSCHE WHEN I WAS SEVENTEEN, following the usual trail of existential candies—Camus, Sartre, Beckett—that unsuspecting teenagers find in the woods. The effect was more like a drug than a philosophy. I was whirled upward—or was it downward?—into a one-man universe, a secret cult demanding that you put a gun to the head of your dearest habits and beliefs. That intoxicating whiff of half-conscious madness; that casually hair-rising evisceration of everything moral, responsible and parentally approved—these waves overwhelmed my adolescent dinghy. And even more than by his ideas—many of which I didn't understand at all, but some of which I perhaps grasped better than I do now—I was seduced by his prose. At the end of his sentences you could hear an electric crack, like the whip of a steel blade being tested in the air. He might have been the Devil, but he had better lines than God.

I was sold. Like those German soldiers in World War I who were found dead with copies of *Thus Spake Zarathustra* in their pockets, I hauled my tattered purple-covered copy of the Viking Portable Nietzsche with me everywhere. It was with me when I dropped out of college after a semester to go work in a shipyard, with me years later when, sitting on a knoll on a tiny island off Vancouver, I decided to wake up from my dream of total escape and go back to school. I read him to elevate myself, to punish myself, to remind myself of the promises I had broken. He was the closest thing I had to church.

Eventually, I stopped going to church. There were various reasons for this, some of them good and some of them not; I couldn't sort out which was which then, and can't now. Maybe it was just satiation. The philosopher John Searle once told me that reading Nietzsche was like drinking cognac—a sip was good, but you didn't want to drink the whole bottle. I'd been pounding Nietzsche by the case.

So I left Nietzsche alone on his mountaintop. But as every lapsed believer knows, you never wholly escape the church. Nietzsche had come to stand for something absolute and pure, like gilded Byzantium or Ahab's whale; he represented what I imagined I might have been. He had become a permanent horizon.

Oddly, during this long, strange love affair, I avoided learning much about Nietzsche's life. Maybe this was because I had turned him into a shrine—after all, totems have no history. I knew only the superficial: that he was a desperately lonely man, poor and largely unread, plagued by bad health, who went mad at the age of forty-four.

Then, last summer, I planned a trip to Switzerland, As a highlight, I decided to visit Sils Maria—the small village near Saint Moritz where Nietzsche spent seven summers and wrote many of his masterpieces. The tourist soon won out over the iconoclast: now that I was going to stand where the Master stood, I couldn't pretend I didn't care about how he lived, what people he liked, what he wore. So I immersed myself in various biographical accounts: *Nietzsche in Turin*, Lesley Chamberlain's psychologically penetrating book about the philosopher's final year; Ronald Hayman's challenging *Nietzsche: A Critical Life*; and a book that only a Nietzsche cultist would consume, *The Good European: Nietzsche's Work Sites in Word and Image*.

It wasn't the grand narrative of his life but the details that stayed

with me. The joke photograph in which he and his friend Paul
Rée posed in a cart over which Lou Salomé, the twenty-one-year-
old woman with whom he was timidly, desperately in love, held a
whip. Nietzsche in the Caligari-shadowed last days of his sanity,
once again turning himself into a character in an unhappy novel,
lamenting that a journey was "perhaps the most unfortunate I have
made" simply because he had climbed aboard the wrong train. The
fact that he liked "Tom Sawyer." The solicitude of an old female
friend who tried to buck him up but was unable to teach him not
to let everything wound him. The visitor who simply reported
how much he *liked* Herr Nietzsche, the lonely, earnest professor
with bad eyes.

This wasn't the Nietzsche I remembered. The philosopher I had
worshipped was an uncanny hybrid, simultaneously a terrifying
Old Testament prophet and a nineteenth-century free spirit. To be
sure, much of Nietzsche—maybe the best of him—was as lucid,
critical and quick-footed as Stendhal. Yet it was the monstrous
doctrines at the heart of his thought—the Overman, the Eternal
Recurrence—that had drawn me; they hypnotized me because I
couldn't figure out whether they were coming from man or some
frightening gospel. Now that I understood how much of
Nietzsche's work was an attempt to turn his personal torment into
something lasting, I realized that perhaps those enigmatic pro-
nouncements were best seen not as antitruths handed down from
on high, but as words he whispered to himself, beacons he lighted
in the darkness to cheer himself up. What was great in Nietzsche
was not, I began to see, his holiness, maybe not even his wisdom.
It was his courage.

Then I went to Sils.

Sils Maria is a bland, one-horse resort village under spectacular
mountains between two crystalline lakes. Terminally respectable
Swiss burghers polish their vacation homes; tourists ("They climb
mountains like animals, stupid and sweating," Nietzsche wrote) fill
the hotels. The Nietzsche-Haus stands near the center. In his day
it was a tea and spice shop whose owner rented an upstairs room
to Nietzsche; now it is a museum. In front of the tidy white-and-

green buildings stands a sculpture of a large black eagle—one of the companions that consoled Zarathustra in his last loneliness. On a gray afternoon I pulled open the door and climbed the stairs to his room.

No one was there. I looked in. A small, low-ceilinged room, walls of knotty pine. A lumpy-looking bed. A small table with a green silk cover. A wash basin. A single window, looking out onto a patch of forest.

We go to literary shrines to touch things. We run our fingers along the writing table, we furtively step over the red-velvet rope and finger the water jug by the edge of the bed. Yet to feel the pedestal is to call the very idea of the pedestal into question. Which is why there is something comic in all pilgrimages: while Don Quixote holds loftily forth, Sancho Panza steals the ashtray.

But as I ran my fingertips along the knotty pine, it all rose up: the indelible words that had been created here; the misery of the man who had shivered out his life in this room; and all the years I had spent charting my course by a dream. Standing outside in the hallway, I was surprised to find myself beginning to weep, like the most breast-heaving pilgrim.

> There is an indefinable mysterious Power that pervades everything. I feel it, though I do not see it. It is this unseen Power which makes itself felt and yet defies all proof, because it is so unlike all that I perceive through my senses. It transcends the senses. But it is possible to reason out the existence of God to a limited extent.
>
> —Mahatma Gandhi

A familiar voice, very old and once sacred to me, protested. I could not pity Nietzsche. It was a betrayal of everything he had believed. He had railed against pity. Compassion was for the hearth-huddlers, the followers, those who lacked the strength to turn themselves into "dancing stars." The last temptation of the higher man, Nietzsche had taught, was pity; on its far side was a roaring Dionysian, inhuman laughter.

I could recite this chapter and verse, but I had never been able to live it. It was the most alien and terrifying of Nietzsche's teachings. Still, long reverence pulled me up short. Here, of all places, I must feel no pity.

But my heart won the war. Maybe it was resignation—but the final acceptance that I was not going to forge myself into a new shape. Maybe it was weariness with a doctrine, with all doctrines, that sounded delirious but that couldn't be used. Whatever it was, I stopped fighting. Yes, part of Nietzsche would always stand far above the tree line, and I would treasure that iciness. But I had to walk on the paths where I could go.

Still confused, I stood in the doorway. And then, as a gift, the following words came into my head, words spoken by Zarathustra to his disciples, disciples that Nietzsche himself never had. "You revere me; but what if your reverence tumbles one day? Beware lest a statue slay you. You say you believe in Zarathustra? But what matters Zarathustra?…Now I bid you lose me and find yourselves; and only when you have all denied me will I return to you."

I took a last look at the room. Then I walked out the door.

Gary Kamiya, formerly a film and media critic for the San Francisco Examiner, *is now the executive editor of the online magazine,* Salon. *His work has appeared in* Art Forum, The New York Times, Sports Illustrated, Hippocrates, California *and many other publications. He lives on Nob Hill in San Francisco.*

PAUL WILLIAM ROBERTS

✦ ✦ ✦

I Am Always with You

*Avatar or not, this Indian holy man
is lodged in the author's heart.*

ONE DAY, SEVERAL MONTHS AFTER ARRIVING IN PUTTAPARTHI, I
suddenly felt it was time for me to leave, that I'd learned all I could
in Sathya Sai Baba's ashram, and that the path of devotion was not
to be my path. From all I now understood, God lay within, and *that*
was where one ought to start looking for any truth. The holy
man's presence seemed to stand in the way of this. Here *he* was
God. I'd decided to travel around the country next, to study, to listen, and to learn whatever there was to learn from whoever was
willing to teach me. But I was also feeling the seductive pull of the
material world, I must confess. My idyll was over. On the day I
made up my mind to leave, Baba told me he would talk to me. I
was shocked.

Finally I found myself walking over the compound to the door
of the Baba's living quarters. I had wondered for months what was
behind it. I stood, looking into a concrete room scarcely larger
than a pickup truck and virtually bare. It smelled nice, at least,
smelled of the incense that burned in the temple. I've never encountered that fragrance anywhere else.

Several people sat beside me; no one spoke. Baba appeared after
the darshan from the compound outside, as he must have done

every day I'd been there. He stood, looking at us. He said something about seeing God in everyone, and then, rolling up a sleeve, waved his hand and slowly produced a huge rosary of pink stones. It seemed to emerge from a hole in space just below his palm, swinging in a circle until it was all there, all present in its new dimension. I was no more than a yard from his hand. He presented this sparkling *japamala* to an old Chinese woman, beckoning her and her husband to follow him through a door covered by a cloth flap.

Soon—or maybe not soon—the couple emerged in a daze, followed by Baba, who beckoned someone else inside the other room. Muffled grunts could be heard, and then this person would emerge as if stunned. What was he going to say to me? I didn't want to leave anymore.

Finally I was inside that room. I recall being amazed by how small and bare it was, too. My room at Nagamma's was bigger and more comfortable, and I had regarded my room as a penance. This was also the first time I had ever really stood beside Baba. Like the room, he was unbelievably small. As I looked down into his eyes, trying to think of something to say, I began to shake, gasping with emotion. Quite involuntarily, I said, "I love you, Baba," over and over and over again.

> Seeing the rose, separating it from the thorn and the shrub, is Concentration.
> Plucking the rose, separating the heart from the mind and all else, is Contemplation. Offering the rose at the Lord's feet is Meditation.
> —Sathya Sai Baba

He hugged me, his hair soft as lamb's wool in my face. This surprised me. I'd imagined it would be wiry. *Ba-ba,* I thought absurdly, *the Lamb of God.* Looking down at him, though, I had the odd impression that I was really looking up at him.

"Baba love you, too," he said.

He meant it—I could *feel* it. To *be loved*: That was not the same as to *love*. I had never let myself *be loved* before, I realized.

And I was so grateful that I merely wept more. It was all I could do.

Baba then proceeded to basically deliver a summary of my life and a breakdown of my personality in machine-gun bursts that had me reeling, nodding humbly, speechless. With all my faults, there I was, "the thing itself." It seemed to be his way of reassuring me that there was nothing he did not know about me, and that none of it bothered him. The sum total was, as he usefully confided, "much confusion." I had to agree. He reassured me that he would sort things out. It was a workmanlike statement.

"Thanks," I managed.

He'd moved back by now, and was circling his hand in the space between us. Expecting some trinket, I was surprised to see a white, oily substance appear in his palm. Somehow, I knew what he wanted to do, so I lifted my shirt and let him rub this substance into my chest.

I kept thanking him profusely. Then he said, "Don't worry. I am always with you. Baba love you."

Next thing I knew, I was back in the antechamber.

The subsequent few days are a blur. I recall walking around in a daze, so happy that I couldn't speak. It once crossed my mind to start walking out across the great subcontinent and never stop, never question again what was undeniably true.

Perhaps I should have done that, but I didn't. When I eventually tried to tell people what had happened, I found I was not even sure what *had* happened. Words failed, simply did not adapt to the feelings I wished to express. A week later, I could no longer return my consciousness to wherever it had been at all. It was like waking from a beautiful dream and realizing that you could never ever explain *why* the dream was beautiful. I was certain of only one thing again: I should leave Puttaparthi. As soon as possible.

As my bus finally turned onto the Bangalore road, I felt an enormous sense of relief. As if I'd survived some dreadful test, as if I'd passed through the fire. I hardly knew that person who had arrived there the previous September. Something of him had been burned away, some part I didn't miss. Even the searing air now seemed kinder and cooler. As many have attested, before and since, Puttaparthi is a crucible. It would be twenty years before I physically saw the place again, although in dreams I returned often.

Paul William Roberts has written for many magazines and newspapers, including The Toronto Star, Saturday Night, Toronto Life, *and* Harper's, *and is an award-winning writer-producer for Canadian television. Born in Britain and educated at Oxford, he currently lives in Toronto. He is the author of* In Search of the Birth of Jesus: The Real Journey of the Magi, River in the Desert: Modern Travels in Ancient Egypt, The Demonic Comedy: Some Detours in the Baghdad of Saddam Hussein, *and* Empire of the Soul: Some Journeys in India, *from which this story was excerpted.*

Recommended Reading

Atwater, P. M. H. *Future Memory: How Those Who "See the Future" Shed New Light on the Workings of the Human Mind*. New York: Birch Lane Press, 1996.

Aurobindo, Sri. *The Life Divine, Vol. 19*. India: Sri Aurobindo Ashram, 1970.

Bender, Sue. *Everyday Sacred: A Woman's Journey Home*. San Francisco: HarperSan Francisco, 1995.

Bernardin, Joseph Louis. *The Gift of Peace: Personal Reflections*. Chicago: Loyola Press, 1997.

Bolen, Jean Shinoda, M.D. *Crossing to Avalon: A Woman's Midlife Pilgrimage*. San Francisco: HarperSan Francisco, 1995.

Brown, Mick. *The Spiritual Tourist: A Personal Odyssey through the Outer Reaches of Belief*. New York: Bloomsbury, 1998.

Chernin, Kim. *Reinventing Eve: Modern Woman in Search of Herself*. New York: HarperPerennial, 1994; New York: Times Books, 1987.

Cooper, Rabbi David A. *Entering the Sacred Mountain: Exploring the Mystical Practices of Judaism, Buddhism, and Sufism*. New York: Bell Tower, 1994.

Davies, Paul. *God and the New Physics*. New York: Simon & Schuster, 1983.

Deming, Alison Hawthorne. *Temporary Homelands: Essays on Nature, Spirit and Place*. New York: Picador, 1996.

Dossey, Larry, M.D. *Recovering the Soul*. New York: Bantam Books, 1989.

Ehrlich, Gretel. *Questions of Heaven: The Chinese Journeys of an American Buddhist*. Boston: Beacon Press, 1997.

Eliade, Mircea, ed. *The Encyclopedia of Religion, Vol. 13*. New York: Macmillan, 1987.

Elliott, William. *Tying Rocks to Clouds: Meetings and Conversations with Wise and Spiritual People*. Wheaton, Ill.: Quest Books, 1995.

Frankl, Viktor. *Man's Search for Meaning*. Seattle: University of Washington Press, 1959.

Gallagher, Nora. *Things Seen and Unseen: A Year Lived in Faith*. New York: Vintage, 1999.

Gallup, George, Jr. *Adventures in Immortality*. New York: McGraw-Hill, 1982.

Goldberg, Natalie. *Long Quiet Highway: Waking Up in America*. New York: Bantam, 1993.

Gonzalez-Crussi, F. *Suspended Animation: Six Essays on the Preservation of Bodily Parts*. Orlando: Harvest, 1995.

Gruber, Mark, O.S.B. *Wounded by Love: Intimations of an Outpouring Heart*. Latrobe, Pa.: Saint Vincent Archabbey, 1993.

Hogan, Linda. *Dwellings: A Spiritual History of the Living World*. New York: Touchstone, 1995.

Housden, Roger. *Sacred Journeys in a Modern World*. New York: Simon & Schuster, 1998.

Houston, James D. *In the Ring of Fire: A Pacific Basin Journey*. San Francisco: Mercury House, 1997.

Huxley, Aldous. *The Doors of Perception*. New York: Colophon Books, 1954.

Jung, C. G. *Man and His Symbols*. New York: Doubleday, 1964.

Kaku, Michio. *Hyperspace*. New York: Anchor Doubleday, 1994.

Kingsolver, Barbara. *High Tide in Tucson: Essays from Now or Never*. New York: HarperPerennial, 1995.

Kubler-Ross, Elisabeth. *On Death and Dying*. New York: Simon & Schuster Inc., 1997.

Lamott, Anne. *Traveling Mercies: Some Thoughts on Faith*. New York: Pantheon, 1999.

Lane, Belden C. *The Solace of Fierce Landscapes: Exploring Desert and Mountain Spirituality*. New York: Oxford University Press, 1998.

Lash, Jennifer. *On Pilgrimage: A Time to Seek*. London: Bloomsbury Publishing, 1991.

Lewis, C. S. *A Grief Observed*. New York: Bantam Books, 1983.

Lindbergh, Anne Morrow. *Gift from the Sea*. New York: Pantheon, 1992.

Livingston, Patricia H. *Lessons of the Heart: Celebrating the Rhythms of Life*. Notre Dame, Ind.: Ave Maria Press, 1992.

Matousek, Mark. *Sex, Death, Enlightenment: A True Story*. New York: Riverhead Books, 1996.

Matthiessen, Peter. *The Tree Where Man Was Born*. New York: Penguin, 1995.

Mayorga, Nancy Pope. *The Hunger of the Soul: A Spiritual Diary*. Studio City, Calif.: Vedanta, 1981.

Morton, H. V. *In the Steps of the Master*. New York: Dodd, Mead & Company, 1934.

Norris, Kathleen. *The Cloister Walk*. New York: Riverhead Books, 1997.

Norris, Kathleen. *Dakota: A Spiritual Geography*. New York: Houghton Mifflin, 1993.

Olsen, W. Scott, and Scott Cairns, eds. *The Sacred Place: Witnessing the Holy in the Physical World*. Salt Lake City: University of Utah Press, 1996.

Remen, Rachel Naomi, M.D. *Kitchen Table Wisdom: Stories That Heal*. New York: Riverhead Books, 1996.

Rinpoche, Sogyal, Patrick Gaffney, and Andrew Harvey (eds.). *The Tibetan Book of Living and Dying*. San Francisco: HarperSan Francisco, 1992.

Roberts, Paul William. *Empire of the Soul: Some Journeys in India*. New York: Riverhead Books, 1996.

Shrady, Nicholas. *Sacred Roads: Adventures from the Pilgrimage Trail*. San Francisco: HarperSan Francisco, 1999.

Somé, Malidoma Patrice. *Of Water and the Spirit: Ritual, Magic, and Initiation in the Life on an African Shaman*. New York: Jeremy P. Tarcher, 1994.

Talbot, Michael. *The Holographic Universe*. New York: HarperCollins, 1992.

Tipler, Frank J. *The Physics of Immortality.* New York: Doubleday, 1994.

Tóibín, Colm. *The Sign of the Cross: Travels in Catholic Europe.* London: Random House UK, 1994.

Wolf, Fred Allen. *Star Wave: Mind, Consciousness, and Quantum Physics.* New York: Macmillan, 1984.

Wolfe, Michael. *The Hadj: An American's Pilgrimage to Mecca.* New York: Grove Press, 1993.

Index

Index of Contributors

Acknowledgments

We would like to thank our families and friends for their usual forbearance while we are putting a book together. Thanks also to Larry Habegger, Lisa Bach, Susan Brady, Raj Khadka, Jennifer Leo, Natanya Pearlman, Tara Austen Weaver, Cynthia Lamb, Trisha Schwartz, Judy Johnson, Tim O'Reilly, Michele Wetherbee, and to Sleeping Lady Retreat and Conference Center in Leavenworth, Washington, for a wonderful and supportive creative environment.

Introduction by Phil Cousineau published with permission from the author. Copyright © 2000 by Phil Cousineau.

"Old City, Jerusalem" by Rabbi David A. Cooper excerpted from *Entering the Sacred Mountain: Exploring the Mystical Practices of Judaism, Buddhism, and Sufism* by Rabbi David A. Cooper. Copyright © 1994 by David Hanoch Cooper. Reprinted by permission of Bell Tower, a division of Random House, Inc.

"On the Road to Santiago de Compostela" by Jack Hitt reprinted from the August 1994 issue of *The New York Times*. Copyright © 1994 by Jack Hitt. Reprinted by permission of International Creative Management, Inc.

"In Search of Miracles" by Ann Hood copyright © 1998 by Ann Hood. Originally published in the Winter 1999 issue of *DoubleTake Magazine*. Reprinted by permission of Brandt & Brandt Literary Agents, Inc.

"Darshan with Mother Meera" by Mark Matousek excerpted from *Sex, Death, Enlightenment* by Mark Matousek. Copyright © 1996 by Mark Matousek. Used by permission of Riverhead Books, a division of Penguin Putnam, Inc.

"In the Footsteps of the Buddha" by Nicholas Shrady excerpted from *Sacred Roads: Adventures from the Pilgrimage Trail* by Nicholas Shrady. Copyright © 1999 by Nicholas Shrady. Reprinted by permission of HarperCollins Publishers, Inc. and Penguin Books, Ltd.

"Making the Hadj to Mecca" by Michael Wolfe excerpted from *The Hadj: An American's Pilgrimage to Mecca* by Michael Wolfe. Copyright © 1993 by Michael Wolfe. Used by permission of Grove/Atlantic, Inc.

"The Fruitful Void" by Roger Housden excerpted from *Sacred Journeys in a*

Modern World by Roger Housden. Copyright © 1998 by Roger Housden. Reprinted by permission of Simon & Schuster, Inc., and the author.

"The Road to Bethlehem" by H. V. Morton excerpted from *In the Steps of the Master* by H. V. Morton. Copyright © 1934 by H. V. Morton. Reprinted by permission of Methuen Publishing Limited.

"Pilgrimage to Glastonbury" by Jean Shinoda Bolen, M.D. excerpted from *Crossing to Avalon: A Woman's Midlife Pilgrimage* by Jean Shinoda Bolen, M.D. Copyright © 1994 by Jean Shinoda Bolen. Reprinted by permission of HarperCollins Publishers, Inc. .

"The Devil's Wind" by Kent E. St. John published with permission from the author. Copyright © 2000 by Kent E. St. John.

"Naked on Mount Sinai" by Michael Tobias excerpted from *A Vision of Nature: Traces of the Original World* (Kent State University Press, 1995) by Michael Tobias. Reprinted by permission of the Kent State University Press. Copyright © 1995 by Michael Tobias.

"Black Stones, Ancient Voices" by James D. Houston excerpted from *In the Ring of Fire: A Pacific Basin Journey* by James D. Houston, published by Mercury House. Reprinted by permission of the author. Copyright © 1997 by James D. Houston.

"Thin Places" by Ann Armbrecht Forbes reprinted from the February 1998 issue of *Terra Nova: Nature and Culture*. Copyright © 1998 by The Massachusetts Institute of Technology. Reprinted by permission of MIT Press Journals.

"Shikoku Pilgrimage" by Tara Austen Weaver published with permission from the author. Copyright © 2000 by Tara Austen Weaver.

"In the Dust of His Peacock's Feathers" by Ruth Kamnitzer published with permission from the author. Copyright © 2000 by Ruth Kamnitzer.

"My Father's House" by Mary McHugh published with permission from the author. Copyright © 2000 by Mary McHugh.

"Mount Kailash, the Throne of Shiva" by Tom Joyce published with permission from the author. Copyright © 2000 by Tom Joyce.

"Falling Out with Superman" by Gary Kamiya reprinted from the January 23, 2000 issue of *The New York Times Book Review*. Copyright © 2000 by Gary Kamiya. Reprinted by permission of the author.

"I Am Always with You" by Paul William Roberts excerpted from *Empire of the Soul: Some Journeys In India* by Paul William Roberts. Copyright © 1994 by Paul William Roberts. Used by permission of Putnam Berkley, a division of Penguin Putnam Inc. and Stoddart Publishing Co. Limited

Additional Credits (Arranged alphabetically by title)

Selection from "Decaf" by Moss Campion published with permission from the author. Copyright © 2000 by Peter Cohen.

About the Editors

Sean O'Reilly is a former seminarian, stockbroker, and prison instructor who lives in Arizona with his wife Brenda and their five young boys. He's had a life-long interest in philosophy and theology, and is at work on a book called *How to Manage Your Dick: A Guide for the Soul,* which makes the proposition that classic Greek, Roman, and Christian moral philosophies, allied with post-quantum physics, form the building blocks of a new ethics and psychology. Widely traveled, Sean most recently completed an 18,000-mile van journey around the United States, sharing the treasures of the open road with his family. He is editor-at-large and director of international sales for Travelers' Tales.

James O'Reilly, president and co-publisher of Travelers' Tales, wrote mystery serials before becoming a travel writer in the early 1980s. He's visited more than forty countries, along the way meditating with monks in Tibet, participating in West African voodoo rituals, and hanging out the laundry with nuns in Florence. He travels extensively with his wife Wenda and their three daughters. They live in Palo Alto, California when they're not in Leavenworth, Washington.

TRAVELERS' TALES

THE SOUL OF TRAVEL

Footsteps Series

KITE STRINGS OF THE SOUTHERN CROSS
A Woman's Travel Odyssey
By Laurie Gough
ISBN 1-885211-54-6
$14.95

"Gough's poetic and sensual string of tales richly evokes the unexpected rewards—and perils—of the traveler's life. A striking, moving debut." – *Salon.com*

— ★ ★ ★ —

*ForeWord Silver Medal Winner
– Travel Book of the Year*

THE SWORD OF HEAVEN
A Five Continent Odyssey to Save the World
By Mikkel Aaland
ISBN 1-885211-44-9
$24.00 (cloth)

"Few books capture the soul of the road like *The Sword of Heaven*, a sharp-edged, beautifully rendered memoir that will inspire anyone."
– Phil Cousineau, author of *The Art of Pilgrimage*

STORM
A Motorcycle Journey of Love, Endurance, and Transformation
By Allen Noren
ISBN 1-885211-45-7
$24.00 (cloth)

"Beautiful, tumultuous, deeply engaging, and very satisfying."
– Ted Simon, author of *Jupiter's Travels*

TAKE ME WITH YOU
A Round-the-World Journey to Invite a Stranger Home
By Brad Newsham
ISBN 1-885211-51-1
$24.00 (cloth)

"Newsham is an ideal guide. His journey, at heart, is into humanity."
– Pico Iyer, author of *Video Night in Kathmandu*

Travelers' Tales Classics

THE ROYAL ROAD TO ROMANCE
By Richard Halliburton
ISBN 1-885211-53-8
$14.95

"Laughing at hardships, dreaming of beauty, ardent for adventure, Halliburton has managed to sing into the pages of this glorious book his own exultant spirit of youth and freedom."
– *Chicago Post*

UNBEATEN TRACKS IN JAPAN
By Isabella L. Bird
ISBN 1-885211-57-0
$14.95

Isabella Bird gained a reputation as one of the most adventurous women travelers of the 19th century with her unconventional journeys to Tibet, Canada, Korea, Turkey, Hawaii, and Japan. A fascinating read for anyone interested in women's travel, spirituality, and Asian culture.

Europe

GREECE
True Stories of Life on the Road
Edited by Larry Habegger, Sean O'Reilly & Brian Alexander
ISBN 1-885211-52-X
$17.95
"This is the stuff memories can be duplicated from."
—*Foreign Service Journal*

IRELAND
True Stories of Life on the Emerald Isle
Edited by James O'Reilly, Larry Habegger & Sean O'Reilly
ISBN 1-885211-46-5
$17.95
Discover the wonder of Ireland with Frank McCourt, Thomas Flanagan, Nuala O'Faolain, Rosemary Mahoney, Colm Tóibín, and many more.

FRANCE
True Stories of Life on the Road
Edited by James O'Reilly, Larry Habegger & Sean O'Reilly
ISBN 1-885211-02-3
$17.95
The French passion for life bursts forth from every page of this invaluable guide, featuring stories by Peter Mayle, M.F.K. Fisher, Ina Caro, Jan Morris, Jon Krakauer and many more.

PARIS
True Stories of Life on the Road
Edited by James O'Reilly, Larry Habegger & Sean O'Reilly
ISBN 1-885211-10-4
$17.95
"If Paris is the main dish, here is a rich and fascinating assortment of hors d'oeuvres."
– Peter Mayle, author of *A Year in Provence*

ITALY
True Stories of Life on the Road
Edited by Anne Calcagno Introduction by Jan Morris
ISBN 1-885211-16-3
$17.95

—— ★ ★ ★ ——
ForeWord Silver Medal Winner – Travel Book of the Year

SPAIN
True Stories of Life on the Road
Edited by Lucy McCauley
ISBN 1-885211-07-4
$17.95
"A superb, eclectic collection that reeks wonderfully of gazpacho and paella, and resonates with sounds of heel-clicking and flamenco singing."
– Barnaby Conrad, author of *Matador*

For a complete list of titles, visit our website at www.travelerstales.com

Asia/Pacific

AUSTRALIA
True Stories of Life Down Under
Edited by Larry Habegger
ISBN 1-885211-40-6
$17.95
Explore Australia with authors Paul Theroux, Robyn Davidson, Bruce Chatwin, Pico Iyer, Tim Cahill, and many more.

JAPAN
True Stories of Life on the Road
Edited by Donald W. George & Amy Greimann Carlson
ISBN 1-885211-04-X
$17.95
"Readers of this entertaining anthology will be better equipped to plot a rewarding course through the marvelously bewildering, bewitching cultural landscape of Japan." – *Time* (Asia)

INDIA
True Stories of Life on the Road
Edited by James O'Reilly & Larry Habegger
ISBN 1-885211-01-5
$17.95
"The Travelers' Tales series should become required reading for anyone visiting a foreign country." – *St. Petersburg Times*

NEPAL
True Stories of Life on the Road
Edited by Rajendra S. Khadka
ISBN 1-885211-14-7
$17.95
"If there's one thing traditional guidebooks lack, it's the really juicy travel information, the personal stories about back alleys and brief encounters. This series fills this gap." – *Diversion*

THAILAND
True Stories of Life on the Road
Edited by James O'Reilly & Larry Habegger
ISBN 1-885211-05-8
$17.95

——— ★ ★ ★ ———
Winner of the Lowell Thomas Award for Best Travel Book – Society of American Travel Writers

HONG KONG
True Stories of Life on the Road
Edited by James O'Reilly, Larry Habegger & Sean O'Reilly
ISBN 1-885211-03-1
$17.95
"Travelers' Tales Hong Kong will delight the senses and heighten the sensibilities, whether you are an armchair traveler or an old China hand."
– *Profiles*

The Americas

AMERICA
True Stories of Life on the Road
Edited by Fred Setterberg
ISBN 1-885211-28-7
$19.95
"Look no further. This book is America."
— David Yeadon, author of *Lost Worlds*

HAWAI'I
True Stories of the Island Spirit
Edited by Rick & Marcie Carroll
ISBN 1-885211-35-X
$17.95
"Travelers' Tales aims to convey the excitement of voyaging through exotic territory with a vivacity that guidebooks can only hint at." — *Millenium Whole Earth Catalog*

GRAND CANYON
True Stories of Life Below the Rim
Edited by Sean O'Reilly, James O'Reilly & Larry Habegger
ISBN 1-885211-34-1
$17.95
"Travelers' Tales should be required reading for anyone who wants to truly step off the tourist track."
— *St. Petersburg Times*

SAN FRANCISCO
True Stories of Life on the Road
Edited by James O'Reilly, Larry Habegger & Sean O'Reilly
ISBN 1-885211-08-2
$17.95
"Like spying on the natives."
— *San Francisco Chronicle*

BRAZIL
True Stories of Life on the Road
Edited by Annette Haddad & Scott Doggett
Introduction by Alex Shoumatoff
ISBN 1-885211-11-2
$17.95

— ★ ★ ★ —
Benjamin Franklin Silver Award Winner

MEXICO
True Stories of Life on the Road
Edited by James O'Reilly & Larry Habegger
ISBN 1-885211-00-7
$17.95

— ★ ★ ★ —
One of the Year's Best Travel Books on Mexico
— *The New York Times*

For a complete list of titles, visit our website at www.travelerstales.com

Women's Travel

A WOMAN'S PASSION FOR TRAVEL
More True Stories from A Woman's World
Edited by Marybeth Bond & Pamela Michael
ISBN 1-885211-36-8
$17.95

"A diverse and gripping series of stories!" – Arlene Blum, author of *Annapurna: A Woman's Place*

A WOMAN'S WORLD
True Stories of Life on the Road
Edited by Marybeth Bond
Introduction by Dervla Murphy
ISBN 1-885211-06-6
$17.95

— ★ ★ ★ —

Winner of the Lowell Thomas Award for Best Travel Book – Society of American Travel Writers

WOMEN IN THE WILD
True Stories of Adventure and Connection
Edited by Lucy McCauley
ISBN 1-885211-21-X
$17.95

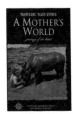

"A spiritual, moving, and totally female book to take you around the world and back." – *Mademoiselle*

A MOTHER'S WORLD
Journeys of the Heart
Edited by Marybeth Bond & Pamela Michael
ISBN 1-885211-26-0
$14.95

"These stories remind us that motherhood is one of the great unifying forces in the world" – *San Francisco Examiner*

Spiritual Travel

A WOMAN'S PATH
Women's Best Spiritual Travel Writing
Edited by Lucy McCauley, Amy G. Carlson & Jennifer Leo
ISBN 1-885211-48-1
$16.95

"A sensitive exploration of women's lives that have been unexpectedly and spiritually touched by travel experiences... highly recommended."
– *Library Journal*

THE ULTIMATE JOURNEY
Inspiring Stories of Living and Dying
James O'Reilly, Sean O'Reilly & Richard Sterling
ISBN 1-885211-38-4
$17.95

"A glorious collection of writings about the ultimate adventure. A book to keep by one's bedside—and close to one's heart." – Philip Zaleski, editor, *The Best Spiritual Writing* series

THE ROAD WITHIN:
True Stories of Transformation and the Soul
Edited by Sean O'Reilly, James O'Reilly & Tim O'Reilly
ISBN 1-885211-19-8
$17.95

— ★ ★ ★ —

Best Spiritual Book – Independent Publisher's Book Award

PILGRIMAGE
Adventures of the spirit
Edited by Sean O'Reilly & James O'Reilly
Introduction by Phil Cousineau
ISBN 1-885211-56-2
$16.95

A diverse array of spirit-renewing journeys—trips to world-famous sites as well as places sacred, related by pilgrims of all kinds.

Adventure

TESTOSTERONE PLANET
True Stories from a Man's World
Edited by Sean O'Reilly, Larry Habegger & James O'Reilly
ISBN 1-885211-43-0
$17.95

Thrills and laughter with some of today's best writers: Sebastian Junger, Tim Cahill, Bill Bryson, Jon Krakauer, and Frank McCourt.

DANGER!
True Stories of Trouble and Survival
Edited by James O'Reilly, Larry Habegger & Sean O'Reilly
ISBN 1-885211-32-5
$17.95

"Exciting...for those who enjoy living on the edge or prefer to read the survival stories of others, this is a good pick." – *Library Journal*

Travel Humor

NOT SO FUNNY WHEN IT HAPPENED
The Best of Travel Humor and Misadventure
Edited by Tim Cahill
ISBN 1-885211-55-4
$12.95

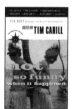

Laugh with Bill Bryson, Dave Barry, Anne Lamott, Adair Lara, Doug Lansky, and many more.

THERE'S NO TOILET PAPER...ON THE ROAD LESS TRAVELED
The Best of Travel Humor and Misadventure
Edited by Doug Lansky
ISBN 1-885211-27-9
$12.95

— ★ ★ ★ —
Humor Book of the Year
– Independent
Publisher's Book Award

Food

THE ADVENTURE OF FOOD
True Stories of Eating Everything
Edited by Richard Sterling
ISBN 1-885211-37-6
$17.95

"These stories are bound to whet appetites for more than food."
– *Publishers Weekly*

FOOD
A Taste of the Road
Edited by Richard Sterling
Introduction by Margo True
ISBN 1-885211-09-0
$17.95

Sumptious stories by M.F.K. Fisher, David Yeadon, P.J. O'Rourke, Colin Thubron, and many more.

— ★ ★ ★ —
Silver Medal Winner of the Lowell Thomas Award for Best Travel Book—Society of American Travel Writers

Special Interest

THE GIFT OF RIVERS
True Stories of Life on the Water
Edited by Pamela Michael
Introduction by Robert Hass
ISBN 1-885211-42-2
$14.95

"The Gift of Rivers is a soulful fact- and image-filled compendium of wonderful stories that illuminate, educate, inspire and delight. One cannot read this compelling anthology without coming away in awe of the strong hold rivers exert on human imagination and history."
– David Brower, Chairman of Earth Island Institute

THE GIFT OF TRAVEL
The Best of Travelers' Tales
Edited by Larry Habegger, James O'Reilly & Sean O'Reilly
ISBN 1-885211-25-2
$14.95

"Like gourmet chefs in a French market, the editors of Travelers' Tales pick, sift, and prod their way through the weighty shelves of contemporary travel writing, creaming off the very best."
– William Dalrymple, author of *City of Djinns*

FAMILY TRAVEL
The Farther You Go, the Closer You Get
Edited by Laura Manske
ISBN 1-885211-33-3
$17.95

"This is family travel at its finest." – *Working Mother*

LOVE & ROMANCE
True Stories of Passion on the Road
Edited by Judith Babcock Wylie
ISBN 1-885211-18-X
$17.95

"A wonderful book to read by a crackling fire."
– *Romantic Traveling*

THE GIFT OF BIRDS
True Encounters with Avian Spirits
Edited by Larry Habegger & Amy G. Carlson
ISBN 1-885211-41-4
$17.95

"These are all wonderful, entertaining stories offering a *birds-eye view!* of our avian friends."
– *Booklist*

A DOG'S WORLD
True Stories of Man's Best Friend on the Road
Edited by Christine Hunsicker
ISBN 1-885211-23-6
$12.95

This extraordinary collection includes stories by John Steinbeck, Helen Thayer, James Herriot, Pico Iyer, and many others. A must for any dog and travel lover.

Submit Your Own Travel Tale

Do you have a tale of your own that you would like to submit to Travelers' Tales? For submission guidelines and a list of titles in the works, send a SASE to:

Travelers' Tales Submission Guidelines
330 Townsend Street, Suite 208, San Francisco, CA 94107

You may also send email to *guidelines@travelerstales.com* or visit our Web site at *www.travelerstales.com*

Travel Advice

SHITTING PRETTY
How to Stay Clean and Healthy While Traveling
By Dr. Jane Wilson-Howarth
ISBN 1-885211-47-3
$12.95

A light-hearted book about a serious subject for millions of travelers—staying healthy on the road—written by international health expert, Dr. Jane Wilson-Howarth.

THE FEARLESS SHOPPER
How to Get the Best Deals on the Planet
By Kathy Borrus
ISBN 1-885211-39-2
$14.95

"Anyone who reads *The Fearless Shopper* will come away a smarter, more responsible shopper and a more curious, culturally attuned traveler."
— Jo Mancuso, *The Shopologist*

THE PENNY PINCHER'S PASSPORT TO LUXURY TRAVEL
The Art of Cultivating Preferred Customer Status
By Joel L. Widzer
ISBN 1-885211-31-7
$12.95

World travel expert Joel Widzer shares his proven techniques on how to travel First Class at discount prices, even if you're not a frequent flyer.

SAFETY AND SECURITY FOR WOMEN WHO TRAVEL
By Sheila Swan & Peter Laufer
ISBN 1-885211-29-5
$12.95

A must for every woman traveler!

THE FEARLESS DINER
Travel Tips and Wisdom for Eating around the World
By Richard Sterling
ISBN 1-885211-22-8
$7.95

Combines practical advice on foodstuffs, habits, & etiquette, with hilarious accounts of others' eating adventures.

GUTSY WOMEN
Travel Tips and Wisdom for the Road
By Marybeth Bond
ISBN 1-885211-15-5
$7.95

Packed with funny, instructive, and inspiring advice for women heading out to see the world.

GUTSY MAMAS:
Travel Tips and Wisdom for Mothers on the Road
By Marybeth Bond
ISBN 1-885211-20-1
$7.95

A delightful guide for mothers traveling with their children—or without them!